Harmonious Petals

True Journey of the Soul

Rose A. Chylek

ARPress
ILLUMINATING IDEAS.
EMPOWERING VOICES

ARPress
45 Dan Road Suite 5
Canton MA 02021
Hotline: 1(888) 821-0229
Fax: 1(508) 545-7580

Ordering Information:

Quantity sales. Special discounts are available on quantity purchases by corporations, associations, and others. For details, contact the publisher at the address above.

Printed in the United States of America.

ISBN-13:   Softcover   979-8-89389-213-0
             eBook   979-8-89389-214-7
Library of Congress Control Number: 2024905899

Table Of Contents

Part 2

Book Reviews

"Change must occur to heal each and every one of us and creation itself. Faith must come to help and transform us and the world."

Expressing her views on a wide range of spiritual subjects, author Chylek offers numerous fresh ways to approach life's happenings and renew the reader's sense that one should rejoice in being able to access and appreciate what the Creator has given. Interspersing her narrative with graphic depictions and explanations of such illuminating images as the Hebrew alphabet, she encourages readers to be ruled neither by their physical bodies nor by ever-present limited agendas but by the beatific spirit infused in nature, good deeds, and loving thoughts. She advises that all have the task of building wings of the spirit to soar beyond the bodily existence while warning that people will be "detained at the port of entry" and their wings disabled if they act wrongly. Every aspect of experience—beliefs, trials, marriage, family—offers the opportunity to let the King dwell within, cast off one's physical chains, and see God in all.

Chylek's writings read like a correspondence with other, like-minded aspirants while including the proviso that she does not expect everyone to agree with her. Her belief system encompasses the world's great religions: Old Testament teachings, Christ-centered ideals, recognition of Islam, and Eastern spiritual wisdom. All are based around a solidly monotheistic view. She passionately urges readers to seek harmony, cherish life (even so tiny a life as that of an ant), and seek an end to war and destruction of one another and the planet. She begins many paragraphs with the introductory phrase "My Soulful thought today…," which makes the work come across as a journal created over a period of years. Her book includes many pithy, pertinent metaphors and aphorisms, emphasizing serious attention to spirituality in almost every life situation. Chylek's work could provide a medium for study and discussion among open-minded people of any God-centered faith.

- US Review of Books

I

As a person begins to awake spiritually, they begin to view the world around them with a fresh perspective. They discover that their existence on Earth is temporary to enable their souls to achieve their true purpose through experiences before returning back to the source. When mankind becomes enlightened, they seek knowledge and answers around their existence and life's meaning. Throughout this collection of thoughts, quotes, visions, and instructions, Harmonious Petals by Rose A Chylek aims to guide the spiritually awakened toward their true path of self-actualization. Discover why humanity often succumbs to a dark and overwhelming power that draws them to negative emotions and behaviors. Why does man seem determined to destroy the perfection God has created and identify themselves by self-limiting thoughts? How can we exist together in harmony and peace and how would this affect the world in the future? What happens when we allow our ego and self-righteousness to rule our minds and how can we move toward a life of spiritual and physical abundance? Through spiritual knowledge and understanding, you are invited to examine and analyze the myths we have been conditioned to believe as reality. Only when you understand why God placed you in his Creation of perfection can you begin to live in accordance with your true authentic self and move away from the chaos. Harmonious Petals by Rose A Chylek is a powerful and thought-provoking read that is sometimes uncomfortable to digest. There are many harsh truths but intelligent observations throughout which provide true enlightenment for anyone searching for answers. I absolutely loved the second chapter which analyzes the science type and how we limit ourselves to the five senses when in reality this only limits our spiritual journey. The chapters around the destructive and harmful human behavior toward each other and the world were superb and really make you reflect on your beliefs and actions. I found such enlightenment and knowledge from every chapter, especially around ego, perceived reality, and how our minds have been conditioned so others can retain their power over us. I have gained a true understanding of why I am here, what my purpose is, and how I can live more in alignment with my soul. This is a highly recommended read.

- Lesley Jones (Readers'
Favorite)

Harmonious Petals: True Journey of the Soul is a work of non-fiction in the self-help genre. It is suitable for the general reading audience and was penned by author Rose A. Chylek. The book serves as a guide to spiritual enlightenment through the discussion of souls; how souls enter the world, how they grow and develop, and how their journey concludes. Following a spiritual exploration of the role of the soul guided by visions the author has been receiving for some time, the book seeks to help its readers capitalize on their good fortune of being born as human beings.

I've got a lot of time for spiritualists and gurus who focus their practice and message on spreading and exploring love and the importance of living life fully. There are a lot of would-be guides out there that try to present spiritualism as a cure for all life's problems rather than as a framework for exploring those problems and finding solutions. Author Rose A. Chylek's writing on the subject of the soul is passionate, wise, and knowledgeable in equal measure. Her writing style is very accessible for readers of all ages and the concepts discussed in the book are broken down into manageable pieces so that even the uninitiated can understand and appreciate the guidance this work offers. Harmonious Petals is an essential book for those wishing to undertake a spiritual reflection on their life. I highly encourage anyone with an interest in spiritualism to acquire a copy, read what it has to say, then reflect on its message whilst meditating.

- K.C. Finn (★★★★★)

- - -

Harmonious Petals: True Journey of the Soul by Rose A. Chylek is about the power of spiritual awareness and ascending and how you can do it. It is a dynamic contribution to a better understanding of nurturing our souls in relation to our corporeal existence. Chylek asserts that you should pay attention to what is good for your soul. In doing so, she divides her book into two parts. The first part operates on the premise that human society needs a better understanding of ourselves and our relationship to others to engender a more sustainable culture based on love. The second part operates on the premise that nourishing our soul with its spiritual needs is based on what we say, think, and do; in return, it will serve as our guide for an enriching human life.

In Harmonious Petals, you'll find a narrative of how you and your soul can grow whole by earning your rights through living. With your soul as your wisest and most trustworthy guide, this self-help for individual human development does have common teachings that you've heard before, as they are Scripture-based, and Chylek alludes to the wisdom of the sages to drive her point. But what is original about Rose A. Chylek's discourse is her exploration of our unique relationship with God and our souls and the practical conscious discovery of cultivating a healthy body-mind-soul relationship. In a busy world, we think of nothing but hard work, material gains, and becoming great providers. In our spiritual affiliation with God and ourselves, a soul-infused existence becomes the core of our self-transformation. If you feel burdened by society's demands and feel the need to take a break, consider reading Harmonious Petals as part of your R&R.

- *Vincent Dublado* (★★★★)

- - -

Harmonious Petals: True Journey of the Soul by Rose A. Chylek is a compelling book that explores the nature of the soul from the moment it enters into the world and its ultimate destiny. The author writes about how the soul learns, develops, and acquires wisdom and understanding and its journey to Universal Love. Examining multiple topics, the author explains the growth of the human soul. The reader will learn lessons and insights about love as the ultimate reality, relationships, human potential, hardships, the language of nature, prayer, sex, marriage, seeing with the soul's eye, family, and more. This book presents the idea we are more than the physical world. Our physical body is just a home to the Soul. The author identifies the centrality of Christ's message of Love, which enables humankind to complete God's work of creation and bring it to its fulfillment in Him. This book is one of the most powerful Christian books I have ever read. Readers will enjoy how the author writes about her personal experience of God, her spiritual insights, and her visions in the book. Deeply researched, it features the concepts discussed herein in other traditions. It is a book about spiritual enlightenment, and it contains diagrams and symbolic illustrations. I loved the analogy of the frog and the author's reflections on the symbolism of the garden. Harmonious Petals: True Journey of the Soul will infuse readers with a fresh consciousness about who they are and what they are called to be. A book with strong lessons on love as the ultimate reality we are called to experience; it is inspiring and informative.

- *Romuald Dzemo* (★★★★★)

- - -

Harmonious Petals: True Journey of the Soul by Rose A. Chylek opens a portal through which we can gaze into the world of our soul, understand its journey, and steer it toward higher realms of consciousness. The author captures the soul's journey into this life with vividness and discusses its ultimate destination and purpose, sharing spiritual insights rooted in her personal and spiritual experience, and showing readers that there is far more to the spiritual world than our religious beliefs suggest. This is a book about purpose and the meaningful connection with the spiritual world. In this book, readers will encounter energy that gives meaning to things that can seem mundane; the author invites readers to look at the world through the eyes of the soul and to pierce the veil that limits our gaze through the art of universal love and informed faith. Rose A. Chylek talks about complex topics in a style that is simple and compelling, making the message accessible to all readers. She discusses a wide range of topics and sheds a lot of light on topics such as sexuality, actions, and reactions, the cosmos, love for others, marriage, procreation, the language of nature, being connected, the dual nature of life, dealing with hardships and a lot, lot more. This book features the wisdom of the sages, the different dimensions of life, the implications of physical death, and the place of spiritual practice. This is a book from someone with a lot of spiritual experience, even as a child. Harmonious Petals: True Journey of the Soul is the book you need for real spiritual awakening. As a Christian, I can relate to most of what the author discusses without seeing any contradiction to my faith; it provides a deepening and enriching experience that will shift the way we think about life, death, love, and existence.

- *Christian Sia* (★★★★★)

Amazon Reviews

The magical vibrations of Rose's painting and insights for our Soul/Spirit Journey in this current civilization has a blessed profound communication with the Spirit World. If people would open their minds in their religious view, they would get a new aspect of divine spirituality.

- Tessbah

- - -

Finding the true essence of the soul is so hard to discover and understand without knowing its purpose. Going beyond the fads, opinions, and false hopes of "expert" self-help books, Harmonious Petals explores the incredible connection between purposeful living and quality of life. Rose Chylek have discussed thoroughly in this book the connectivity of life, the world and the universe. There will be a lot of understandable aspect in the book that can help us realize the value of life, exploring our purpose and radiating it towards the other being and the universe. Rose has a vast knowledge about the topic she is discussing. The things that we seek to learn and understand is in this book. Illuminating, accessible, and authentically grounded in experiences, knowledge and wisdom, the book is essential reading for everyone seeking lasting improvement and understanding in their lives and souls. This should be a "must-buy" for everyone.

- M. Lee DYOMC Manager
for Operations

- - -

Harmonious Petals, This gorgeous book, filled with inspiring full-color illustrations by the author, is dedicated to helping everyone to become "harmonious petals" and to live and prosper on all levels with all beings. Rose asks us to rise above our baser concerns, to be better. She shows us many ways to accomplish this, and gives many signposts along the way, based on her lifetime of spiritual work and study. You can turn to any page and find inspiration and instruction. If you want to get serious about your work in this world, this thought-provoking work is a good place to begin.

- Clarke Fountain

- - -

In this heartfelt book, Rose offers her astute, enlightened observations on the journey of the soul through life on earth, and the urgent need of every spiritual seeker to assume personal responsibility for his or her individual transformation and become a willing and essential contributor to a harmonious earthly existence. Born from Rose's spiritual and life experiences as well as the richness of her dreams, Harmonious Petals lays out a framework for this crucial work, and the challenging but necessary task of balancing the dual natures - spiritual and physical - that exist in every human. With chapters and discussions focusing on essential qualities such as empathy, compassion, heart, love, and right action, Rose encourages each of us to be an instrument of change, to summon the strength and courage to unlock our potential richness and master our lower natures for the benefit of all beings. Only through this mastery, she suggests, through discipline and by directing ourselves away from worldly selfishness, can we protect the precious beauty of life on earth, and create the possibility of our spiritual ascension to the realm of the divine. Open ourselves to nature and its creatures, her work states, for every animal, plant, and being is infused with the sacred spark of God. Do not allow innocents of any form to suffer. Ask ourselves always: what role we are playing in this earthly drama? Are we contributing to peace, or to its opposite? Let us not, Rose tells us, miss the opportunities that this exquisite life provides us to grow, to experience the beauty of creation. Harmonious Petals is beautifully illustrated with Rose's vibrant, dynamic paintings of nature, of her expansive celestial visions, of the Kabbalistic Tree of Life, as well as sacred images from other spiritual traditions. Achieving that unity is Rose's urgent prayer for us all, and for the remarkable realm of earth, whose future, she reminds us, is in our hands, and needs us to act boldly on its behalf.

- Heidi Schulman

This is a very interesting read. The book touches on many aspects of daily life. The stream of consciousness writing style is particularly absorbing. I recommend this book for anyone who is looking for spiritual guidance.

- Benjamin Kanter (★★★★★)

This is the most profound information regarding a connection with spirit and soul. It is necessary to open our minds and reconnect to our Mother Earth Spirit. This western civilization needs a commitment of individuals to respect and protect all living creatures as well as the human population. It is our duty to secure our future generations. Everyone is born with creativity and should apply their intellect in making a beautiful life for themselves and others. Blessings. Thank you Rose for giving us this divine gift and knowledge.

- Terry B (★★★★★)

This books gives you a better understanding of what is real and spiritual; a grandeur understanding of the path of light, and truth and a much bigger understanding of the universe and god than any religion on earth could ever tell.

-Timothy Douget (★★★★★)

I am really touched by this book. God bless 🐾

-Jebes Ramachandran (★★★★★)

This is one of my visions where I saw this light. I asked myself. what is this? And perceived the answer as "Light of God." (God Is Light).

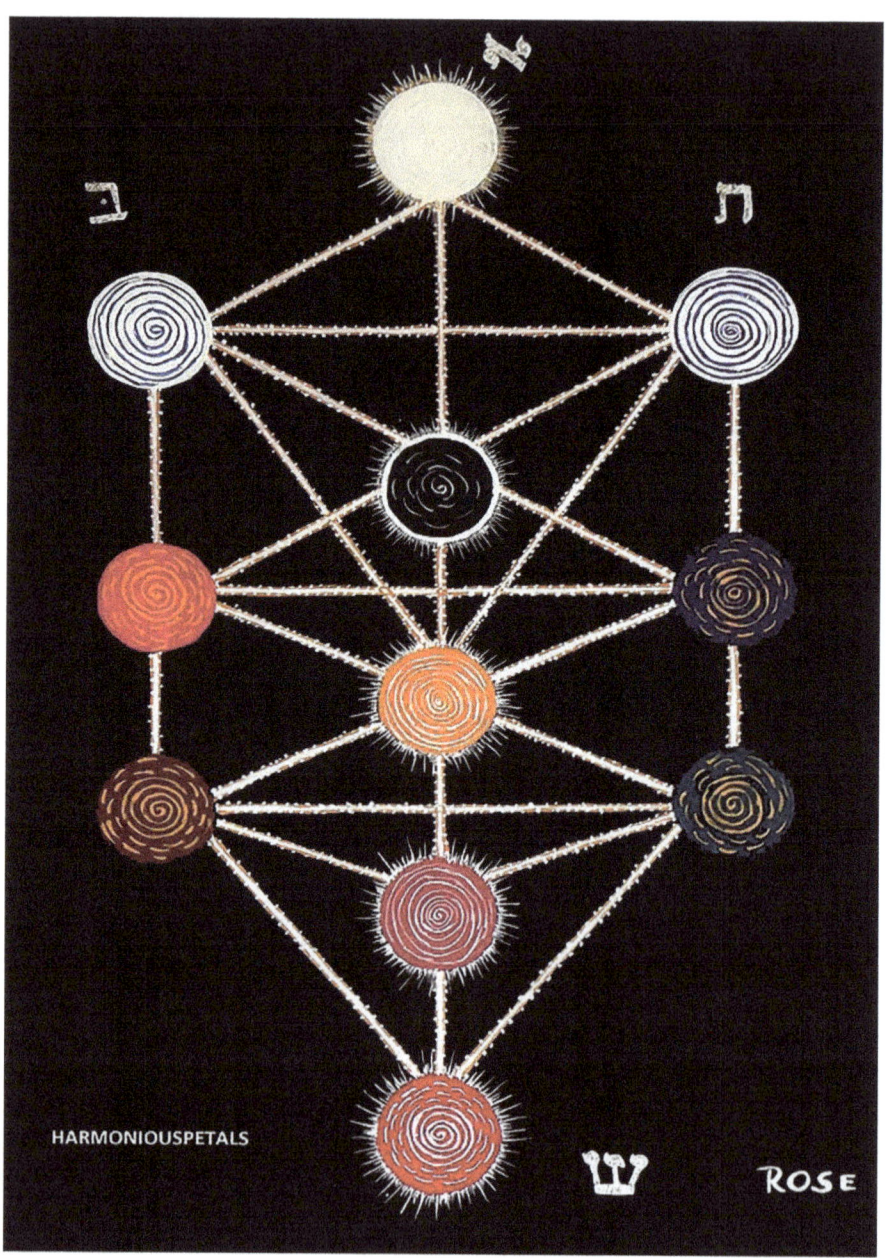

HARMONIOUSPETALS

ROSE

X

This book is dedicated to my beloved departed brother, Joseph

Introduction Harmonious Petals

At a very early age, I was experiencing spiritual dreams/ visions/ images of all religions. As a young person, I never paid any attention to anything. I used to see always continuously in dreams, the departed friends, relatives, discussion with them etc. Also, lots of the Saints, sages of all religions. As I was growing up like anyone else went through trials. However, my inner knowing was kept growing about life, souls, spirits, etc.

As born and raised Catholic it was fine for a while as my inner knowing kept asking all sorts of questions and I was looking for more and more answers to the physical existence, our roles, in the collective. About 20 years ago, I joined the Mystical Path called Kabbalah I found that to be the Best way to understand the story of the Spirit/Souls/ Physical Creation/Spiritual Dimension and the Great Dimension where No one Can have access to it from which all forces of nature, worlds undreamed all come to exist. This Mystical Path satisfied me greatly. This is our journey.

As Time went by, I finally fully awakened in spirit Once that happened, my inner life and outer life, changed completely. I cannot stand the suffering of any beings. I cannot stand violence I seek unity and peace with all creation. I recognized I am Part of All and All is Part of me. I was forced to give up all of what is was pleasurable and pleasing. I did it happily With spiritual awakening, I cannot stand all what was happening on the earth by us, humans I start to write to some few members. I sit and I write whosoever's souls that received my writing liked and appreciated it. They were suggesting that, I should save those writings and write a book, etc. It was not in my mind at all.

However, a beautiful soul [Teesbah] came into my life and she appreciated very much what I am doing. With her help I decided to put it together some of my writings. They are tough to read, because it is for the ardent and true spiritual seekers that is the work we all souls have to follow. In my book I have shared images, visions, quotes, instructions, etc. They all came to me and as I saw them, I just wrote it down or painted it. I have few books full of down pouring of the higher worlds. In this book, I am only sharing very little of what I have If I have to put all into one book, the book will be huge and it may not be pleasing. So, I chose very little. Throughout the book whatever images are shared are my own soul experiences I am not saying to anyone to take it or reject it. The God's Universe is Vast and Beyond anyone's Comprehensions. I would like to mention a few people in my life who are dear to me and participated in creating this book.

1. Dr. Petr, my dear husband, who is my strength and pillar of support.

2. To my daughter, Dr. Ann, who is my sunshine. She is very wise, intelligent, kind, compassionate and a blessing from God.

3. Tessbah, she's a beautiful soul and happened to visit me at my home and saw my work. She was taken with a wonderful feeling and insisted I share the work with the world, if I don't do, once I pass from this world all will go to the trash. So, I agreed with her. She created a website, Facebook, and she cooperated with this book. And without her help, it would not have been possible for me to finish this book. I am forever grateful to her.

Also, I have to mention a dear soul, Mr. Clarke Fountain. He is very wise and knowledgeable in philosophical subjects. He was my past life friend and we met in this life (it is my experience, not his). He wanted to edit the book for me; however, circumstances were beyond his control. His love and best wishes go with this book. God Bless them and guide them all.

FOREWORD

It is a privilege, an opportunity, a chance to be a soul being born as human being in the physical existence. We must spend the time wisely in order to progress soulfully with wisdom and understanding ... a Higher calling. Since my inner awakening, I became aware of a million things that I did not pay any attention to before ... so I started to write and share these with some groups, they all liked what I was doing and encouraged me to create a journal of them all. So many people told me to write a book, so this book is a fraction of what I have been writing.

If One understood the sacredness and impermanence of physical existence and the purpose of the soul's existence, we all would treat each being as moving temples.

> "Some wandered in deserts wastes, finding no road to a residence city. Hungry and thirsty, their souls faint within them."
>
> -Psalms

> "When you are lonely and sad, see Me as your companion. I see you. I am with you. You don't see Me. I am your companion FOREVER."
>
> -(The God Within, Rose).

> "One who can register a feeling of love, empathy, and compassion towards other beings, he or she has

taken the steps to know the forces and sources of ALL."

-Rose

"Honest and open communication brings harmony and peace. Love and light will enter their hearts and dwell with them".

-Rose

"Earth is the mother of ALL physical creation. She nourishes us all. She heals us. Pay attention to her plea; not to destroy HER!"

-Rose

"If one loves one's life and wants to live, if so; love all life. They too love their life and want to live, and it is pleasing to the Creator, Giver of all life."

-Rose

"I romance, I mate, I hate, I fight, I leave, I love, I cherish, I sacrifice, I seek, I find, I race AND I cross over. I am HUMANITY."

-Rose

"When I wore garments of glitters and the world was around me. When I wore sackcloth, my friends and their world disappeared."

-Rose

"Noble writings are greater than guns. Guns terrorize the souls, burn the bodies. Noble writings penetrate & transform hearts and souls."

-Rose

Physical creation is the garment of the eternal. All creation is part of it. Preserve and respect; it is our duty as humans."

-Rose

"Do not find reason to fight. Find reason to love, cherish and live.

-Rose

I am the tree of life and my roots are established in heaven."

-Rose

"What one do not cherish will perish in time."

-Rose

"What is not negotiated is negated and unsettled."

-Rose

"Do not look at one's garment and fascinate. Garment will get old and fade. Learn to look inside, so that one may not be deceived."

-Rose

"Wise learn from the mistakes and go forward and upward. Others repeat it and go backward until they hit the rock bottom. Which is better?"

-Rose

"Prisons and jails should be a place for soul's or human's transformation. Rather than a physical enclosure with high walls and wire."

-Rose

"Law enforcements, prison walls will not prevent crime or criminals. Practice of Moral, Ethics and Disciplined Existence Will."

-Rose

"Do not say one has done everything legally correct. May be morally wrong. Do all morally right. Moral and legal run parallel."

-Rose

"Share your wealth, share your joy and share your unconditional love. Whatever one shared will multiply in here and hereafter."

-Rose

"God created the world and humans. Humans created divisions, destruction and suffering for all on the Earth."

-Rose

"Do not worry about others judging you or praising you. These are two sides of the same coin. They have done that to all."

-Rose

"Practice empathy, compassion and love and your soul will be blessed. Heaven will take delight in you."

-Rose

"If someone trusts you with something precious, guard them with your life, until you have returned it back to them safely."

-Rose

"Why God gave us the big heart, so, God can make its habitation in our heart by helping us to be loving & compassionate to all."

-Rose

"ONE who practices, moral, ethics, compassion, that being is in love and is in a perpetual meditative state and constantly the channel for Universal Love."

-Rose

"What is displayed will be misplaced or replaced. What one cherished will be kept in the archives of the hearts as memories."

-Rose

"If one is hungry for physical food, Earth will feed you. If one is hungry for wisdom, Heaven will feed you."

-Rose

"When you are in the dark place, light your candle, so that others can light theirs from yours or they can trace their steps by your candlelight."

-Rose

"Do and say the right thing all the time, so that; one's soul will not regret at the wrong time at the wrong place."

-Rose

"If one stretched out one arm to receive, stretch out the other arm to give, this way one is balanced on the ground."

-Rose

"I am the Life of All. I dwell in all forms. If one tried to kill a being, I take leave of that form and give life to another. I am deathless and eternal. Know this and live." (The Life Force- God Force)

-Rose

"Empathy, compassion and love is the way for the seeker of the spiritual path."

-Rose

"Do not desire to have what belongs to others."

-Rose

"Learn to live and tolerate others and other beings and their place in creation. If one would do, will spare many bad outcomes in the journey of the soul life."

-Rose

"If one will impose the will on other being, that being fails to recognize the will of the other and the imposer is in error and accountable."

-Rose

"If I am your friend, I will tell you what you need to hear, not what you want to hear. It may not be pleasing."

-Rose

"If one hears or reads a word of wisdom, a good word, do not bother to ask who spoke it, rather allow those words to sink into one's life and be part of one's daily living. That person will be a happy soul."

-Rose

"In my vision, I was in an existence where no word can describe the beauty, enchantment, the ecstasy, and glory of the existence. I asked myself, 'Where am I?'," the Voice said, 'This is consciousness.' I said to myself, I never want to leave this place. I was so happy."

-Rose

"In my vision, one day I was beyond the veil of the physical and I saw happy souls, suffering souls, and I was given a fraction of a minute, if I did not get out of that place, the veil would fall, and I would not get back into my body. So, I entered my body."

-Rose

"Countless times, the voice said, 'Do not try to understand the Infinite God and Infinite Creation, it is not our job'".

-Rose

"To the readers, these are all my experiences, I have nothing to prove, and you can draw your own conclusion that pleases you."

-Rose

"This book is only for the people who are spiritually awakened, who believe in creator, soul, spirit and only those who will understand this book and its contents."

-Rose

"I meant no offense to anyone. We have free will and freedom of speech. So, in my awareness I wrote this book. I am not advocating anything to anyone. Humanity has the tenancy to kill the messenger or remove them from the field of action. Look at the humanity from the inception of time, how many wars we fought, invaders, religious division, color, race, male, female, animals, rich, poor, etc. Where is our heart with such capacity to love, cherish and live with one another in peace and unity? So, I say, this is not for everybody. It is for the few who seek God, light, love, unity with all. If we all could realize the existence of others and other beings. We will live in a world where there are no tears, no fears. One happy family of the creator that includes all creation. People may oppose my views, my question to them is: Why do we have religions, spirituality, sages, saints, prophets, scriptures, law and order, jail, police, military and so forth. Why? Are we not humans with heart that can love and consider others and live in peace. Animals do not have any of the above. That means we have problems, and that problem was is created by us due to selfishness, greed, ignorance, etc. I still say, this is only for the souls that seek to ascend the path of love. I am not here to fight with anybody, argue with anybody. My awareness: I wrote it here."

-Rose

HARMONIOUS PETALS

All Noble Teachers

All noble teachers say we are attached to our families. It is true for some and not true for others. If it is true, then no human family would fight divorce, have unwanted children, lose children, or have children born into poverty and suffering. Surely, they are attached to something, and the consequences are disastrous. It is very visible with humans. Christ had and has only one mission in the world, that is love ... so, Jesus is continuously knocking at the door of our hearts to enter. Are we opening the door of our hearts through love, empathy, and compassion, for all creation and each other? This is how we can open the heart to Christ. This is how we can testify to its presence and its rulership among humans and the rest of the creation. People are warring with each other, nations are warring with each other, and humans are creating havoc with other creations and earth as a whole. Does it make any sense? Unless people have self-mastery, self-discipline first ... then love and charity will flow from them to others, other nations, and all other creatures. Each one of us should be John the Baptist with our living and work ... so, Christ can manifest with its glory in its creation. Let us all make this creation a fertile land for all inhabitants under the rulership of the Lord. Jesus says one should not tie a heavy rock onto the neck of a drowning person ... so that they can drown quicker. That is what happens with quarrel and war when people are already suffering for want of the basic necessities of life. We are all one in the body of Christ. Change must occur to heal each and every one of us and creation itself. Faith must come to help and transform us and the world.

The Heavenly Father is continuously working and bringing out creation. Christ is working continuously for the journey and perfection of creation by infusing it with love. We, as humans on the earth, must listen to Christ's call and receive the love and transmit it to all beings on the planet. Preserve what is given to us on earth and all that is with it. That is all of us, humans, the earth, and all its inhabitants whether we—all human beings—recognize the fact that we are spirits/souls and we are temporarily here to experience the majesty of creation. We should recognize the fact that we are spirits/souls, and we are temporarily here to experience the majesty of the creator and we have to leave this earth to return home.

What happened to human spirits? Suffering from forgetfulness? We are so caught up in the flesh and put the spirit to sleep. We are destroying the earth; we are violating all laws and norms. We are causing suffering to all the earth's inhabitants and each other. When we crush the body of a being, who feels the pain, the spirit within that particular being suffers. Are we aware of anything or paying attention to anything? The physical world is the challenger of the spirit, which is dark in its nature by the will of the infinite God. You see, how we become perfect from innocence. By going through all and all suffering. Realizing the good, the evil and the light within. We are all working for one end: Salvation of the soul. The selfish people, the egotists, the killers, the jealous, etc., we will all be forced to take stock when we leave this earth and are forced to face the music. Why are we so silly? Have we not learned enough? The true seekers of God/light leave this mess behind and practice love, selflessness, charity, simplicity, humility, etc., receive the abundant light from the divine. St. Francis is a great example of our time. Remember, the killing will serve nothing. War, violence, lies, selfishness, greed, irresponsibility, jealousy, etc., the great traps set for humans' spiritual journey. We must pluck these weeds entirely from our lives so that we can see the road that leads to Heaven's existence ... here, and in the hereafter. We each should be the allies for each other.

The Hebrew Letters

It is my greatest privilege to write something about the Hebrew Letters. It was the gift given by my departed brother. He appeared in my dream and said to me, "Hebrew is the language of the soul." So, I put effort to learn to write the Hebrew letters and the meaning. What a profound wisdom. So, I am very delighted to share with you this profound gift given by the Hebrew Sages to humanity. It is wonderful. I love them and respect them. The Great Sages who created the Hebrew Letters and assigned the meaning to each letter were divinely inspired and guided. Through Hebrew Letters, they suggest how creation came to be and the journey of the spirits/souls through many levels and finally entering the physical creation. Through learning and transformation, the soul/spirits enter the Realm of the Divine world, from whence they descended into the physical word as souls to learn and achieve perfection through physical living. I will be posting images of each letter and the meaning assigned to it, will explain our existence and purpose, etc.—I will be very, very brief, because I am not a scholar.

Harmonious Petals

The letter represents "Sacrificial OX" and "One Thousand." As the first letter of all the Holy Letters and symbol of the God's oneness and Omnipotence, ALEPH is a three-in-one presentation. Its upper right-hand segment consists of a "YOD," the first letter in the name of the "Divine." A second "YOD" in the lower left segment signifies the creator's resident with its creation. The center diagonal connecting the pillar is the "VAV" symbol of transformation. "ALEPH" thus represents the process of transformation from human to superhuman. It represents that there is one true living God ... and much more.

Harmonious existence. There is no other way. We have to turn back and take the correct road of spirit and soul. If we realize there are spirits/souls, then we do what is right and take the trail that leads to the Mountain of the Lord. Do not waste time and allow the spirit to sink further into the depths of mire by making excuses or pretending. Take the beautiful inner journey and do not cause others to stumble as well. This is our task. Accept one creation, the brotherhood of humans and the rest of all beings. [Creation]

The Scientist

The scientist type who is materialistic, who cannot see anything beyond the five senses, argues that there is nothing beyond the physical. Science has not yet understood what the reality of the whole physical creation is. There are billions of galaxies and as many spiritual dimensions. Our Earth is only a small mustard seed in the grand scheme of physical existence. What is the spiritual dimension of the earth? Many mansions/ many spheres. Nobody has a clue about the spiritual mansions around the earthly mansion. Do these scientists know how many cells are in the human body? Maybe doctors do. All the intricacies and functions of it all. Our senses allow us to do certain acts such as eating, doing other stuff, all relating to physical gratification and satisfaction, wealth, power, etc. Do humans know how many millions of living sperms are released with one action? They are all living organisms and have only one purpose: To reach the egg and create a life ... whether it is animal or human. When it did not get the opportunity to unite with the egg, it survives outside the body for a short while and dies physically. But the spirit in it won't die. That is why people say abortion is bad. One lady, a long time ago, argued with me that abortion is bad. I agree. I go one step further down ... every sperm wasted and that doesn't get the chance to create a life through union with egg ... is a sin. People may argue as if it has no life, there are sperm banks, and they freeze the sperm for whosoever cannot have a baby. This is the primordial sin.

Harmonious Petals

"BET" Translating literally as "House." "BET" is the first word in the Hebrew Bible. (Bereshit - "In the Beginning"). Also, the first letter in the first word of any Jewish Blessing. Baruch ("Blessed") as in Baruch Ha Shem ("Blessed is The Name of God"). "BET" symbolizes the Duality and Plurality of creation. Also, is represents fullness and emptiness, spiritual and mundane; but all such polarities are ultimately illusory within the light of eternal unity … and much more. Also Bet represent our Physical Body where in dwell the spirit of God. Bet is the Cosmic House for all creation.

But without this, no physical life will be here on the Earth. Creator in ITS Wisdom has done everything but we humans lost all sense of control. The generative force is a storm raging in humans hence, rape, violation of children, great suffering in immense proportion. No one taught us anything the great forefathers handed down to us what they did the Physical, all its aspects of evil/good/suffering, and death. Heaven functions independently from humans. It is Pure Light, Pure Love, Pure Wisdom, if we have to enter heaven, we need the light of Christ pure love, pure wisdom, empathy, compassion to live in the physical. Once the Physical is worn off, we enter the place of our earning and choosing. Christ showed us the way. So, scientists and laymen, all have to go through the learning process. I am no exception. I am going through it. We all are going through it. Our attachment to the power of the physical is far greater than the desire for the Soul/Spirit within. If I am wrong, I invite anyone of you to correct me. We do not want to face reality to see if there is a reality of the soul. We love to talk and talk more.

We must totally empty ourselves of preconceived ideas, notions, etc., with a humble heart of the desire for the knowledge to fill this open vessel. It will be tough but it will be filled. It may take time. Jesus was tempted for forty days, a long time. Jews walked through the desert for forty years. ALL humans must realize that we are creating barren land as far the Spirit/Soul is concerned. We must learn to water it and make it fertile soil so that God can plant the Seed of the Spirit through love, empathy, compassion, and LOVE for all.

We are all connected to the Center. But the creators of wind, storm, lightning, etc., with their actions are trouble makers who ignore the connection to the Center and recognize only the periphery. To keep that imaginary periphery solid, they create havoc. They are that evil through whom suffering, destruction, and chaos takes place. It is really unfortunate humans behave in such a selfish way and cause such torments for other inhabitants to live in pain, fear, and sorrow. This is the cause of ignorant parents, ignorant children, from the very beginning of our existence on the Earth. This can only change when human homes are in order and harmony and bring forth children (like little seedlings) which must be nourished with good tidings that allow them to experience the goodness of their Spirit/Soul. It takes many efforts, much understanding and wisdom on the parents' part. The failed parents' portion is going to be heavy.

Harmonious Petals

"GIMEL" reflects the key qualities of both kindness and growth. It depicts a person running after one person who is needy, in order to be of true help and service. "GIMEL" represents love and kindness. "Right work and diligence will bring out the hidden reward." "GIMEL" teaches us how apparently opposing forces must be blended to form a third, more complete and perfect entity ... and more.

It is a lack of wisdom and understanding on the part of humanity that we face today. Destruction and unrest among all inhabitants of the earth. People want to be leaders and have authority, but they have not taken authority over their own impulses and out of control habits and nature. The person who has mastered themselves is wise and can be a leader in any way.

Lack of understanding of the wholeness of the creator ... humankind fragmented everything. We misuse all our potential richness as humans because we connect ourselves totally with physical existence and all its wants and unending desires of the flesh. If we are seeking something beyond, we must choose to act responsibly. There is no free lunch. When self-righteousness and ego rules, there is no room for patience or to have the heart that can feel or the ear that can hear anything or do anything from somebody else's point of view. Hence, the infinite problems we endure: Broken relationships, broken homes, disorderly children, war, and violence. It is useless talking about it. Even the spiritual (the so-called) cannot do anything reasonable or right in harmony with their environments, people, etc. People will have to work and earn everything ... i.e., self-discipline, self-mastery, and all other soulful matters and aspects. Wise are those who do and think rightly, do the right thing to avoid the entanglements of the karmic crucifixion of souls together. So, be on guard. We must live a mask-free life that is pleasing to the Spirit within.

Harmonious Petals

"DALED" means literally, "Door", also meaning weakness. It represents dimensions in space and time. The four physical directions—north, south, east, west and the metaphysical "four worlds"—emanation, creation, formation, and action. Also, this "DALED" is an entry into the divine world through our desire, work, and transformation... and more.

Unfortunately, it only reaches few and out of the few, fewer will read it and very few will comprehend it and still, fewer will practice it.

Jesus said, "God is Love.," out of the love of the creator; all creations were brought forth. Jesus understood this phenomenon, so he came to teach humanity the importance of love. If we love something, we cherish it. No matter whether it is human, animal, flower, or anything and everything. When one's heart is filled with all that is in creation, we are one with the creator. You see, there is a great magnetism with fleshly existence ... a great power, trap, attraction, and distraction. If there was no such pull, all humans would turn to the spirit and there would not be much activity of reproduction per se. But we lost all purpose and entered the futility of the power of flesh and lost the love so that we worship lust/skin. In the majority of the human family, between husband and wives, between brothers and sisters ... there is only a war of jealousy waiting for an opportunity to shed blood and laugh loud with pride.

Men and women kill each other. However, there are lots of people who live in harmony and have good children. Where men and women fight, the majority of children from their family will be doomed. Some turn out to be great souls. But because of these human egos and evil, His blood will continue to pour from the cross from the top of the mountain. Why are we so slow to learn? What great power of ego and flesh!

In today's terror, eighty people were killed and many wounded. What a folly. It is useless for me to write about it, but if I do not express my feeling, my spirit within will cringe. Most of us act like hyenas. I think the sooner we act like humans; the sooner healing will start.

Harmonious Petals

The letter "HEI" is found twice in the sacred name of "GOD" known as the tetragrammaton. "YOD HEI VOV HEI" and IT connotes divine revelation. The letter "HEI" represents "GOD's" effortless breath in forming Adam Kadmon (The Primal Human). The divine presence here and now … and more.

Royalty

Royalty: "This is the fool's paradise where fools parade with golden garb who wears a crown and tell others to bow down." In the truest sense, they are impostors and slaves unto themselves. Yeshua was the real prince who overcame the lower kingdom and taught humanity to overcome it likewise and thus partake of the heritage of the Heavenly Kingdom. God formed man out of clay and breathed into his nostrils and he became a living being and was imbued with potential for inheriting the heavenly heritage. What are the potentials? To become wise, intelligent, thoughtful, kind, compassionate, empathetic. These are the qualities, the means by which humans can ascend to the Father's home. There have been few who have understood these mysteries: One of those is St. Francis of Assisi.

He was a normal human being touched by war, violence, and chaos, yet right then and there he was touched by the noble light, and he became a transformed being. From then on, he was the friend of all that is on the blessed earth. Watch the movie on the internet: *Brother Sun, Sister Moon*. Our faith must come to aid us in transforming our attitude so that we move to help all beings, easing suffering, cultivating love. Jesus says, "God is Love." Love all creation. Live an entanglement-free life. Do not throw your baggage onto other's shoulders. Clear away the mess we are in. If any of you read this writing and act to the contrary and talk about God, know that your soul will be liable.

As Jesus told the people of that time: "You white-washed tombs!" We must rise above the fleshly tombs and shine forth.

Also, do not cause others to stay buried in their fleshly tombs. See, we have emotions, pains, when we cause others to suffer from our actions. Our souls react, and this way, we become our own stumbling blocks. We have a huge mountain to climb, a stormy ocean to cross. Our faith must be the way-shower for all seekers to help them walk these narrow paths.

Harmonious Petals

Rose

This letter "VAV" represents completion. Also connecting two subjects. Also, in Hebrew, "VAV" stands for confession, or Teshuva [Atonement for our sins against creation and creator as a whole] and more.

There are so many facts I am mentioning with regards to spirit/soul. The forests ... the wing. For the soul and the spirit, earthly existence is a necessary evil. The primordial humans ventured into the forests by the Will of the Absolute. The souls throughout physical existence meander through the hills, valleys, deserts, and all that the blessed earthly existence offers. Through our existence, we will build our wings of the spirit and must fly upward/heavenward. That is the dwelling of our spirit/soul. Each spirit is on a journey in a foreign land. We, as the soul, must realize that our passport/visa expires, and we have to say goodbye to this physical journey. We must never forget the fact that if we do wrong things, we violate the laws of the visa/passport ... we will be detained at the port of entry and our very wings will be broken or fractured and won't be able to fly ... this is what happens to the souls who have lost all concept of God/spirit and indulge in the physical to satisfy the fleshly power. Be on guard. Hold onto the strong trunk of the tree that is our goodness, which is of "God" ... so that no storm can carry us away into the pits.

To have the strength and courage to face everything, we must have the heart to do everything before the light. We must be pure, loving, transparent. If every action we do is transformed by love and purity, we are rising within, and the Holy Spirit descends into our hearts. We may not move the mountain but certainly, we feel strong and do not care for any glamour of this world. We are tuned into the celestial music and enjoy our moments, hours, or even days. We and all humanity could do and experience the Holy Spirit's presence in our heart all the time, and when we do, we will have no time for arguments, violence, falsehood, killing of people or animals alike.

Harmonious Petals

This letter, "ZAYIN," represents time in the physical universe. Remembrance of GOD on Jewish high holiday days. People pray, "Remember us Oh GOD in The Book of Life." When we are completely lost in the world of action try to mediate upon "ZAYIN" to get connected to the Divine... and more.

"Blessed are the peacemakers," Jesus says, "How much peace are we making as humankind?" The moment people say or do anything contrary to love and purity, instead of the Holy Spirit, the dark spirit will take us over for a long ride. So, we always have to be on guard. Many words and mutterings are only noises. The Holy Spirit does not inhabit such places, or such hearts.

Sex

About sex, mystics say ... yes, it is a fire ... fire has the capacity to cook, yet if not watched, it burns. This is what humanity is facing ... burning everything in the human's path. Birth control, abortions, many other practices: They play with the fire's burning (that is, interfere with creative law) so the earth is exploding with overpopulation and suffering. Of course, we have free will—so do all moving creatures, but we supersede all others. We think the little ant has no free will—try to catch one without hurting it. Observe, he tries to avoid you catching it. But the ant's scope is limited in comparison to ours that is all. We throw our free will into the storm, which catches fire and burns everything in its path. The people who read this message are good ones. But they are only a few. From the beginning of time, we humans recognized this fire, but instead of using this ability to our advantage, for each other and in the collective, we humans are abusing it. Messengers are killed. Religions do not help. Everybody has their own agenda. Well, all these agendas will blow up in flame before God's law. We cannot talk it out or manipulate the divine plan. When I read some noble message, I catch fire and I write. Wherever we are in the walk of life, at least few of us can think, act, feel and recognize the fact of the divine plan and law and live and let live.

Harmonious Petals

Rose

This letter, "CHET," represents vitality, health, and relationships with other creations. Also, our relationship of our outer and inner world, dreams, and visions. It also represents wisdom and simplicity. The importance of practicing noble nature ... and more.

Before we do anything, the thought arises from within us, then the action follows. When people do not pay attention to the consequences of their thoughts and actions, they play havoc with creation. We can clearly see what is happening. Before the physical creation and the spiritual world was the self-existing ocean, the Almighty Father, from it comes the thought of creation and the manifestation of all that is. Jesus says, "Even if one did not do a thing, the thought itself is as good as doing it, so be aware of it."

From the very beginning of human existence, if humans lived with good thoughts, good actions, and a desire to live in harmony with God's creation, we would have a better world to pass on and live safely on the Earth. Nobody feels safe. For a normal human being, thinking is part of our existence. We cannot avoid that.

We have to know what we are thinking. Are we planting weeds or good seeds? We sow thinking and reap action ... and re-reap reaction. Everything goes hand in hand. Everything is interlinked. There is no solution to this unless transformation takes place.

INITIATION

All human beings from primitive times to now, and all major religions as well, practice initiation. This is an outward expression of affiliation with the particular religions in regard to the relationship with God. Here comes the interesting part: No outward practices and bodily mortification can connect individuals to God. On the other hand, each and every individual's hunger and desire to know God and the steps that particular individual will take towards that goal by acknowledging the state they are in, the need to take a different direction, moving toward love, empathy, compassion, unity of all, whereby one truly recognizes the creator within and automatically recognizes the God within all: This is True initiation. All selfless practices with full knowledge of that goal must transcend all other goals in the physical sense.

Yeshua says, "I am in this world, but I am not of this world." Every initiate must be able to say these words that Jesus spoke. This is the true salvation of the soul. If we get lost in the maze of this physical existence and partake in war, violence, killing innocent animals, violating other humans for their physical pleasures ... we are then far from any possibility of initiation. Because of the super free will, we have to work for everything, including physical maintaining, the ascension of the spirit/soul. Money, somebody can hand it over to you ... but soul food you have to earn. Why are thoughtless people fighting to establish their so-called faith by killing and causing havoc? They cannot control themselves. It is easy to control others. animals, humans, etc., for their sins. The primal parents ... what is their sin? Has humanity stopped sinning? They are so stuck in this. Only with knowledge of the divine and spirit/soul, and the work every human should do in order to ascend to the Heavenly Kingdom to inherit the portion we would have earned with our living. We can manipulate everything in the physical by lying, cheating, being clever, eloquent speech, loud screaming, etc.—these all belong to the dark forces. The divine is pure love, pure light, etc. Taste and see the Lord is good. Yes, we can taste this without the use of tongues. We can only taste with the heart. Once one tastes that, one will never be the same. If anybody has had enough of me, let me know. I have no intention of sending these messages to such a person. You all desired that I share this, so I am. Because, while we are seemingly separate, in the divine sense we are one in all.

Harmonious Petals

This letter, "TET," represents the good, spiritual journey of the soul through physical existence. Spiritual word for "TAV" [good] starts with "TET." Scriptures says, God saw everything was good. "TET" suggests goodness is hidden in our universe and in each of us. God is concealed within its creation. It is for us to go deep within and bring out what is hidden through our physical living ... and much more.

Harmonious Petals

Rose

This letter, "YUD," is the tiniest letter from all the twenty-two letters. It represents the cosmic messenger bringing movement and changing into creation. Traversing the entire universe in a micro- instant. The tiny dot bursts into a greater force. "YUD" begins the Hebrew word for "YETZIYRAH"—meaning marching forth. There is more to it, but I decline to write more … and much more.

Actions and Reactions

Somebody's trash can be someone else's treasure. Poison can cure major sickness ... or even cure another poison. Everything has an end and results in something contrary to what we imagine. Humans and all creation are composed of two kinds of DNA: Spiritual DNA and physical DNA, which is limited in scope as far as the family tree goes. What happens on the surface of the physical existence for us may have spiritual implications or spiritual importance. However, standing in the physical, to experience the calamity and suffering that is happening in the creation through humankind is beyond any spiritual being's desire to watch and go through. The question to ask is: Why do we have this "free will," and super ability to comprehend things? Are we so stuck in the physical that we do not even recognize that we are spirits/souls, and we are sojourners here. Do we have to pack our conduct here as soul memories and return from where we came? People speak of God. The Creator is infinite, and no finite can speak of God in its full potential.

If one says that we can say and understand the infinite, we pretend to make the infinite into a finite form, which is not the infinite. We have to be careful with what we think about the Creator. We can do one thing; we live under the domain of divine law and order, and we as spirits will have to comply with the law until perfection is achieved. It is a good thing to have a natural forest fire, all the old trees and weeds will burn off, and new fresh seedlings will sprout. But if somebody purposely lights a forest fire and burns the trees and all else, there are going to be consequences. We as humans must realize and recognize the role we are playing at any given moment. Whether we are contributing to peaceful coexistence of all that is, or division and destruction. Each spirit/soul will go through a furnace of purification whether we like it or not. In the physical, the trials, temptations, wants, cravings, desires, etc., these are all entrapping our souls, which will eventually make us realize we are trapped. When does the awareness of our doing good or evil come and when does the true soul journey begin? Spiritual DNA is connected to the Creator, to creation. No human on the face of the Earth or any force in hell or heaven can break spiritual DNA. We believe in appearances, that is why we see I and they, the small, big, rich, poor, etc. We must try to overcome all these divisions and work collectively, live for one another, live justly, simply. Do not shake the tree of life in general, to cause suffering. If I am wrong, your correction is requested.

This word, "KAF," represents intention, willpower, one pointedness, etc. "KAF" begins the letter for "KETTER" (Crown). The highest of the Ten Divine energy, etc. "KETTER" is the topmost Sephiroth in the tree of life from which began the spiritual creation and physical creation.

My Loving Friends: Sorry, I did not send this yesterday. Something within me did not nudge me to send it. So, I did not. Yes, we make great plans, hope for great things etc., this is the human story. This is Creation's story. We may accomplish many things, or we may accomplish nothing much in the physical sense. But one thing we must be sure of is that at all given times, we do our best.

LOVE, THE ULTIMATE REALITY

No matter what the outcome may be. This is for the ultimate reality, love. By the *love* for Creation, the father force created everything, and all continue to exist through this mighty love, which animates all things. Let no one take this love lightly ... it is in the absence of true love that Earthly inhabitants suffer physical, emotional, and true spiritual suffering. We cannot take love and put it in a little container and close it, saying, "I have love and I share it with nobody." If it is not shared, it diminishes, and finally, it loses its lustre, like salt, which loses its saltiness.

Humans are the caretakers of all the inhabitants of the Earth. And we are the wellbeing of the Earth itself. Let no one take this responsibility lightly. "Love shared is multiplied," hence we all must love and multiply the Creator's love. If that happens, we all live in peace and harmony. It all starts with good relationships between men and women, then children love their parents, and they will love and respect everything outside of their homes. They must get their first training from their homes. A failed home environment leads to failed villages, failed nations. In turn, all creation is in turmoil. Don't take my word for it. Open your eyes and see: People forgot to love, and they worshiped lust, so there is great suffering.

Jesus said, "Love one another as I have Loved you." If we can realize the meaning of that, we will do what we were created to do.

Our failure to do what was placed in us, and then everything becomes a mere outward expression. Through love for all, we can testify to the Lord and all its attributes. This is the Law of Creation. This is the ultimate reality, and this is the journey of the soul.

Harmonious Petals

This letter, "LAMED," represents our desire for learning and teaching from the heart about spiritual knowledge and much more.

Religions

"MEM" represents water, also intuitive knowledge. The word stands for angels and celestial dream. "MEM" also signifies the length of time necessary for a cycle to reach fruition.

To perfect Judaism, Christianity came. To perfect Christianity, Islam came. From the above faiths, many sub-branches emerged.

Everybody proclaims , "We got it and ours is the only way." We have to think, what is the way and where does it lead? From the results, one can realize where all these lead to. Is the world better off now than it was two thousand years ago? Observe what the Mystics write about perfection, religions, etc. We have achieved so much progress in science and technology, but what has happened to our soul and spiritual evolution? In the soul sense, are we better off? Or are we going down the tubes?

We will hit rock bottom and from there, we will wake up and listen to the call of the divine. But before that, so much pain, sorrow, suffering of all sorts among humans at each other's hands and for all other creatures. This is what will happen unless and until we recognize our potential or know God's love and take responsibility and transform from within and manifest our transformation in the collective for the wellbeing of all and the harmonious existence of all in the Blessed Earth. We continue to crucify the love (Christ). When we allow others and other beings to bleed emotionally or otherwise physically, we allow Christ to Bleed.

We must take control of our animalistic nature and replace it with "God's" love and nature or there won't be any peace in creation. People and nations will make war and kill each other. Also, billions upon billions of innocent animals will suffer abuse and be killed. All that most of us are doing is paying lip service to the Good/GOD. We must recognize the fact that we have to take control of our lower nature: Lust, gluttony, aggression, selfishness, jealousy, and all other vile tendencies that cause us to destroy one another and Creation. Humans are made with two natures: "God" nature and animal nature. When humans act from within our animal nature, we are far worse than any other animal due to our high intellect. So, we twist everything in nature to feed the flesh, attain wealth, and give to our self-centred nature. I am not accusing anybody. I am, too, a part of this calamity. If we have to have salvation for our spirit/soul, we have to desire it sincerely and work towards it. Then light will show the way. Tragedies and suffering are happening to humans by the hands of humans and the rest of all creation suffers, too. Everybody is trying to do good, yet one doing good is going to hurt other beings, no matter whether its humans or animals. We have to really recognize what exactly is happening with us about our doing good. Why, then, is there so much division, why so much suffering?

This Hebrew letter, "Nun," symbolizes faith and its vibrancy in spiritual life and more.

Trials

In the physical sense, we study, memorize, write and take exams, and pass or take whatever kinds of tests. We are done with tests and are ready to start our careers. However, in the spiritual sense, if one understood anything such as the Creator—creation, spirit, soul—how all things work, what is our purpose? Where we are going? Whether there is a life after death—if one understands such things then, one will automatically live by it and with it to make sure we live and prepare our soul journey so that we will minimize the trials of the soul after the physical existence. If one knows there is a great mountain called Mount Everest and we have the map, we study thoroughly how to reach it, the highways, byways, and dangers we may face in order to reach the top. It is far simpler to hike Mount Everest; compared to climbing the Mountain of the Lord. It takes absolute self-discipline and physical restraint to prevent many pitfalls arising due to physical wants, desires, cravings, etc. The one who understands things for what they are will do them lovingly. All faiths (religions) in the world say we are in the physical world for a period of time, we get old, worn out, and then our souls depart from the physical.

But we are too busy talking of faith and physical wants and we are slaves to its power. All things work in the physical, by physical laws, and all things work in the spiritual by the spiritual laws. When Jesus was on Earth, He saw the so-called spiritual people who talked about high spiritual things, God, etc. He called them white-washed tombs. You hold the keys to the kingdom, yet you do not enter, and you do not allow others to enter. We must walk the talk , not the other way around. We must be caring, kind towards all beings and experience others suffering. We all try our best to satisfy our bodily desires at all costs. If animals need to be killed, or somebody has to suffer physically or emotionally, so be it. This attitude will definitely have its own reaping. If one says, "I understand," then practice it. In the absence of true practice, we are betraying the very essence—God within, God is love. If I am wrong, I invite you to correct me. We all must be instruments of change in accordance with the Bread of Life that comes down from Heaven! Love and Wisdom.

Letter SAMECH, this is a closed letter which signifies divine protection in our daily life. Everything we experience is illuminated by the "SAMECH." Its radiance and presence connote the hidden realms around us. It also means, divine presence is in the heart of all creation and more.

Analogy of the Frog

The collective is like a frog in a well. That frog only knows the well: he does not know there is a stream, a lake, a sea, an ocean. Even if you try to tell the frog there is an ocean out there, he will not believe you. This is how humans have existed, are existing. It is indeed a sad story.

Our body is like the well. And in the well dwells the spirit. The spark of the mighty ocean of universal love/light/spirit. I am only a tiny drop. Still, once I leave the well, I become part of that mighty ocean of love/light. It is not going to be a trip directly from well to ocean for the soul. There is sowing and reaping. The soul does not come on the Earth in the physical sense, to die for the flesh; rather it comes to do some sowing and reaping—growing, etc . Magic will not work. Our upbringing and faith, all must help us to abstain from doing a lot of glamour, which binds the spirit/soul to the physical. The physical is not our permanent dwelling. As Yeshua said, "I am in the world ... but not of the world." We have to understand what that means. Establishments do not insist on or teach the importance of transformation. No organization can establish the order of heavens/journey for the soul, the destiny of the soul, but the indwelling spirit only. We have to earn our dwelling places. We have to acknowledge all moving things, the Earth, and all that is in it. Everything has a place in the universe before the Creator. If we think chiefly of the pleasures of the body by killing animals to eat, violating others, making war, committing acts of violence, know that these are born out of selfishness, self-power, and ignorance of the spirit/ soul. In the Old Testament, Genesis Chapter

One, verses twenty-one and twenty-two, etc. God says, "I gave to man, the beasts and the birds of the air, what is grown on the tree and earth." Go read it if you want. Then comes the flood, people can eat all moving things, except pigs—clean, unclean. Does one honestly think, God changes his mind according to the whims of man? This is slavery.

Humans are attached to our physical pleasures of eating, mating, etc. That is, the physically oriented living. God—they spend ages talking about God and their actions prove otherwise. God was, is, and will be without our talking about God. We all have our beings in God. We have to realize that. All things have their being in God. So, we must think collectively, live and have our living in the collective sense. We must do our best to walk the path, not talk. How powerfully people speak of God. No one will never get to know God fully, because God is infinite. If I am wrong, correction is requested. I am truly angry at the suffering of humans, children, animals, and the destruction of the Earth. The self-righteousness of humans!

Letter AYIN, This letter symbolizes the qualities for perception and insight. It begins the Hebrew word for "Eyes." True discernment, "AYIN" also represent the interconnectedness of all things. "AYIN" starts the Hebrew word for tree. In Kabbalah, every form in the universe, including ourselves is regarded as part of the great "tree of life," filled with ineffable radiance of God and more.

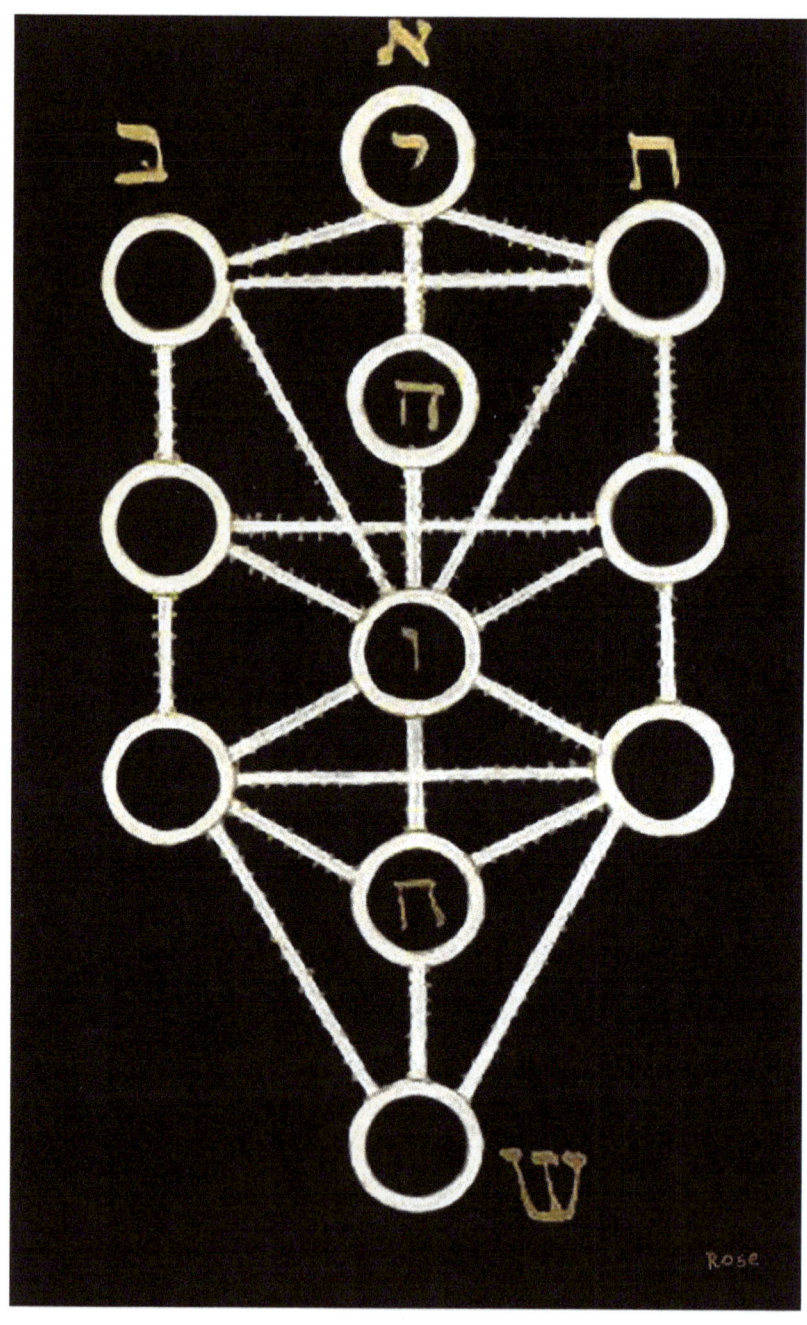

To See with Soul's Eye

This Hebrew letter, "PEI," represents the power of human speech. Saints and Sages believe that when people speak, visible and invisible energy is released (light or dark energy depending on what we speak from the heart). It is a double letter representing negative and positive. For example, if one insults somebody in public or private to show off one's ego-centered nature—it is equal to murder and much more.

If we can open our eyes of the Soul and see each being, we will see something so different from the physical. But we are not trained to see the soul of a person. We see the wrappings and make certain decisions and most of the time, it proves to be disastrous, and that decision may be the heaviest cross we are forced to carry.

Well, everything on the Earth is to expiate our spirit/soul. Blessed are those who see the soul and make decisions and live. Blessings in disguise. While I was writing, I felt something, so I had to stop. What I want to say about the trees ... without trees and plants, there wouldn't be life. Without the sun, there wouldn't be any greenery. Without water, there won't be any life either. This is purely natural and understood by science/biology, sociology, etc. So, one has to realize the interconnectedness of all. So, the responsibility lies with every one of us to maintain and keep balance with all creation. We cannot tip the scale of balance either way. We are doing it with overpopulation, and our destruction of everything. Nobody wants to think or hear about anything like this. Because it doesn't fit into their concept of living. That is all for now. I am not saying anything to fill the pocket of my ego or anything. I am just concerned.

Learn to Climb the Mountain

Dear friends in faith and travelers of the path: I did not send the writing yesterday because sometimes I feel it is pointless and it does not serve any purposes to anyone... Writing and reading sometimes feel pointless and most of us read tons of books. If one reads a book and if there is some wisdom imparted for our soul progression, then we must apply that and live our lives accordingly. In the absence of an application, it is intellectual gymnastics, and it is only good for debate. But talking about God and the path will not take anyone to God, but if one uses the map and starts to walk towards the mountain, surely, we will reach the mountaintop sometime in our long and arduous journey of the soul. Today's writing is very important because I added two people who are Catholic. Saying of Saints are solely for Catholics. It does not mean that others do not have saints. We are all on the way to sainthood, some are just thinking of starting their journey, some have started their journey, some are midway, and some started it and went back to the comfort of the old way of life. But it will happen. Eternity has eternity available to all its Creation. For us, as humans, because of our free will and the ability to comprehend, we have to work to achieve it. All the saints in Catholicism and all religions have the light of God, which was earlier covered with worldly things, but the power love and light ignited in their hearts and they have become empathetic; they have become the friends of the Creator and creation. They abstain from killing any living beings. They recognize the life force animating them and in all creatures.

Harmonious Petals

Rose

This letter, "TZADI," represents the Hebrew word for "Righteous." One who is on the highest level of righteousness can only convey the true perception of the divine in all its radiance. According to the sage Isaac Luria, God created the cosmos through a process known as Tzimtzum using the letter "TZADI." The Hebrew terms refer to withdrawal or contraction of the divine and much more...

They will never ever worship the fleshly desires of lust, sex, eating. They eat to live. They do not need much of anything. They eat to survive. The glamour of this physical state is their burden. They are here and they go through it as an expiation. Generally, they will face lots of trials and persecution because of their stand. Finally, they die, then we will realize who they were and declare them saints. The saints do not care whether we declare them saints or not. They are down to earth and such things are beneath them. Now what we do, we pray to them: "Help me, help...," and in that way, we are the ones who try to eat crumbs while heaven is waiting with a feast of glory and beauty of the soul journey. We have to make the same journey, do what the saints did to reach the place where they are.

The saints do not make displays to prove their faith. They know who they are. Jesus says, "When you want to pray, go into your room, close the door and pray in secret, the Father sees you and will reward you."

"Where one or two gathered in my name, there I will be among them." Church is one of those places, provided our heart is in tune with the light of Christ. Trials are many, so keep moving.

This Hebrew letter, "KUF," composed of "ZAYIN" and "RIESH." "KUF" referred to Kedusha, which means holiness. "KUF" also opens the Hebrew word "Korban," meaning Sacrifice. Which means to attend holiness and walk the spiritual path. We may have to sacrifice our many animal natures, especially when it hurts other beings or harms others. We must be willing to give up anything and everything in order to receive God's Light and much more.

Be honest in all that we do, say, "Remember, once we leave the Earth physically, the book of life will open before us, and we will see all we have written during our physical journey." We may have to rewrite many things.

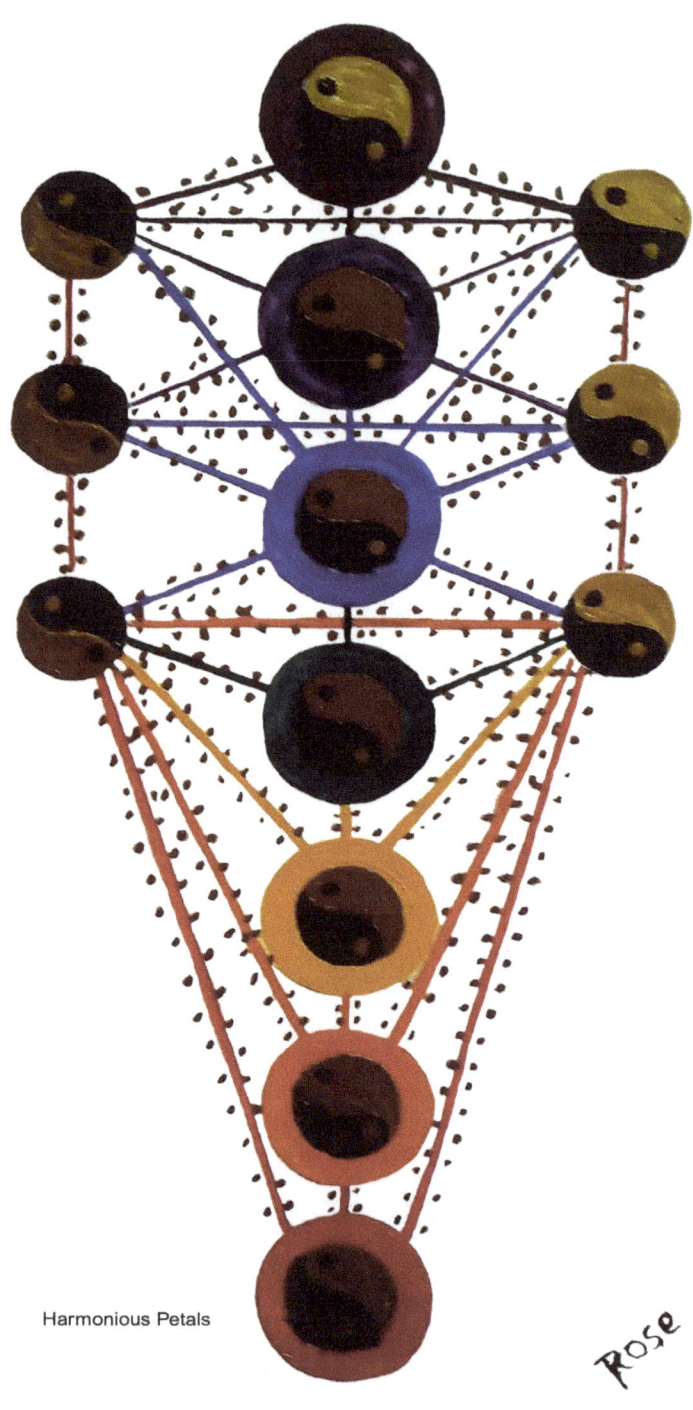

Harmonious Petals

Rose

Religious Beliefs

This is how life is, we fall and rise again like little babies. If anybody has other things to say or does not want to receive any more, please let me know. I am only sharing my awareness with you. We have met in this lifetime talking about spirituality, etc. I am not putting anything down anyone's throat. Why we humans fractured the whole creation with our beliefs, religions, non-religions. Beliefs about God. Above all, we believe we are such superior beings; the rest of Creation is for our pleasures, and the other human next to us.

Look at the rising sun, the magnificent sun. Who is behind the sun? Has anyone thought about it? Maybe a few. The sun is the mighty light, which shines within the hearts of all beings. The physical sun shines on all creation. What we have done to the precious creations. What a calamity befalls on all creation by way of humans. Deception and ignorance are the masters ruling humanity. We must practice God's love. The way humanity is reproducing, the time will come that the Earth won't be capable of producing enough food for all. Animals are increasingly infested with toxins that cause heavy sickness to animals and humans. We have trashed the procreative power, sent it to the gutter. There is no virtue in it. Marriage, divorces, countless relationships. We, most of us, have totally betrayed the divine plan. Our generation will die.

Harmonious Petals

This letter, "REISH," is associated with higher consciousness. It begins the word (in Hebrew) for Holy Spirit (Ruach Ha-Kadosh). The letter "REISH" reminds us of the Creator's intention that all humanity gains the knowledge of the divine and its ultimate purpose for creation—Union with the divine and much more...

What is going to be there for the following ones, and many generations after that? Did we and our religions plant the seeds of character, seeds of love, unity and so on for the following generation? Is there discipline among children, or just hormone storms? It is really sickening to observe all this. The Bible says, "What you have bound on the Earth is bound in Heaven." What kind of heaven will we, our soul, occupy after the physical? I know it is annoying to read what I write. We might think it was the job of founding fathers, parents, and religions to teach the people how to live and be caring toward all creation. They did not do that. We are all endowed with the ability to think and act in a way that will fulfill the divine law of nature and God. But religious establishments decided from the very beginning that if you do this, all will be okay. Heaven is wide open.

The Cosmos

If we take the cosmos, the visible and the invisible, our Earth and all its inhabitants are a tiny drop in the cosmic ocean. Can one imagine the immensity of the Creator? No, nobody can. What we little humans are doing here on the Earth, the fighting, killing, struggles, suffering of all kinds to each other and all others. Pause for a minute and consider what is going on. The majority of humans have faith, religions, and belief systems. Where did it all go wrong? This little ego mind, this is the problem. Humans are capable of achieving great things on both the physical level and spiritual level. Talking about God is not working. What will work? In my opinion, very probably, we, the humans, and all other inhabitants of the earth will physically perish from the deeds by human hands. It is just a matter of time: A thousand years or many thousands of years, and then it will take a long time for the earth to restore itself from all toxins we left behind. Then the Creator will, hopefully, send a new swamp of beings who will inhabit the Earth and hopefully, they will not kill each other, or any other inhabitants, then they will be living in peace and love will guide them.

Recently, one fellow reading the news said that in one country, once a year, they kill ten thousand dogs and before killing them they make them suffer to the maximum. They believe these dogs' suffering will enhance their sexuality. That is what they believe. It is very painful to listen and comprehend. Uncontrolled sexuality has caused all the overpopulation, selfishness, war, evils, etc. Nobody will talk about it or think about it.

There is nobody safe on the earth from crime and suffering. My friends, I have no intention of putting you all in an off mood. We are all in this. It would be good if as soon as possible, we speak and take action and guide our spirit/soul into the love of God as Christ expected us to do. That is where our spirit/soul dwelling place is. Everything else is just made up of stories to hold onto power and everything else the lower kingdom can offer. At the University in Minnesota (I believe) they started a program of educating students about the suffering of animals, encouraging vegan diets or vegetarian diets, etc. I was like any of you, I was forced by Christ to leave my old lifestyle behind and take a new road. It is not easy. Yeshua never said it was easy. No spiritual path is easy. We have to leave our comfort zones and follow the light. I do not know how long I will write, it is very difficult to move on with these kinds of burdens on one's soul. Jesus said, "If you gain everything in the world and lose your soul, what will be your profit? Nothing but sorrows."

Yesterday, a fellow came to my house holding the Bible asking me, "People say the Bible was written by men, what do you think?" I said, "All the good things in the Bible were written by men and were inspired by God." We had about twenty minutes of conversation and he left. God exists.

This Hebrew letter, "SHIN," begins with the word Shalom referred to wholeness complete. Also, the Hebrew word for Joy (SIMCHA) begins with SHIN. To better experience peacefulness and harmony, meditate on "SHIN" and much more.

All kinds of fundamentalism has frozen human spirits and souls into eternity per se. Somebody has invented and done all the jobs for us and you just do what they tell you to do. How long we will remain in infancy? Why did the Creator give us the ability to comprehend? To think?

Wisdom can be gained by ardent practice and understanding the potentiality of the soul ... yet we surrendered to some phantom.

Of course, we do not have time to pay attention to anything. We are so busy. I read somewhere saying we live as if we will never die and will die as if we never lived. Our intelligence is comparable to cosmic intelligence, but very imperfect. Of course, it has to be. To perfect it is our job. That is why we have this physical existence. Humankind is not working on our character/moral/ethical improvement; rather we are so busy with self-deception and self-glorification. What a misguided idea. Eating the right food, keeping peaceful, healthy psychic, noble thoughts, feelings, etc., these are the soul food. Above all, having gratitude for whatever we are, whatever we have, or don't have; all these are good things. Yet we do not apply this in our daily lives, and our relationships with the rest of the creation. So, what we have is an eternal mess. What is missing in us? We have all the necessary things and faculties. Are we using them for the development of the whole psyche? Not at all, every day we are crucifying the good and noble with our self-service.

Recently, I was talking to somebody about loving your neighbor—whether it is the person one lives with, next door, in the next village, or neighboring nations. Instead of loving, we declare war. We are all warring with each other, with nations. Of course, we all go to worship places and worship something outside. God is out there somewhere as if God demands our worship and praise. No! The Almighty Creator wishes that we all practice love, empathy, and compassion, but mostly love and that we travel the road that will take every part of creation towards the unification with the Creator in perfection. We must praise and worship the Creator with actions of love and charity. Words without practical application are noise and are an abomination to the loving God. We should stand above the Earth to look down on it and see what's going on. That is how the Creator views things. We are all chained from the very beginning with an unbroken link, which connects us to the lower physical kingdom, which belongs to the animal kingdom. And we forgot all our inheritance of the Heavenly Kingdom. Unless we realize we are bound by fleshly demands and need to break free, otherwise we will not inherit the Heavenly Kingdom. Creation is the divine in action. So, work towards purification, unification, perfection of all. Let all creation praise and worship the living God within. We are hurting all creatures, including us. Life is more than flesh. There is life after flesh for the souls.

Harmonious Petals

This letter, "TAV," is the last letter in the Hebrew alphabet. "TAV" symbolizing that our universe is marked by cycles in all things. The Ultimate end of the cycle is joyful, complete redemption. It begins the word "Tikkun," meaning to rectify—"Redeem." Also "TAV" begins the Hebrew word for Tefilla (Prayer), and much more...

Suppose you give the most precious gift, for example to a baby, for instance, the highest quality diamond ring? What will the baby do? They will just discard it and look for a plastic toy because a child does not understand the value of a diamond and he cannot do anything with it. So, he has no value for it.

This is a purely physical analogy. It is the same for spiritual growth. Young souls do not seek a deep understanding of divine existence. They are satisfied with a few rituals and prayers and their life goes on. They are baby souls, and they go to sleep with that. But one day, something arises and ignites in them, then the slumbering spirit will ignite and rise, and then it will be a whole new story. Then they are not satisfied with rituals, talk, and some surface activities. Once that happens, no one can stop them, they are on a mission, a journey, which will be guided by the divine force. They will try to connect with all Creation. They cannot stand the abuse of animals, bloodshed, war, children suffering, women suffering, injustice. All humans, have to honestly know the God force for ourselves. Let no one tell you about universal love. Initially, all is a preparation of the ground for the manifestation of the sprouting of the slumbering seed within. Once the seed has sprouted, it must be allowed to grow. If we do not act on the desire for the inner tree to grow, it will wither within and then one has to start all over again, as spirit/soul. No one can manipulate the law of God. We have learned to earn in the physical and also have to earn the spiritual food. If anybody has had enough of my words, let me know.

Harmonious Petals

The above picture is Four Letter Word for GOD… YUD HEY VAV HEY. ADONAI, TETRAGRAMMATON OR Ha Shem (The Name). The Ancient Jewish sages created these words and assigned their meanings. It is profound indeed.

For the love of Creation, the creative force brought forth all creation. That means Creation is the offspring of the Creator, who is the parent for all that is and that was and that will be. So, in the recess of each of us lays dormant the potential seed of God's love. To wake up and make it active is our job throughout our physical lives. That is how we can be one with Creator.

We are endowed with the ability to bring forth what is hidden beneath. It is as if we are a bird in a cage made of gold, but still, a cage is a cage. This is the story of the spirit and soul.

Our soul's cage is our physical existence, and it demands—wants— character, or lack of character.

Everyone has to bring forth what is within through desire for love, love in action, abstains from the millions of glittering forces of the physical. There is no quick fix. Love is the link that connects all creation to each other and the Creator. When we can practice love, this world and all its inhabitants will bleed less, all wounds will be healed, and there will be peace and joy for all.

I know, I am dreaming.

Think of Others

Everything humans do should be with others in mind. It does not mean we have to ignore ourselves. It is the self-serving selfishness that we have to look out for. If we do everything on the Earth for our soul's progress and purposes, the divine law will manifest, and we won't be able to escape. It may take time but surely it will come to pass.

Today, while taking a shower, a thought came to me about the Garden of Eden with the tree of the knowledge of good and evil, the snake, the main characters, Adam and Eve. Based on the story, Adam and Eve and all forms of life exist in the spiritual world. The snake (lust) represents the desire for union between the male and female. The tree of knowledge of good and evil. Their desire causes them to become physical human beings (God gave them a coat of skin that is the physical body as male and female, and they desired each other). Like a snake, we eat from the dust, crawl with our lowest nature for procreation or for pleasure. It continues and continues, there is no end to it. Finally, from this, the serpent rises up (representing wisdom intellect). It has power, it has the truth.

Once it rises within us, we try to climb the tree of knowledge, which is through the hollow column in the vertebrate and reaches the top of the head (the element Kundalini) rising. Even today, we use this process as a symbol for medicine. Now, what is rising? When we don't use or abuse sexual energy, it has creative power. Last time, I said there are countless entities working within our body. One should know, every time what comes out of a male's body in orgasm is millions of living organisms. If it is not wasted and with the diversion of love and knowledge, they will help us ascend spiritually. There are so many mysteries in creation. We do not know far more than we know. The Library of Alexandria was burned. That was a tragedy for all humanity. Also, Nalanda and Thakshashila. These places were seats of wisdom and invaders burnt it out. That was where we should have found all the wisdom—teachings of self-mastery, spirit/soul, etc. We humans tried to burn the tree of knowledge of good and evil (by which we will travel and get into knowledge of the tree of life. Knowledge is Power.

All those who cause suffering to other beings are called the agents of darkness. Darkness covers the Earth and suffering is the portion for all beings in physical existence. The forces that cause pain to other beings may come to realize the importance of seeking to benefit from the existence of all. There is a saying, "When you dig a grave for others, dig one for the digger as well."

We, humankind, have taken our eating habits to a whole new level. It is not new anymore. This behavior is probably as old as humans. There is hardly any sanity in the way we humans eat. Not all of us. We habitually eat to entertain; we eat when we are sad, happy, even if we are not hungry. We love to eat. One has to ask a question, why do we do what we do? Food is to nourish the body. By doing so, the God force, the soul and spirit living in the body serves their purpose. Who is happy? Who is learning? Who is suffering? It is the spirit within. So, we have to be aware: Whatever we do in the physical, positively or negatively, affects the spirit within. The bulk production of food, all these cheap restaurants like fast food, etc., are sickness-producing businesses. People pray for it. It is cheap.

It is a lot. They are not even aware of what they do. What are the results? Sickness? Anything done without awareness itself is falling into the power of darkness. Overproduction of humans, in turn, killing, eating, destroying the habitat of poor animals, the saga of misused life goes on. Nobody can say anything. It offends them. So, preachers and pastors are failing, parents are failing—they do not know anything. If one does not know anything, how can you give? In countless places in the world, there is overpopulation, suffering from lack of food, lack of everything. We humans are doing a great job! Of course, God knows everything, so we do not have to worry much.

Chapter 16

The Point

The point within the circle. This point we are talking about is beyond anyone's comprehension. What is that point, what is the depth of this point? Every point starts from this point: All spiritual universes, all physical universes. This is the self-existing, unborn state. This is the dwelling place; this is the secret chamber of the highest. There is a point in every living, moving, non-moving thing in creation. Just imagine, we as humans began our physical journey from this tiny point smaller than a pinhead, which, however, is visible. One can measure it and it contains a tiny center point of the spiritual center as well. You may dissect it into millions of pieces, but one will not find the spiritual point. But we are all struggling to get in touch with that point. We try any method; physically by using drugs, and other substances, and overdoing many physical pleasures. Reading a countless number of books. Still, we are where we started. No made-up story is going to open this channel to reach this point. Travel through the universe of physical existence or travel through the spiritual dimensions by virtue of love, then one may come to the periphery of this existence. If it is the will of the indweller, then one may enter this point of no return. It is like a tiny stream that starts from the top of the mountain, meanders through hills, valleys, plains, and forests, watering and nourishing and giving life to all on the way and finally reaches the ocean.

This is the Soul Journey, the destiny of Spirits, to reach the Point of NO Return.

Hence, my friends, be still, cause no one to stumble. Treat all creation with love. The giver of life of the spirit is the same in all. Let no theory misguide us. Stay firm and embrace love, honesty, compassion, empathy. Let all live and finish their journey according to the will of the absolute. Make your comments if you have suggestions. I write what flows through me. It may be nothing or something.

We have to ask this question: What is the psyche? What is its function and where did it come from? When I write, something goes through me, and I write. This is what I feel, subconscious-conscious, or soul stuff. It cannot be touched by the hand. It is mind-stuff. It is mind-being with the brain as the receptor, which receives.

When chemicals are produced in the brain and are imperfect or underproduced, our mind goes wacky, and we become out of control. We get crazy, violent, quiet, killers, and harmful to ourselves and others. We do all these because it affects our psyche negatively or positively. Psyche is the pathway created by the God force mind for its Creation. When people take substances, it destroys our brain cells and it affects our psyche, and we become paranoid, depressed, violent, and self-destructive and we cause others to suffer as well. When we love and do kind things, it affects our psyche positively and it will affect our spirit/soul positively.

Think for a moment, when I think of doing something wrong to others it affects my psyche and not the other person whom I had in mind to hurt. If I really do some harm, it affects my psyche seriously and it affects the other person as well. I allow that person to be deeply upset and something will start in his mind that is negative and it creates a vicious circle, unless this person is Christ or Buddha. If we are Christ, we would not be on the Earth physically.

Harmonious Petals

The above pictures… YUD HEY VAV HEY. People who read the Old Testament Realize that there is a saying, God created Man in his image. The Spirit of Man.

We are here to expiate the millions of shortcomings dating from the inception of our soul journey. Doctors treat mental patients with drugs, so his brain does not produce the harmful chemical which will, in turn, affect his psyche and in turn, he will be quiet. Yet this is only a mask. He needs something far deeper to heal his psyche. One has to know what caused him to be in this condition in the first place. Doctors are not equipped to study the psyche. It is a mysterious part of existence. When you kill an animal, torture or cause pain and suffering to a human or animal, emotionally or physically, it affects the human psyche of both animals and far more with humans, both the causer and the caused.

So, now we have what Christ said, "When you think of harming somebody, you have already done it." That means that thoughts affect the psyche. If one has loving thoughts towards others, it affects ours and theirs positively. Selfishness, egotism, pride, etc., affect the psyche very negatively. When you go to a war zone, a dark cloud of injured psyche hovers around those areas. Humility makes the psyche beautiful. The Bible says, Jesus washed the feet of His disciples, which means He is showing the importance of humility. My friends, we are in bondage from all these psychic dramas affecting Creation. Everything created has its psyche, no matter whether it is humans, animals, Earth or stars, or plants. Of course, it varies in many ways. See, the sages and Masters knew all this. Religions and establishments do not know or do not teach this. Socrates said, "Know thyself." What this means is that we have to know all aspects of creation/ us and not invade other's psyche.

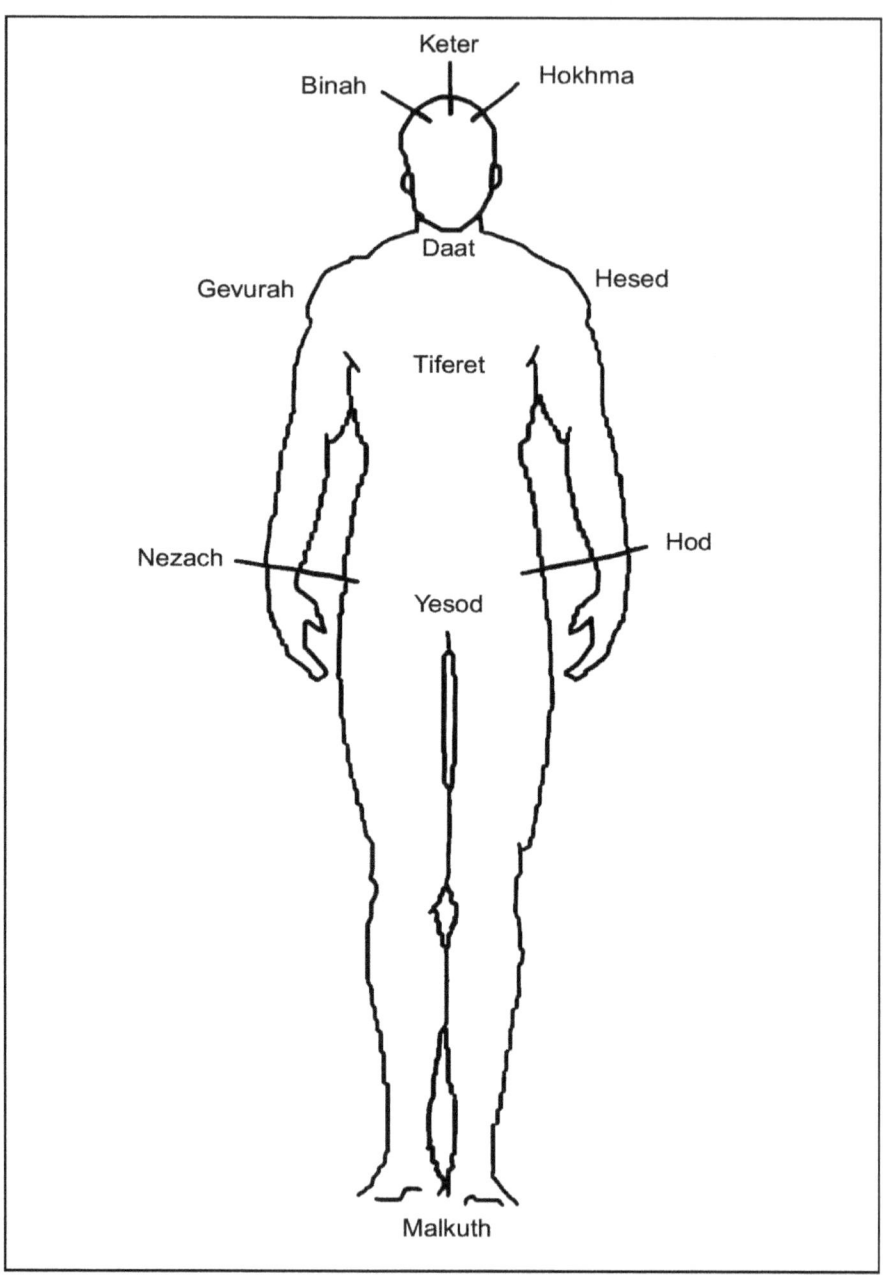

The Spirit of Man. There is a saying, God made man its image. This image represents all the divine qualities descending through many dimensions and born on the Earth as human.

If we do, it has a sowing and reaping effect. That is why Jesus said, "Before you partake of my supper, if you have a problem with your brother, go and resolve it." This will dissolve and free you from psychic darkness. Your psyche will then be clear of impurity. Did the church father tell us anything? We need solid food to grow. Knowledge of God comes through life and just living in accordance with the creative law of love. What I am writing is nothing or something important to take on things. If you read it and forget it, you are not involved in this understanding. So, I would appreciate your comments.

The Scriptures we read, or anything, we must put into practice in our daily lives to enhance our psyche and the force around us. Pastors and preachers make noise, they are not allowing each one to grow spiritually. Jesus said, "When you are a baby, you were fed by mothers, or by spoon." When you grow up you must prepare your own food. This is the desire to grow spiritually and to know oneself. Your whole self. The universal self. If you seek God, seek wisdom, and share love, grow. That which glitters will pass away with physical death. Then psyche/soul memory will follow us to the afterlife. My fellow sisters and brothers and children, read this. Seek God in its beauty, wonder, awe with love, empathy, selflessness. Do not miss the opportunities presented while we are alive.

In my vision, I was asked to climb a very tall white wall. There was nothing to hold onto and to climb. But I did climb in my vision and on completing the wall, there comes down from high the ladder, it is suspended in mid-air and again, I was asked climb that ladder … Oh, my God, how it is possible, and I got up. This is the description of the ladder.

All the Best

Rose

Human Potentialities

I would like to write about human potential—possibilities. Here, I compare with what Jesus said in the Bible. There was a rich man who handed over his garden/vineyard to some hired hands (employees) and went for a long trip. Then, sent his son to see what was going on and to take charge of his property. For many years, the owner did not return to take charge of his property, the employees thought, "This is the owner's son. Let us kill him and the property will be ours." So, they did and were having a good time, and then the actual owner came and destroyed the evil caretakers and took over the property.

The Earth is our garden given to us by the Creator. We are the caretakers of this garden. What we are doing to it, subduing all, destroying all and causing pain and suffering to all inhabitants of the Earth, which is in our hands. We have lost all sense of purpose and are totally immersed in the five senses of the flesh. We live for it, work for it, and kill for it. Our souls and spirits are in shock and in an awful state. Nobody is listening to its wants, purpose. On top of it, they are completely oblivious to any and all parts of the divine calling. Participating in rituals, saying a few prayers and being content with it, while the Earth and all its inhabitants are going through immense suffering due to our behavior caught up with the five senses. Nobody has any time to listen to the inner calling. One is in the Garden, and it is filled with multicolored lives. All are important in their own right. Do we give damn about it? All that we care about is to look down on one another, subdue, kill, eat, mate. Surely, when we meet with the owner of the garden, we will have to account for it.

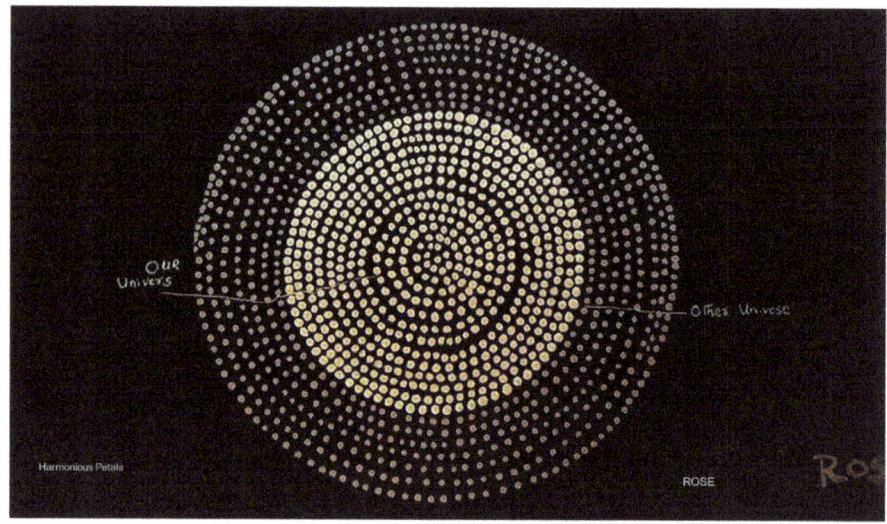

Universes

I saw this vision. Everything was filled with golden bright lights in the center and little faded lights outside. The stars were all twinkling. I perceived the voice saying, "The bright lights are Our Universe and the faded is another Universe." I have nothing to say about it further. I always see luminaries in the space. One thing I must say that, No One can comprehend the Magnitude and Immensity of Physical and Spiritual existence. And the Power of the Creator.

I am writing about hope. It is an interesting subject. It is a wonderful thing, which drives humans to the depth of all. Hope and faith must be followed by sincere action. Desire to take the journey towards achieving the things hoped for. We hope God will set all things right. Truly, what is the purpose of our existence? The majority of us work very hard to make money and acquire riches, and make children, care for them, don't care for them, spoil them, abandon them, or whatever.

This all remains on the surface and is physical only. We are spiritual beings. We are the indwelling place of the infinite. Are we able to stop for a minute and think? It seldom happens. We have to expand our awareness beyond our fleshly needs. We have to think: One Creator, one creation. Think and work collectively for the wellbeing of all. We must be sensitive towards all life forms. We are making hopelessness out of humanity and are bringing that to all other inhabitants of the Earth as well. We all are God's love made visible and put into action. We must live and act in such a way that we are participating in the continuum of all that is through creation. We must collectively work for peace and tranquility in creation. Then selfishness, crime and evil will have no place in creation. Humans have misused and abused our God-given talent and slain our divine presence in us and in all by overpopulation and indulgence of the five senses.

Truth and Prana

What is the truth? We claim we have it and try to impose it on others. But what we claim we have is handed down by others of the past. So, until today and until tomorrow and millions of years to come, we will be battling to establish the truth. First of all, we have to battle for truth. The truth, the God force is ever present, ever flowing, ever living in its tangibility and multiversity. This is Creator and creation. We have to ask ourselves why and what we are trying to establish by fighting. Truth must be discovered by every human by connecting with its source within and realize that source is within all. Love, respect it, care for it and allow it to have its being in the cosmic vibration of all. Stop killing, abusing. Imagine, the Earth is our worship place, and the worshipers are all the living beings, then who will have time to fight, kill, and abuse other beings, or go to war, destroy other nations. No, we humans have lost every connection in its true sense and are enslaving ourselves with lower senses and what we are doing to others. The result is bloodbaths, discord, and disharmony. We kill the messengers. Blessed are the peacemakers. Jesus said, "How many people are trying to make peace even with their little world?" Very few. So, where do we go from here? It is for all humans to think and act to keep creation going. Renounce the untrue. Experience truth, love, and connectedness with all creation. Live a life where there is no desire to harm any other being mentally or physically. We will experience truth. We are carried away by our ego, longing for glory, which is an actor playing a role to take the soul away from the truth. God seeks our hearts, allow that to happen. God seeks and dwells in the hearts of all.

I write about harmony. Harmony is becoming an illusion for most humans and in turn, with the animal kingdoms as well. I am not making this up. If this precious gift was understood and practiced with sensitivity, what would have been our world today? The infinite creator through its love of creation created the infinite world. What are we doing to bring about harmony?

Harmonious Creation

Since I know how to write Hebrew letters and I created the Circles [Four Worlds], and I believe in unity and oneness with all creation, with this desire in my heart I created this circle of creation in using current existing religious symbols. I meant to offend nobody. That's my prayer.

The Force, the deathless force, brought forth creation and order. Humans brought disorder and chaos to the Earth. We as souls will be subject to immutable law. That, too, is the great law of God. Darkness must be swallowed by the light. Until that happens for all creatures, including humans, sowing and reaping will continue for the spirit/soul. To bring about change in the world, we have to stop for a moment and think about what we are doing with our blessed gift of birth and life. Are we participating in the peaceful co-existence or participating in anarchy for all God's creation?

We all—who have some sense of goodwill—will fulfill something with our lives. We are and we will stay put how we are, what we do, how we conduct our life on earth and everything else that goes with it. If we do not practice the love connection of the creator, children will suffer, animals will suffer, women will suffer, creation will suffer. God has given us this physical body, it is not for suffering by abuse and excesses, but to use the physical body to navigate through physical existence, to learn, accept what is good for the soul, reject what is hindering the soul ascension, love, lend a hand to other beings, be kind, care for the mind and body of all. The physical bodies of all are not the object for the pleasure of eating, or for the abuse by another human. This is the sacred temple/the dwelling place of the divine Spirit/the Christ spirit.

Let us all work together, shed evil, accept the light of Christ and let the light shine within and outside and let all creation praise and give thanks for the gift of life. If anybody participates in hindering other forms of life, be it of humans or otherwise, in any form either mentally, emotionally, or physically, our soul will be liable. I know, I am wasting my time. So be it. My God within me nudges me to write, hence I write, I know it falls by the wayside. Some do read, think, some read and there is no thinking. We are busy.

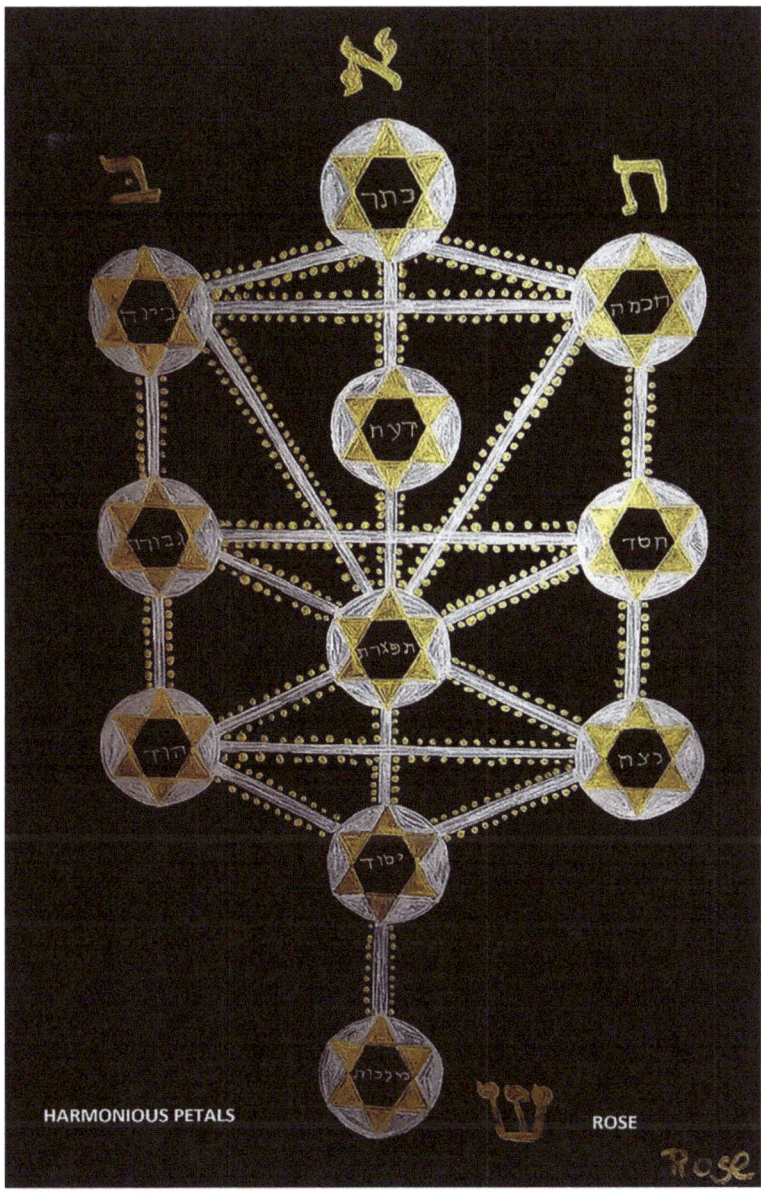

HARMONIOUS PETALS

ROSE

This is a little information about the Tree of Life. I would like to write something about the tree of life, in turn the Kabbalah. The ancient divinely inspired sages created this tree of life as an analogy for the spirit of life, descending through the tree of life. From the divine existence, the spirits descend through many invisible worlds and finally enter the store house of the soul where the spirits get the soul and all its attributes and enter the physical world (First, it enters the womb and then finally manifest as a human being).

I will talk about the Prana (the breath of life). Christians and Jews have this creation story. God formed the man from the clay and breathed into his nostrils and he became a living being. When we stop breathing for more than a few minutes or so, then we are pronounced dead. Through God's Breath, it imparted his law through to its creation as well. If one notices in Genesis Chapter One it says, "I give to man the beasts and fowls of the air, what is grown on the tree and what is gown on the earth." See, the plant does not breathe oxygen, rather it breathes out oxygen for moving beings, including us. It does not mean we can destroy what is grown on the earth thoughtlessly. We have this tremendous ability to comprehend, feel sense, experience, etc. We must put all those faculties into use while living. We are God's law unto ourselves. When we kill humans or animals, we are taking the breath away from the creature. Everything has a time to live and to leave. All must fulfil their purpose. Interfering with any natural function is wrong. Birth control, abortion, etc., are all problems but self-restraint for the love of God, that's not a problem. The ancient yogis and all Mystics understood this, they live among us, but they live far away from this mundane life of ours. Why? Because they open the channel of God directly and they are satisfied with the love connection with God. They will not permit the suffering of any humans or animals. They are one with law and lord. Practice, if possible. Have a blessed day.

Hardships

Hardships are unavoidable for all physical creatures. Knowingly or unknowingly, hardships are always there to show us the way. That is why Jeshuva says, do not cause others to stumble and so many other advice given to people. Hindus believe if they take a dip in the Ganges, their sins will be forgiven, and they will achieve Nirvana (Heaven). Islam believes every Muslim should visit Mecca and they are guaranteed to go to heaven. Others have other beliefs. If one allows other brothers, sisters, or others of God's creation to bleed and suffer and if I believe in something and do nothing about the atrocities towards fellow creatures or other beings, how can it be possible? We justify suffering by saying it is good for the soul, maybe. We have to practice not causing suffering to others. If someone falls or gets some disease and suffers, if that situation can be taken into a kind of purgation, the sufferer may find comfort in the suffering. Homes are being devastated, children are ruined, mental, emotional, and physical suffering is the case for the majority of humans. Children are born randomly out of ignorance of people. Before this civilization existed, other civilizations existed; for us, they are mythology. Some were very peaceful; others were barbaric and destroyed those who were peaceful. We do not believe there were other civilizations before us, twenty thousand years from now, we will also be mythology for the then existing civilization. They will find remnants of one or more charred civilizations. We are absolutely not doing well in the eyes of the Creator. We do not need a judge, just sit silently and be the good judge for ourselves and see ourselves for who we are by the power of truth. Are we instrumental for others' suffering? Have we caused others to stumble through our action or inaction? How much pain and suffering have we caused to other beings including human brothers, sisters, husbands, wives, children, animals? If God were to physically stand before us and see us for who we are, where we stand, and what then? That is why Jesus said, "If anyone of you is free of sin, cast the first stone towards the woman caught in adultery."

What about animals? What crime they have done to us so that we cause them to suffer? Nations are uprooted and brought to dust. The amount of suffering is inconceivable. Whoever is alive, instead of playing noble games, do what is right to avoid causing suffering whether it is of children, husbands, wives, mothers, fathers, nations, etc. We must always do our part fairly. We all make mistakes, but one who continues to live in falsehood is not right. We must act like responsible humans to all other humans. The divine is present everywhere so rejoice and be glad and humble. This is the divine calling. Teshuva. Have a great journey.

Harmonious Petals

The Tree of life…is mentioned in the Upanishads, the oldest spiritual practice in human history. People may differ in their opinions. My purpose is not to argue but to get some glimpse of what the tree of life is and how it applies to our spiritual journey as spirits/souls. The Sages say, "Roots of the tree of life is established in the primordial existence."

The tree of life is the microcosmic expression of the macrocosm, which nobody has any access to. Macrocosm is the self-existing phenomenon, the infinite God force; from its desire, the physical world came into being. This tree of life contains all spiritual worlds and physical creation, which means all solar systems, galaxies, planets, Earth and all its inhabitants. nothing is excluded. Wonderful indeed.

Above this tree of life, there are circles within the circles. In the center of the circle, there is a dark space representing AIN. Which is the unknowable, the self-existing God force. The blue circle represents the impregnation of fullness of creation that is called AINSOF. The outer circle represents the manifestation of fullness of creation and that is called The Ain Sof Aur and by showing the lightening flash, the fullness of creation and entering the tree of life. The single circle is called Sephirah. Each Sephirah represents a particular character. For example, wisdom on one side, understanding on the other side, etc. This is nature; the spirits take as they descend towards physical existence. Upon incarnating on the Earth, spirits/souls learn to fulfill its tasks, learning, mastering it and then the spirits take their ascension back to the God force. It may take many hundreds of soul times as physical beings before it gets perfected. If you are interested, you can buy a book or go to the internet to get a full understanding of it. There is no religious dogma involved in it. True seekers of light go through this. A Mystic, a Sage, a good human being will automatically practice all these. Only Kabbalah (the tree of life gives us the perspective). Every time, we do something angry or lovingly, we can look into the tree and know, from where we are functioning and from which place of the tree of life. If you notice, you will see, there is an expression of spiraling motion. As one should know, in the universe, there is nothing static.

This tree of life is the path of the mystic. The spiritual journey for all humans. Have a safe journey through the tree of life.

I decided to do this because I see where humanity, the rest of the creation, and Mother Earth is heading towards. Indeed, it is heading towards major destruction and suffering of all inhabitants by humans and humanity along with the rest.

We are living thoughtlessly, no thought of the future generations. No thought of the depletion of resources and earth becoming barren due to deforestation, overpopulation, abuse of the animal kingdom. We are not thinking about anybody else. Some of us believe in the soul/spirit, a formless beyond the existence of space and time. For such people, it is painful to watch how we are conducting our business.

We are infringing on each other's peace, protection, other life forms, etc. If we do not take a different course, seeking less of ours and more of common wealth and wellbeing of all, we will and our future generation will pay dearly.

I write about double agents, money, etc. Double agents, double standards will do poorly in the long run. It projects no character of the high human standards. Double agents cause havoc for all concerned. In the end, having such a character will swallow the person. Shame will be their portion. Money, we gave value to money a very long time ago. Now, money is virtually the ruler of humanity.

Without money, we seemingly cannot move one second. To get money, we choose to do anything.

Money is a good ally when used with restraint and respect. When we use money to get power, enslave other beings, gain votes, conquer others/nations, it is a fire and it burns. We humans must train this power to be our best friend who will serve us. This power has put humanity into a spin. We are reeling from its power.

We have to serve this master with force. If we do not do it, we are the castaway. People of God learn to have balance in all things, and not using money for their power or to gain reputation.

Marriage

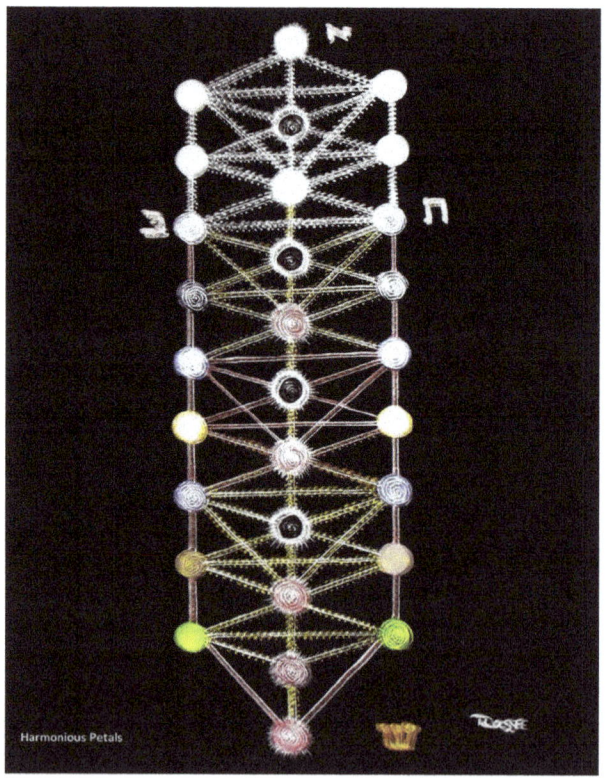

This image of the Trees is called the extended Tree of Life. The ancient Sages say, "Each world has its own tree. So, this tree is a combination of all four worlds. This tree represents each world with this one diagram."

In physical creation, there are two aspects played out to bring forth creation. It is from the Holy Union of the two aspects that the world comes to exist. In the physical, there is one thing we know: men and women. Marriage between a man and a woman is truly a holy sacrament and from this union of the two comes forth a spark of the great parents manifested as a living being. We call it a child.

So likewise, the whole creation in its order and qualities of its kind. This holy sacrament for the majority of humans remains holy during the ceremony yet even that is doubtful.

Humans created money and gave it power and it is our Pharaoh, an evil king. Animals do not have money. They still live. Similarly, sex has been made into an Almighty Pharaoh by which great hell comes to life on the earth and beyond. See, we have put aside our preconceived ideas and desire to know all and meditate. Abstain from many powers that this physical life can offer. We know something, and by that something, we may know more as time goes by. We have conditioned mind, body and thinking for some acts. Hence our scope of knowledge is limited. We have to take off the mask that we are wearing, recognize our blindness, our ignorance and desire to know divine parents and its attributes.

Finally, humankind created hellish life from sex, and any man or woman may abuse this power, enslave this power for uses other than for procreation and their souls are liable to suffer the effect of this. Sex slavery, rape, prostitution, violence against women, those who do this are serving the evil king? Humanity lost all sense of the holiness about marriage, sex, procreation. Everybody is a victim of this. There is no divinity at all. Hence, we have chaos, crime, and killing. Animals are produced recklessly to be killed, abused, and all life forms suffer. Animals also create their children the same way we create babies. Animals seldom take birth control, they procreate and have their babies, care for them, and teach how to fend for life. We, as superior humans, what are we doing? What have we done with our life purpose?

I am part of the universe, and the universe is part of me. We all have a long way to go. But we have to take our first steps. I am no exception. But I have understood many things during my journey and life. I only wish that we would act like humans as our heavenly parents intended for each one of us in the divine plan. Who can understand the universe in its full scope? No one! So, debating about God is a futile endeavor. All we can do is to love each other and the rest of the creation, shed evil and allow darkness to be dispelled by the power of heavenly light.

Today I write about Human Justice and Divine Justice.

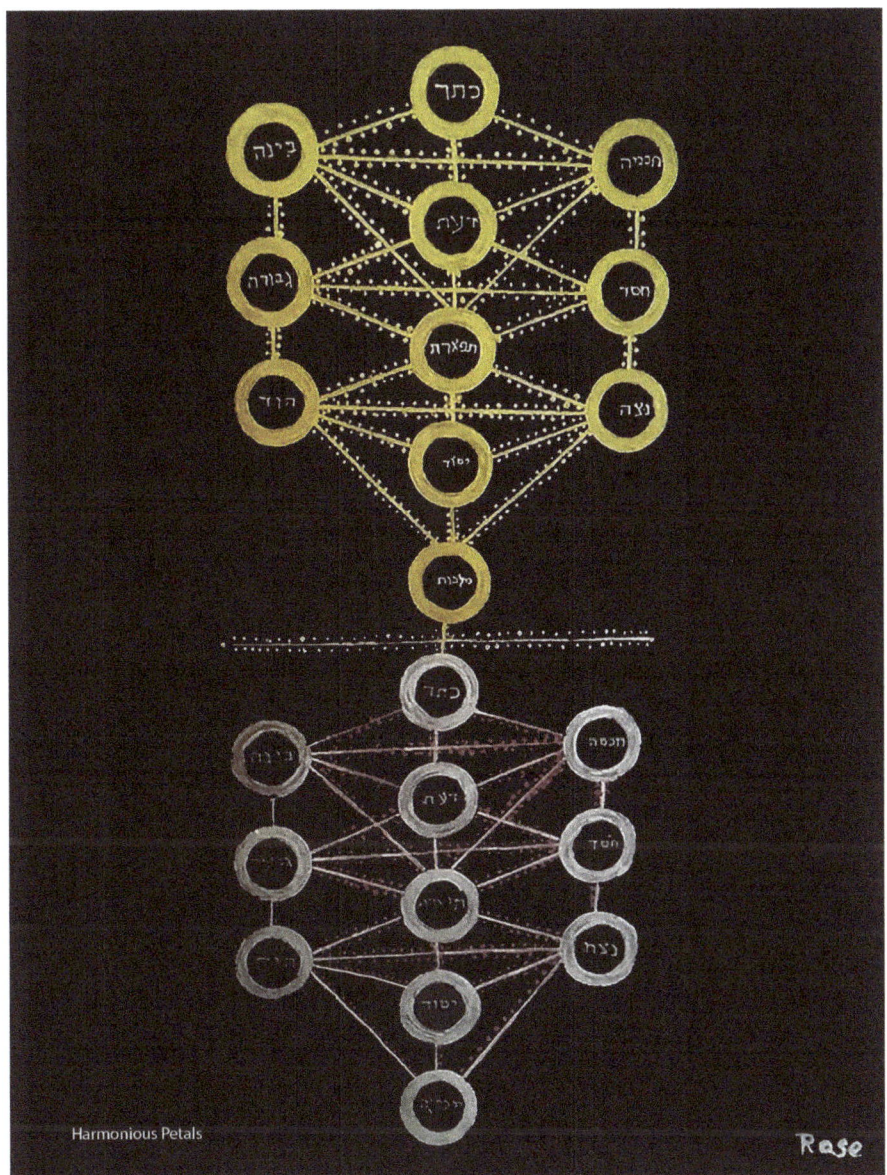

Upper Tree of Life

The first top of the tree represents the creation of spiritual and physical world ending at Malkuth. That is to say, the spirit/soul descends through the tree of life going through many dimensions and manifests on the physical earth. And here we are, spirit/soul in the body experiencing physical existence.

This is the school where we learn our lessons and we are spirit/soul climbing upward towards God. This is the journey of the spirit/soul

However, the majority of humanity during their sojourn often forgets about our origin as spirit/soul and we completely immerse ourselves into the physical existence of glamour, glory, crime, violence and do everything to satisfy our physical senses. In the process, we reach old age, and we never realize that we have caused so much suffering to other humans and other inhabitants of the earth without any atonement, we, the spirit/soul depart from the physical body. Once we are physically dead, all of our doings will be our soul memory and we will realize how we have failed our purpose of living in the physical. Such souls have to go down to the lower tree instead of going up to the light. They have to go through their experiences and by the mercy of God's providence, they can realize their failures in the tree below. And once they done with their spirit/soul search, the desire for God and light, they can go upward to the tree of life and rectify and strive for light, union with the divine through physical life.

The people who committed a grievous crime—torturing animals, mass murders—such souls who have to descend down to the bottom of the lower tree. From there, they have to work their way up. This is my take on the journey of the spirit/soul. If I have offended anybody, I am sorry. This is my opinion only. I must say even Heaven, Hell everything is the domain of the Creator, providence is available to all who seek and desire.

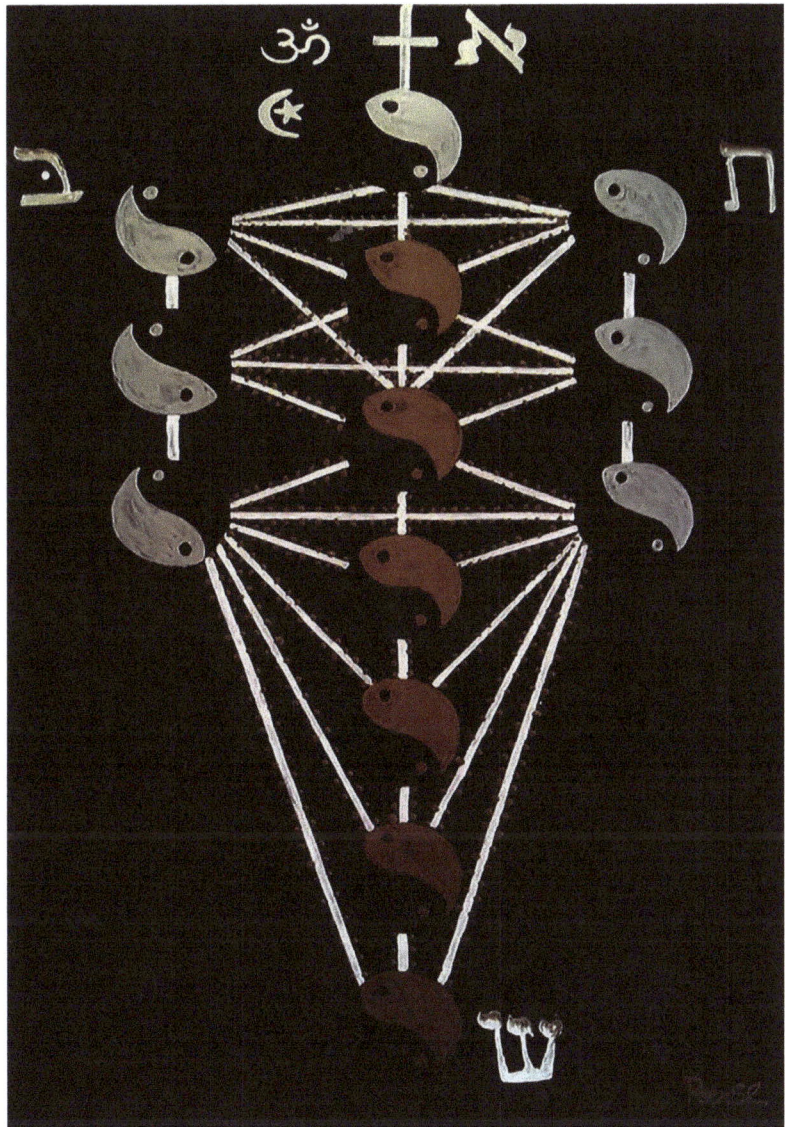

Unification Trees

I had a vision of Yin and Yang in the Chakras in the rainbow colors. Since I know how to draw the Kabbalistic Tree, I incorporated these images into the tree. I placed the other religious images on the top of the tree. So, I do believe all religions seek unity with the divinity. Please look with an open heart and love.

Human justice is partially blind in the eyes of divine justice. A judge gives death sentences to someone who committed a crime. What it does with that human: The body dies, the soul departs without getting an opportunity to realize the pain and suffering he has caused.

Also, there are countless people who escape the law and continue to live a life of crime and no punishments in the eyes of the law. Also, there are countless crimes people commit to each other and other inhabitants of the world, yet in the eyes of human justice, they are not crimes, and one cannot prove it there. For example, emotional suffering, physical abuse, isolation, selfishness, cruelty to each other and creation, sexual abuse, verbal abuse. We cannot establish before the law many of these crimes. Still, so many people and animals are suffering and dying each day. Can we honestly think our souls will escape punishment for these crimes? No. That is why we have a soul and soulful laws given by the divine. Everything that we do or fail to do causes discomfort to other beings, and all our deeds are imprinted in our soul memory and it will reveal them to us, once we leave our physical body and enter into the spirit realm. People without their spirit awakened within them, for them, nothing worries them. They go about and do all kinds of things, enjoy, and live for physical pleasures. At all costs, they achieve that. One can honestly say they believe there is no eye watching. They are blind in that state, it does not mean others are blind or the divine law is blind. That is why Yeshua says, "Stay awake and pray." To pray means what? Not that one utters many words or reads the prayers written by somebody.

Tune in with your God within and live in accordance with God's law. Practice love, empathy, compassion. Treat all who are God's creation, live and let live.

One wonders why and what and where it all leads to. We cannot give a full answer. The infinite Creator is in love with forms, and it creates according to its will. For example, an artist makes many paintings with many colors. Can any of the painted pictures ask, why did you make me?

Chapter 21

Garden

The garden. I write about fruit-bearing trees and visits by the angels into the human garden. First of all, for each one of us, life and existence is our garden, and we are trees, which produce good fruits, bad fruits, etc.

This is the story of the soul's existence in the physical body and the soul's journey through the physical and its accomplishments by the soul, yielding awareness, progress, etc. This is the purpose of human existence. Yesterday, in our group, we read about the tiny mustard seed planted and grown to become a big plant and birds come to nest in it and enjoy the shade. This story is similar. I have to stress here a story in the church said by the Assistant of the Father (Deacon/Cantor) during his sermon he told a story, "A guy was at the beach throwing the Star Fish one at a time back into the ocean, which was beached by the waves. Then another man was walking at the beach and saw the man who is throwing the beached starfish back to the ocean and asked him what are you doing?"

Harmonious Petals

Rose

FOUR WORLDS

The good man said, "These starfish are beached and if I do not throw the fish back to the ocean, they will die." Then the man said, "There are millions of beached starfish, how can you throw all these fish back into the ocean?" The kind man said, "If I can save a life of one starfish at a time, that is what I am doing."

From this, I take the following: The man who threw the starfish into the ocean recognizes the life in this little fish and desires to save it from perishing. This little life is important for that little starfish. His kindness surpasses human pride. All life longs for its life to exist in Creation. So, this kind man is doing whatever he can to recognize the importance of life even in small things. Good for him. The world needs such people. He is an awakened spirit. The other man is a slumbering spirit in his physical body; hence he cannot see what this good man sees. He has no clue. All that he recognizes is his ego: No one exists except him. He cannot see pain and suffering in others, or another of

God's Creation. He has a long way to go before he realizes Creator/ Creation/purpose. We must practice compassion, love, and respect for all life. We have been given these amazing talents. If one expects the seed within to grow, first we have to recognize, there is a seed within us, we must desire to grow through living with only the desire to grow this seed, a soul spark with love. Through love, we unite with the lover.

Procreation

Here, I write about the most fundamental principle of Procreation, the abuse of it and the implications of that. So, what we have here, some faiths believe we are born in sin and the rest of it. How in the world we can say we are born in sin? It is the Creator's plan that creation should continue through male and female interaction.

This becomes a sin when we abuse it. Say; we use this for carnal pleasure, take precautions so that no child is born using all the ways we have to prevent pregnancy. Once a female is pregnant, then she cannot get pregnant again the next day or two days later. So, the life force is brutally wasted. This is half of the story, plus interfering with the peace of the fetus growing in the womb by violence.

Boy! What we have here is ignorance. There are millions of unwanted children who never get to see their parents or enjoy their childhood. They are put into foster homes and experience abuse. Shelter for women, rape, violence, etc. It sounds unpleasant. This is what humans have. Women are mere commodities for men, they have no voice. At least in the western world, things are sometimes different.

Boys and others are even abused in the spiritual kingdoms. Even one child is too much. Nowadays, nobody is safe, not even babies. Terror is everywhere. Women cannot walk outside in the dark. On top of that, people carved out stories about God, how it functions and what to do. How can one carve out stories about these matters when they cannot figure out how to contain the dark force and its power? Ignorant people attract ignorant souls. Criminals attract evil souls. So, the world is filled with crime, selfishness, useless children, and the saga of human retardation in the spiritual and physical sense. Now, spirituality is concerned with humans only. Because the God force has endowed us with greatest talents, which is able to love, emotions, feelings of different nature, etc. We as spirits/souls must use these talents in the physical existence to navigate our spirit/soul ascension back to from whence we came as a spirit. We; the spirits descend from the purest state into the darkest regions of the physical world to learn, gain wisdom, knowledge, understanding and returned to the God head. It is like a baby growing up to be a responsible human being.

So much suffering and such a very heavy burden to carry. We have excuses for everything. We procreate uselessly and to feed the pleasure of eating, we procreate the animals. They are slaughtered.

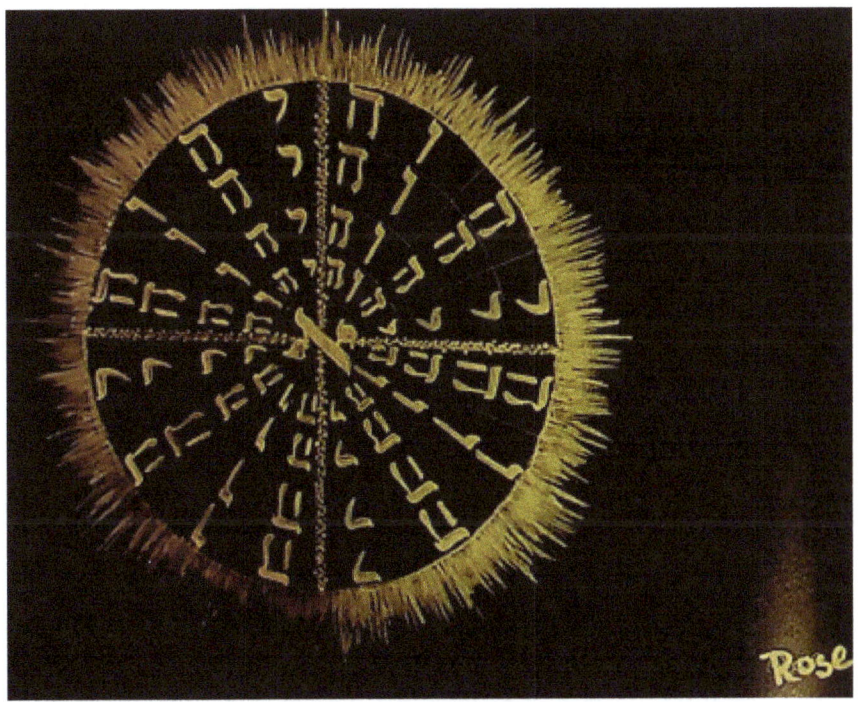

Of Course, they will (the spirit) directly go to the place of the animal spirit world. They have no purgatory or hell. They have no sin, so they go where the divine intended. When people cause suffering to others. Jesus says to them, "Go and resolve one's difference and only then come and partake of the Supper." No confession, no forgiveness of the sin. Because this is very important.

If I have caused some pain to someone, if I am a spiritual and Godly person, I realize my mistake and truly apologize to the affected person. By doing so, I am releasing my bond with that person. Then I go to confession. Forgiving, it is for that person to forgive or not. Another thing I have observed is that people keep dead people as relics and some people keep the body by taking the money and keeping it at sub- zero temperatures, after removing all the internal organs. They think they will come back someday and re-inhabit the body.

There are no organs inside.

How in the world? I think once the spirit/soul departs, the body must return to the Earth and become part of the cosmic dust to be absorbed for whatever may be. When one keeps the body frozen like that, the spirit that inhabited that body will likely hover around for a long time. Ignorance is the mother of all ignorance . We talk plenty of God but let us talk and transform the world in a way the Creator intended. Try to experience God and see what a miracle it will be. If that happens, one will cherish all and will not overpopulate the world. We will be sensitive to everything. There is no quick fix for our issues unless we understand the issues.

There are some great and beautiful people in the world. They live simply, humbly and it is due to them one can still see some sparks flickering in the dark night of the soul. God bless them. I can write a million pages about our ignorance, but what is the point? Enlightenment is the task for each human. Not just to talk about the path but walk the path with spirit/soul awareness and the purpose in creation. We must first learn to unload the heavy garbage bag we are carrying on our souls, which is invisible to most others but is visible to that person if they are spiritual. When we violate the law of God and go about do everything recklessly with no thought of the other beings, whether it human or animal, we forget one thing: The one who has been affected by you is also one of God's creations and this being also came here to co-exist with us. What are we doing with our wisdom, our comprehension of good and evil? We think of nothing but ourselves.

By doing so, we ignore the divine plan and law for us and others. Hence, we create a mess for all. Emotion is strong for all moving beings. We, as superior beings, must recognize this and act accordingly. To avoid pain and suffering to ourselves, avoid causing pain and suffering to other creatures. Mistakes happen due to thoughtlessness. Recognize that fact and go and repair the damage done to others. This is how one sets themselves free of Karma and brings about soul purification. We all physically die one day. Some sooner, some later. Recognize this: We are here as temporary dwellers with a task to learn to manifest love and share with all that comes our way. If I stretch my hands to others with love and the other will cut my hands off, are we practicing love of God or Demons? We must be the ambassador for God's Love and righteousness. If we fail, we fail ourselves, and the Creator itself. We will have our time in the Court of Divine Justice, which is within us. If we try to cover up our harmful/loveless, ego- filled actions, they will manifest once we shed our body and enter the place of the soul. Then the truth will reveal to us with its true ugly color. We have no escape and the torment we will go through will be tenfold. Be mindful of everything. It is our job. We must live with consideration for all. Protect ourselves from the harmful rays of evil lurking everywhere. We are an agent for good or evil. Unfortunately, living in this world is a difficult task for thoughtful people. Because there are so many selfish and thoughtless people who are out there to destroy the good, beautiful, love, and peace.

Crosses

In my vision, I saw this cross. People were standing beneath praying and worshiping. There were a lot of people. So, I decided to paint the cross, putting plants and flowers instead of people. I painted two crosses similar.

SUN

Today, I write about the sun. Of Course, without the sun, there wouldn't be any life on Earth. The question is how many of us are stopping for a moment to marvel at the sun, express gratitude for its blessings. We are all made of star matter that is of the Sun (all are stars). This, our sun, is close to the Earth. Somewhere from the very beginning onwards, humanity turned away from the divinity of all existence. We ignored the sun, stars, earth, wind, air, etc. We took everything for granted. Everything is for our use or abuse, we thought. We walked far away from nature. We give no value to anything, except the power of procreation, pleasures of eating, of making money. This way, we have brought about evil, crime, sorrows of all kinds to the physical Earth.

Oh, you may say, I am talking negatively. No! I am speaking facts. We are all playing a character. I would say, stop playing for a while and live for the truth; love, respect all, and allow all to exist according to the Creator's plan. Pluck evil from the world and prohibit evildoers from functioning or increasing.

Remove the evil from ourselves, in the family and everywhere. Let the sun shine in the darkness so that we see our dark nature, seek love and light in all we do.

Harmonious Petals

Golden Tree with Prayers

I saw this vision of this tree going up in space filled with white cotton balls. And I started asking a question, "What is this?" Then, I perceived the answer saying, "This is the prayers of human and animals going up to God head through this tree."

Here, I write about enjoying the scent of flowers.

Do you pay attention to what I say? See, we have this tendency to pluck flowers and present them to our spouse, the dying, to express our love. Good for them—the giver and the taker. Instead of plucking flowers, present the whole plant (a baby plant with flower). How nice that would be. One can express and show and present the inner flower blossoming through and show love for all: Universal love. The soul/spirit, this aspect of us, is the beautiful flower in nature. If we do not have the quality of scent, tenderness, attraction, beauty, it will be like we are a plastic flower. We must project our spirit/soul/God nature through our living. That is what God asks of us.

Here I am prompted to recollect a story of my daughter. She was merely three years old, and she was at Montessori School. I went to pick her up in the afternoon. In the garden, there are lots of flowers that fell from the tree, and she collected some of those and gave them to me. She never picked any flower by breaking a tree branch. She is kind, wise, and never sought any praise for anything. Living a quiet life. Also, one day when she was a year-old baby, during her bedtime story, I told a story of two children; one does things because he was afraid of the parents; the other one did everything because he loved to do it. I asked, which child is really naturally good? With her baby talk, she said, the one who did everything for the love of doing. I marveled at her answer. I hope the evil world will allow her to live and the merciful God will keep her safe through her sojourn in the physical. It should be human nature to manifest flowers with scent through love, caring, empathy, compassion, truthfulness, etc. May all souls/spirits blossom in the garden of God, which is earthly living.

Book of Life

I had this vision, coming from on high and there is a book through, "Hey" (in Hebrew, it is divine name). The closed book is dangling through the thread from the Hey as the book is coming down. I would say that it is the soul incarnating into the physical world to learn and ascend. That is my impression. Anybody can have their own take.

See, the great Mystics say science and technology have made tremendous progress for the evolution of physical existence and its comforts. Also, the same science and technology are being used to kill and destroy humans and other inhabitants of the Earth. Fire can be used to cook, warm, but can also burn and destroy. Our spirit/soul for some of us is crying aloud for love, peace, unity, and healing on the physical existence for all. The current civilization and many other civilizations as humans did not understand the purpose of existence and went about warring, causing havoc for humans and other inhabitants on the Earth. Ours is doing the worst, due to overpopulation; we are trying to extract all the resources deposited on the Earth, under the ocean, etc. They are being extracted to supply the need and luxury of physical existence using technology. Also, we are using technology for mass farming animals, and other agriculture products using chemicals, which are very harmful to physical bodies, and in turn, it is harmful to the soul. See, when the body suffers, the soul suffers. The one who is experiencing pain, pleasure, joy is not the body; it is the dweller in the body. Humans were never trained or taught to pay attention to the indweller; hence we have this huge dilemma. One against the other, siblings are ready to drink the blood of each other, humans are killing each other and earth's inhabitants. Where is the spirit of God in all of us? I think it stays in the mouth. As long as I have my brain and hand function, I will continue to express my viewpoint about what we are doing. We lost the way to love, joy, and freedom. Seek the light within ours and within all lives. Know that our temporary visit to the Earth will come to an end and the memories of what we have had on the Earth will be in the "Book of Life" to be revealed before our spirit in the afterlife and then we will have no place to hide, everything is naked, and the journey of the spirit/soul continues according to the nature of the life that has just ended.

All Sages plead to humanity to live in peace. Of course, nations are perfecting their weapons to kill brothers and sisters from other nations instead of practicing peace. There is an agenda behind these weapons and killing. Control the population. They never learn to control their impulses of lust. So, however much they try to prevent overpopulation, still the population increases. We never had such a population 2,000 years ago. Now, how many are there? And what is the world population going to be in the future? No one knows. Maybe all will go up in flame. All can then grind and gnash their teeth in hell. In the spirit world, there are neither physical teeth nor a body. It is our soul that experiences its impressions and consequences or blessedness while living.

The Book of Creation

I was given, in my vision, this open book on a golden platter. I did not draw the platter. So, I would say this is the book of Creation and God's teaching. It is for us to read and navigate our lives through this physical world according to the teaching. This is my impression.

Single mothers, single fathers, they want pity from others and support. A single man or woman cannot have a child. Both must join to get one. Irresponsible indeed. Under all laws, it should not be allowed. A couple of months ago, I saw on YouTube, a stray dog found a live baby in the garbage dump in Brazil. He carried the baby alive into a neighboring camp and they called the police. I am almost certain they were Christians. What is the use of this production? We are at odds with each other, each other's religions, nations, innocent animals, and nature as a whole. Where it all leads to is the destruction of all. God created one earth and multitudes of creatures and humans. We divided everything. It is not righteousness. Humanity created evils, pain, and suffering to all. Many homes are war zones, with selfish children and criminal adults, who do everything evil. Jesus says, "I have come to seek the lost, patients needing doctors." He is asking if one has one hundred sheep and loses one … would you not look for that lost one?" A noble teaching for us to consider and live. Remember the self-righteous one who went to the temple and prayed saying, "I am great, and I have followed all the commandments," and boosted himself? On the other hand, there was a sinner who stood outside the temple acknowledging his unworthiness and pleading for redemption. Jesus asked, "Who went home in peace and satisfaction?" We all have to hit the ground with humility and learn to accept our imperfections and need to transform ourselves and help those who are falling. Of course, stay away from criminals who lost the spirit of God by their living. This world is complicated. The selfish and thoughtless people created hell and transfer it to the next person, and to the next.

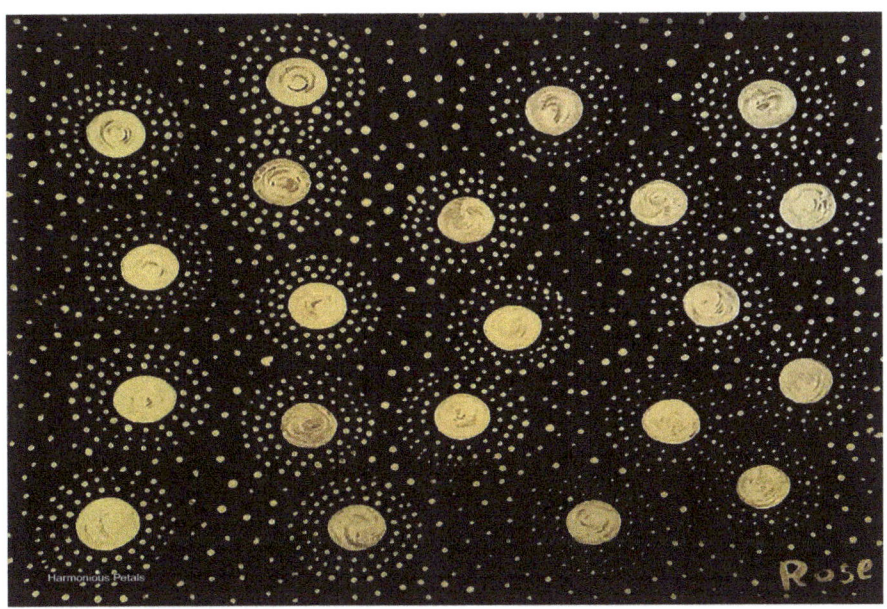

Universe

I saw this vision in which there is a bright golden circle in the center and surrounded by millions of glittering golden stars. They were like moving clusters. I believe it is the soul world. I was so very happy to experience this. You may think whatever you want. One large circle burst into many stars and then exploded and created countless stars. With no time, I saw the entire space was filled with flickering, golden stars. I asked what this is, a voice said, "Creation."

Chapter 24

Language of the Nature

Today I would like to speak about the subtle language of Nature.

Sinking Moon
I saw this vision a moon was sinking into the ocean.

We are all part of nature with distinctive abilities of speech, motion, perception. The one who understands nature, understands the working of the great force called God force, which brought everything into existence. If we understand God, then we will breathe, live, and act accordingly and in harmony with the laws of God and nature. We will then love, respect, and cherish all, from the biggest to the smallest. War, violence, and destruction should never be part of our nature and at least people of God should not partake in such activity. People of God should live for another and be one with all that is. Because all is part of us, and we are part of all. Once we realize that, the healing of our beings and all beings will start. The God in all of us will manifest and guide us and we enjoy the spirit of God and its beauty. We must start somewhere to experience God, not talk about God. In the absence of knowing and experiencing, never-ending talks go on and it becomes a storm in the mind without any transformation.

Thy Kingdom Come. We must act to bring about the Kingdom. We have the power and the ability to do this. It starts in our hearts and goes to all hearts and all beings. Experience the sorrows, suffering of even the little creatures and all beings. Treat all with respect. Give up pride. Because all will come to a screechy halt with our physical deaths when the music of the soul and its memory will overwhelm us. Nobody will fix it. If we want to have mercy from God, be merciful to others and all creation. Do the right thing and seek justice and live justly. Then we can say the Holy Spirit is active in our lives and guiding us. Through love, and only through love for all, will we manifest the presence of the Holy Spirit. The Holy Spirit is *not* the handmaiden of the many who talks about it. Rather, it is the manifestation of the love of the Creator to creation. We can swim in that ocean once we practice love of God in all, and with all. If anybody wishes for a peaceful and safe physical and spiritual existence, this is the way. There is no other way.

This is the Field of the Lord: Creation, the blessed earth, and all its inhabitants. It is the infinite one's will that all came to exist. Then how in the world are we picking and choosing who will live, who will die? It is not the will of the Creator that anyone dies or suffers before their appointed time. We are doing everything against the will of God. We are trying to manipulate everything and saying it is the will of

God. Blessed and called are those who read this message and change the way they live, interact with God's Creation. Everything is beautiful when it is alive. Try to see a chicken or a goat alive and grazing in the field. Then look at the face when its head is cut off to feed our bellies. We do not love God with all our heart, but we love our self-importance, indulgence, lust, power of ego, eloquent speech. These are all hindrances to the ascension of the spirit/soul. Unless we learn to acknowledge the right of existence of other beings, including humans, life in the air, earth, and water, we are in no way allowing the will of God to play out in creation, rather we are challenging the will of God and love, which brought all things into being. Humans are practicing so much cruelty to each other, and the rest of creation. Everything went out of control with this self-serving attitude of humans. There is no us, just me, mine, etc. I know nothing will change. The collective change will not happen. Collective destruction will happen.

One soul at a time, it is the journey of each one of us. Be an instrument for change and peace. Seek justice, protect the weak from criminals. Do not justify evil. See and recognize them for who they are. Let us pray, give us our daily bread, but what is our daily bread? It is wisdom, understanding, and love, this is the true soul food. Not physical bread. When one speaks of the spiritual aspect, then the food is for our soul ... is it not its love? Light? etc. Somehow, we all will get some bread on the Earth for our physical living. Also, see, it is daily bread. Not daily flesh, not daily war, daily evil and all its lies. These will bring sorrow to the soul.

Chapter 25

Angel of the Air

Harmonious Petals

Golden Cross

I saw this cross in the midst of shining golden and white stars. The cross is familiar with Christians because of the crucifixion of Christ. I have a different take about the cross. The parallel pillar represents the physical world. The vertical pillar represents the divine light coming down to creation. Then I saw at the intersection there is a bright light. That means the divine light is always present in the heart of all beings and all creation.

Here, I will talk about the Angel of the Air (the breath of life). Of course, these are all strange teachings for many of us. We are taught to believe something else. Can you imagine if we were taught from the inception of our lives to watch and observe nature, its functions, listen to the wind, the waves, the sunrise and sunset, the birds in the air, the life force of all that inhabits the Earth and water, including us? The life force that goes through our lungs and keeps us alive and also all other life forms.

Primitive humans were savages and all they did was care for their bodies. Then, there was no agriculture. As man developed, we developed agriculture and other farming methods. The primitive hunted animals and went to streams to catch fish. Now, our technology has improved and what we have today is a thoughtless, unethical way of farming and raising moving creatures in very unhealthy environments.

From the beginning of my life on the Earth, I was pushed, pushed, suffocated through experiences, became who I am today, aware of lots of painful things about what is happening on this beautiful Earth. I suffer when a child, women, men, and animals suffer injustice. I am not trying to teach some holy formula. I am just sharing my humble thoughts from my heart. I connect with the great sages. Our Lord, Yeshua, is my Light, so should be for all. May the light shine in the darkness and the healing and transformation of the hearts begin. May we do everything to help and heal the forgotten, the suffering creatures. This world must change; our thoughts and attitudes must change. We have to acknowledge the living God.

This is why I connect with this Christian mystic. We do not have to look any further or anywhere to know God. Listen to this wonderful human's soul who soaks us with this noble truth. Once we experience this, we must set aside our ego self. Who seeks nothing but division and glory? That is the Lucifer at work in us. Instead of acknowledging the divine through its creation, we acknowledge Lucifer and create these monumental problems on Earth. No respect for other creatures, their emotions, their pain, nor their suffering. We are doing the same thing to each other as well. Where is our God when we choose to be blind?

I heard a documentary about some funeral practices somewhere in Asia, Taiwan, or somewhere . When a person dies, they keep the body for some ten to fifteen days. Then, there is a funeral procession with buffalo; they take these poor animals' eyes off, have them walk in the procession with the body and finally, kill the animals and eat them and celebrate. I am writing this not to annoy anybody, but to make one aware, what a terrible superstition is at work with humans. Thus, humans and all their vileness have no boundaries. Our soul in the body seeks to be humble, loving, caring.

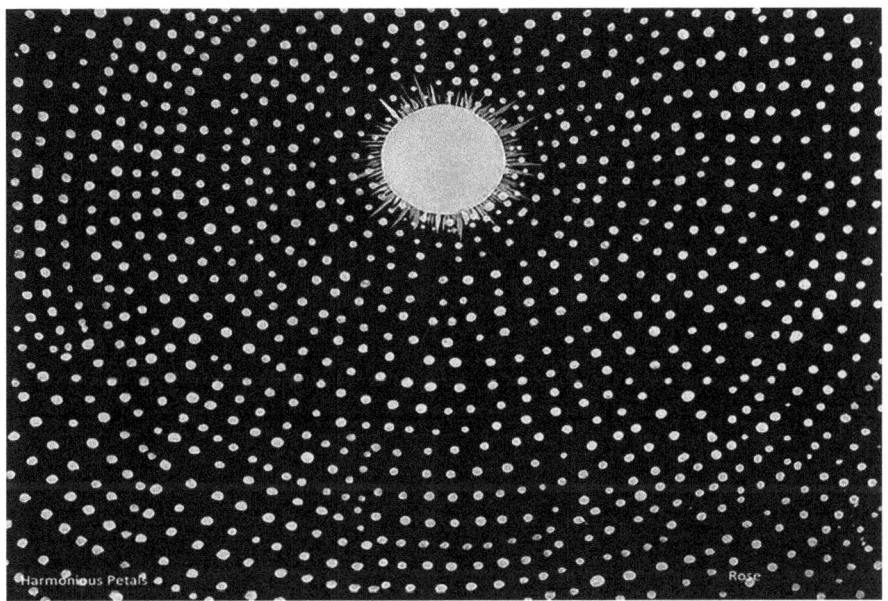

Universe

I saw this vision where very a large, bright, silvery moonlight and its rays were beaming outward into the universe and around was billions of glittering star lights. It was a beautiful scene. I was happy.

Anything else we practice, we are serving the Lord of all lies, the Great Lucifer. When we act with cruelty, we crucify the divine in us. What a mess we humans have made out of this beautiful creation!

Mother Earth prepares and serves all its children with great platters of healthy food, made of plants, seeds, nuts, sunshine, water, and air. Humans, deviated from the wholesomeness, the holy life, and we got sick and suffer. Do not worry, pharmaceutical companies make medicines and enrich themselves with our savings. That is for the rich nations. Poor nations suffer and finally die. So does everyone eventually. We are all sleepwalkers. We are satisfied with something. Creator and Creation, we will never know the depth of it. This little Earth, what have we made out of it? It is soaked with the blood and tears of humans and animals. I sometimes wonder, why in the world I ventured into this writing. It makes no difference to anybody. They hold tight to theirs whatever that may be. Why are we always so caught up in the lower regions of existence? The head is the entry point of the divine light.

It is important to remember this when we are caught up in emotional battles. We lose our sense of light and darkness, which covers the entire universe. Nothing exists but our mental agony.

Once that happens, we allow our body to drown in a mire of pain, sorrow, and finally, sickness.

Our life and relationships with others are all only contributing to others' suffering. Selfish, self-centered people inhabit the Earth. They cannot possibly think of anybody but themselves and their pleasures. To that end, they do not care who they are hurting emotionally or physically. But there are few in the world who think of others as well. Their suffering will be beyond anybody's guess. It is for the wise and thoughtful people to recognize that living on the Earth is not cake walking and it is one step at a time where we learn to climb the thorn-filled step to ascend the top of the ladder to reach the mountain top wherein lies love, light, and strength. If we try to make sense out of nonsense, we become a target for the multitude. Because they have everything ready: Selfishness, greed, lust, and all other fleshy glories. Plus, they have faith in the blood that flows down from calvary to transport them to the lap of the divine. Others have other faiths. Despite that, they do not have to transform or do anything. Think about it. Once we decide to follow the spiritual path, we cannot play the game of fitting everywhere and conforming with everything the world offers and live. Once we commit to the life of the spirit, we have to compromise on many things. We must allow the light, which ignited in us to shine more and more. Once we decide on our path and way of life, lots of the activities of the flesh have to take the back seat.

The lady yesterday was saying we have to leave the driver's seat. No! We stay put in the driver's seat and navigate the vehicle to the pleasure of the spirit. All the people of the world (the majority) left the driver's seat and stayed in the back seat, hence the car goes hither and thither with no control over anything, killing and ambushing many on the way.

One can easily see this kind of thing in the world. The Initiatic school is for willing and disciplined people who only have one aim: To drive the vehicle of their life in the manner of the spiritual path. One must be in charge of the vehicle at all times Humans do not like to exert ourselves or give up our ways of life, go out of our comfort zones. There are people in history who used their compass and navigated their submarine in the infinite ocean (God) because they recognized their soul's purpose and journey.

There are mystics in all religions. In Christianity, there are those like Sister Alphonsa, St. Francis and so many others. They were compassionate, had empathy, loved God and all God's creation equally. They recognized the rights of all in the physical world. The Compass is the recognition of the spirit/soul and the importance of not sinking the ship in the physical existence). Kabbalah is one of such compass. It is a mystical path. It has been formed by the ancients, Jews or some others or combination of all. But officially, it is the mystical path of Judaism. All were not allowed to practice it. Also, they say, until one is forty, they cannot practice Kabbalah. Remember the forty days and nights, forty years in the wilderness, etc. Until forty years of age, aspirants live in the wilderness of the physical, growing up, getting married, having sex, producing babies, seeing to their education and care, making money, acquiring power, riches, etc. For some people, by the time they reach forty, they start asking questions: Who am I? What is the purpose of life? Where am going? Is there a life after my physical death? Then the tree shines in their heart, all the Ten Sephirah, and the pathways. The mustard seed starts sprouting, and soul journey begins. In Genesis, it clearly mentions the tree of life, the garden, the snake, etc. The tree of life is the core of all spiritual practices. They may not recognize it. Jesus said, "No one knows my father except I." Father, the infinite God who is responsible for the infinite creation. Some ignorant people say, Kabbalah is magic. Even to create the magic you have to have a strong mind, a well-trained mind to control the lower spirit and natural phenomenon. Those who do the magic knows how to control all those elements to bring about results.

Harmonious Petals

Crosses

In my vision, I saw this cross. People were standing beneath praying and worshiping. There were a lot of people. So, I decided to paint the Cross, putting plants and flowers instead of people. I painted two Crosses similar.

The ancient Prophets, time and again, cursed this saying for God: "I am sick of your blood-burnt offerings. By killing poor animals and pouring their blood on the Altar." What monster God wants sacrifices and blood? Selfish humans entered the Earth and forgot the spirit of love and ascension. So, they are doing evil things to please the evil/ fleshly force that is in charge of the lower regions of the physical. The Kabbalistic Tree silently calls all spirits to take the journey back home through the narrow path.

Christ is present in the center of the Tree. All roads in Italy lead to Rome. Let us acknowledge the one creation and one creator. There are many branches in the tree, and an independent branch not connected to the tree will not survive. The tree is rooted in the infinite.

Chapter 26

Connectedness

I am writing now about connectedness and the oneness of all. We have to think of how much we practice this connectedness. We do virtually nothing about it. However, the Mystics practice that and live and leave the Earthly life, yet wherever they can speak or make some changes, they do. They are only a very small fragment of humankind. No responsible parents allow their children to go and live a carefree life. If those kinds of parents are rare in the physical, then how in the world can the heavenly father allow a soul to descend into the physical world and not have to earn the kingdom through transformation, by abstaining from the many glamour's of the physical world? The soul is learning, there is no doubt about it. If we do not have to work and earn and all is provided, then all souls would continue to live in infancy and leave the body here having wasted it and then depart. I know it is Lucifer, the part of the Biblical story. He, too, is performing a task for us, providing our trials and temptations. Whatever they may be.

HARMONIOUS PETALS

ROSE

The Golden Rosary

Countless times in my life, I was given Rosaries in my vision. This particular one, I saw a lady figure in golden light and she gave me this. Of course, the rosary represents the Mother Mary and Catholics always say their rosaries, however most of the religions have some kind of beads like rosary and they say their prayers with that. But one must pay attention to the beads that are connected by a single thread. It means that we are all interconnected in creation like the rosary beads. We have one life force connecting all life force. This is my take on the rosary.

Humans, with this heightened awareness, are capable of the greatest achievements. We must practice self-restraint, empathy, compassion, and love. If we can observe these, there is a guarantee for progress in the ascension of the souls. From all the teachings of all religions, something came down to the Earth from the highest region of the cosmic existence. The will of the Creator and the creation... all creation.

Here, I will talk about love.

All religions in the world and spiritual practices say God is Love. What is love? Do humans know how to love? They love themselves. Most people's love lasts for a very short time. Then their love dissipates. Most men and women, once the indulgence of physical love is over, they dump the person they were with and move to the next. Destruction and desolation happen all through such lives. If we say we are moved by God's love and the Holy Spirit is working through us, why can't we recognize that all are manifestations of God's love? Nothing exists outside of God's love, and if that is the case, how many of us are treating each other and the rest of creation with love? In the absence of love, they created dogmas, follow the dogmas and they say all is going to be rosy. Today, all the Earth's life is like arid deserts with no love in sight. Some say, I love my wife, husband, or children. If our life is run by God, then "I" and "Me" must dissolve and we must love all creation and act gently and allow all to exist as God allows. Experience love in its wholeness.

The Bleeding Cross

I saw this vision of the cross in a spiraling kind of existence with golden stars shining. This white cross is dripping with blood. I would say every time anybody hurts any being either man or beast or does any injustice or harm to any living being or any unrighteousness act, the pure spirit will be crucified symbolically. Let us seek healing for all creation.

Prayer

Here, I write about prayer.

We must pray, stay awake, and pray. What does this mean? See, flesh bones and tongues are not us. There is something else animating in us called soul/spirit. But for most of humanity, that which is animating us is in deep slumber because it is caught in the physical world and in its wants, attractions, the ego-driven life, self-concern, the mighty self, its gratification, and bodily needs. When we pursue these all the time, and we seldom remember that there is still something within us that wants something totally different. It wants to experience, overcome obstacles, and move forward. What humankind has done instead is to pray with lips: Prayer by the spirit has been absent or dormant. This physical existence is misunderstood by humans. We want to conquer others, kill everybody, mentally, emotionally, use others and other beings for our pleasure.

Cosmos

In this vision, it is in the Hebrew letters written is "Let there be light." I saw this vision of spiraling brilliance of stars of golden and white. From the top corner, a huge bright light shining out to the universe.

We worship at the places of prayer, thinking that we pray well, but what we have today is this great mess in the physical world. When we are driven by lust, money, greed and desire to subdue others and animals, we are a lost cause. God is not active in such a person but Lucifer. Religions are divided, speaking, and feeling proud, they have the truth and others don't, that is how the majority of all religions behave. We must rise above that and recognize the soul and leave behind all these divisions to connect with each other and the rest of the creation with the unity of love. That should be our prayer. Pray for wisdom and understanding so that we can know how to wake up the slumbering spirit within us. And we should pray for unity, oneness, and love, safe travel for all souls of humans and all other living beings.

A mystic can know what it feels like to see the tears of an animal, a suffering child, an abused woman, and so on. The saints and sages traveled this road to reach where they are and so each one of our journeys should be like that. This is our purpose (the soul's purpose). Stay awake and pray. Kabbalah teaches us that our one soul has two parts: One of animal nature, the other is divine in nature. On observation, we can fully realize this. Caring for the body, seeking pleasure, procreation, making money, getting an education, and holding high positions in society, ruling others, killing other beings, being cruel, not caring for others' feelings, invasion of others' lands. This will take countless pages to say anything about a very little of it. This is the animal soul nature.

On the other hand, the divine part seeks love, honesty, meditation, empathy, and seeks unity, safety for all, the wellbeing of all, respect for all creation, acknowledging our weaknesses, failures and seeks to correct them to the best of our ability and never again to fall back into the trap of the fallen. This is a short description of the divine part of the soul's nature. Higher or highest education will not make anybody wise. Wisdom comes from the God force alone through humility and love. It does not recognize anything but love and purity of the heart. People in power, who are highly educated, walk their heads up for great approval and they demand acknowledgment. On the other hand, the poor and humble sit or walk by the wayside and do their jobs, seeking and they are growing and touching the stars. Theirs is God's kingdom. It will have no end. They progress slowly, quietly. They are the silent walkers, messengers of peace, embodiments of love. They live their physical lives to serve the divine soul factor and their animal souls are under their perfect control. Animal nature does not control them. The infinite God has created us with infinite capacity to traverse through infinite worlds with our ever-growing ability of the mind (God's). But we are so tuned to and caught up in the lower soul nature that we think we are helpless and enslave ourselves to this Luciferic power. In due course of infinite time, the lower and the higher will unite once again and the divine plan for us will be fulfilled. It is for us to understand our ability and capacity and not to mortgage our souls to the animal nature, and succumb to just being content with physical pleasures, killing, doing evil. Try to walk the narrow path and help others to walk it as well. Don't cause others to stumble. Let us all partake of the divine supper and quench our thirst from the infinite well of the infinite God force.

This is our day, our call. Share your thoughts with me.

The Attitude

These great Mystics of all time call all men and humanity to pay attention to their attitudes towards each other. From the inception of human existence, men dominated and subdued women. Because they knew their hormone power—which instead of their practicing to control and balance—they decided to express it to the fullest, resulting in bloodshed, tears, really, all the way until today. I think, there was a time in history when women had a high place, there were hierarchies, and in those times the populations were much less. Women even went to war. I think somewhere in history. Maybe Her-story, now it is History.

Look at the world today, children are born in the streets with no food to eat. Women and children are sold for money—if the fetus is female, in some nations, it is aborted. In the Western world, they are "liberated," acting foolishly. Before their marriages, they have countless relationships, children, etc., when they decide to get married; they have nothing to offer in the marriage. Once they say "I do" and they open their garbage bag and throw their trash all over. There are wonderful men and women who respect each other and live in union and peace as well. But the majority of households are filled with emotional and spiritual bankruptcy and chaos. One is the head, and another is the tail. One has a voice, the other does not. Stupid. When people get involved with the other sex, they should realize, this is the brother or a sister of somebody or is a child of some good parents. One Indian poet even wrote a poem comparing women to a drop of tears. It is very true. Kabbalah really explains this phenomenon, somewhere up in the "Tree of Life," one single light spirit split by the divine law and descended through the "Tree of Life" and entered the world for the soul/spirit purpose of learning. In the Highest spirit world, they are in the innocent state. It is the Creator's will that the spirit descends into the lower regions and take the garments of the soul and descend into the physical Earth, to experience, overcome and ascend. We are soul/ spirit, travelers in God's Universe. God's will be done. Until we realize this, we will travel. In all religions, they talk about it. It is the process.

We, the soul/spirit, entered the valley and came down or were sent out, we have to hike back. It is really hard. Only people who hike the high mountain know how hard it is to hike. That is the physical hike. The spiritual hike is even harder. We have to do this.

We cannot stay stuck here. The sooner we; as souls/spirits realize this, the better it is. It is a soul/spirit journey. Know and strive.

Yeshua went up to the mountain alone to pray, to mediate to commune with the infinite one... The others went into the boat, experiencing the storm, cold, faithlessness, doubt, etc. When our soul and spirits occasionally get into the mode of oneness with ineffable one, we are joyous, with no care in the world. We have to come down from this state of being and face the storm of daily living, and all the forces that we have to reckon with. The selfish forces that surround us will shake our faith, destroy our joy. The boat of our souls will be tossed hither and thither. So, it is very important that we hold on to what we have in the face of the storm that surrounds us. Religion does not teach us the anatomy of the spirit and soul. It is not an easy task. People must practice love. This will be the ladder we can use to ascend the mountain of the Lord. Blessed be the infinite one who brought all things into existence and sustains them all. We must care for all beings. Do not kill physically or emotionally any beings or creatures. Everything belongs to the Creator. It is the will of the Creator that all life returns to the upper world in its given time.

I saw on the Internet in one country, a zoo filled with all kinds of animals. It is called the death zoo. The animals there get no food, no care, animals die of disease and malnutrition. Animals even eat plastics and another awful things. It is a horrible scene. Why in the world do governments and people allow such zoos, or any zoos? We must free the animal kingdom to live freely in their world. We (our souls) will never be in communion with the divine as long as we live in selfishness and misuse the procreative power. Children all over the world are suffering. Religions did nothing to educate these people, since the beginning of time. They held on to their power. This power will stay here. The spirit/souls seek liberation from all power and all earthly glory. Mean spirits will never enter the light. It is the gentle, the peace seekers, the humble ones who do. Nobody has access to the spirit world, except the pure in heart.

Harmonious Petals   Rose

Here, I write about perfume in different bottles. This is quite interesting. It is important for true seekers to check and examine their hearts. That is where we store the perfume of the Lord or the foul smell of Lucifer. We do not have to talk or perform on stage about our relationship with the lover. Our lives and actions will prove by themselves what are our convictions and life. Of course, Earth is a stage, and we are performers here. While performing, true seekers examine themselves to see how genuine their love is, which is the divine and the path we have to travel requires purity, loving, truthful hearts, and prayers. While on the Earth, we must be empathetic. If we are empathetic, we will be able to feel what other beings feel. Without all these attributes of the divine, no one can commune with the divine. It is ever present and yet is inaccessible to the profane. People have devised many formulas, and they are all okay, provided our hearts are pure and filled with empathy and compassion.

We even refuse to be harmonious in our homes. And our homes are the breeding ground for all the good or evil and from there, we fill the earth with whatever . If we can prevent evil from spreading so that the good is not affected, it is all worth doing. We must take our responsibility seriously, so that the good must survive. If we cannot uproot the evil in ourselves, how can we speak of the divine to others?

Creation is the field of the Lord, including us. We are given the highest capacity to perceive everything in creation and be part of it, rather than keeping ourselves excluded from it. If we exclude ourselves from the rest of Creation, we are trying to exclude the author of all, which can never happen. So, let us all play in the field of the Creator, embracing, caring, and loving everything. Do our best to cherish the big, the small, and tiny. I know we excluded ourselves from the rest; hence the field is suffering due to our self-centered exclusivity. Be sensitive to all and in all. If we do, we partake of the love-filled supper from the field. Then, the Lord will say to our soul journey: "Job well done through your journey in the field of action."

Stress

Here, I write about stress. Some very important issues among humans. Running away from responsibility, not being willing to do the right thing, knowing full well it is the right thing. Irresponsibility, allowing evil to prevail, no matter who will be in danger because of that. We are put on the earth not to be irresponsible and squander opportunities. We all must play our part to live and let live all the beings in the world. Those who escape responsibility and refuse to soul-search and do the right thing for the ascension of the soul, are willing to descend into the chaos of the soul and bring others also with them. Unless one searches their souls and transforms from within, all talking about god, spirit, soul, etc., is kind of whitewash and that "whitewash" will be blackwash for the soul! They think they have escaped from fulfilling their duty as humans, but not so fast!

After the transition from the physical, they have already made arrangements for the soul to spin into the lower regions, along with the same kinds of soul/spirit. People who rob, cheat, do evil, allow others to suffer due to their action, are evil. Everyone must do their very best to not allow innocent beings and people to suffer, mentally, emotionally, or physically. People read millions of books and it does not work to transform their inner lives, so why do they read spiritual teachings. God is not in the books. We must recognize that God's spark dwells within each of us and wants to express outward in the collective for the betterment and joy for all. If we are blind to this truth, then there is no truth for such people. It would have been better if they had not been born. Look at the world today: In Adam and Eve, a male and female caused all these problems. They created monsters and monsters that devour the peace and tranquility of all. It is high time humans take a good look at these issues and correct for their own sake and for the sake of all the rest.

Here, I will write about the fundamental principle of how one becomes a spiritual teacher/guide. I wrote many times for the last few years about this subject. One can see people are all over pretending to be teachers and guides. They are all over the world. In some places, some do get a glimpse of the higher dimensions. Wasting no time, they declared themselves as God incarnate and gathered disciples, set up temples and sit on golden thrones and demand worship. Countless of them are there and they travel to the Western world. In the Western world, people are hungry for enlightenment, and they fall for these cons. In the Western world and the rest of the world, they speak, speak, and speak louder about God. Their God remains in their mouths. Their lives and hearts are totally engrossed in the three-dimensional world with five senses. They are very busy with that. They are arid deserts, and no seed ever grows from their actions, for goodness sake. If you want to travel to some far country, you have to know how to get there, make arrangements, get passports, visas, buy tickets, take the proper plane and arrive there, know the language and customs, etc., and be there as long as your visa lasts or whatever time you intended to spend time there. This is the story of our soul/spirit here on the Earth.

We are spirits/souls that have descended from the highest dimension and were sent here out by the Creator. Our physical parents sent us to school to learn and grow capable of living an accomplished life in the true physical sense. Similarly, our Heavenly father/parents created our spirits/souls and sent them out to the physical universe to learn and mature as spirits/souls and become partakers or coworkers with our heavenly parents. The Heavenly being did not send us here for a lifetime's supply of spiritual food and water; rather, it is hidden in the physical universe, covered in narrow pathways throughout fleshly existence. This physical universe is powered by negative forces. Even in the deep core of the negative, one will find the spark of the infinite light. Even on the Earth, see how people scan the deep ocean to get one precious pearl. Similarly, in the very core, the deep recesses of our existence are these sparks. We have to sojourn through many lives' hurdles and dangers to get the precious pearl. Once we have it, it is our duty to cherish it. Getting it is one thing, cherishing it is another. Effort, effort! What efforts one must make, learning honesty, love, empathy, compassion, overcoming the power of lust, no seeking self-glory, false pretenses, etc. If one has self-mastery over all the five-sense existence and can practice with love, then they can be teachers/ guides, etc. The Glory of Heaven will be theirs.

One must be always on guard against tempters. That is the only thing widely available here richly, without much effort. Love all beings. Do not cause any harm to anyone. Kill no moving beings. Live in harmony and peace. If one seriously looks at human history, one can see clearly how messy our attitudes and existence are. Death, lies, and destruction is everywhere. Dogmas will never take any soul/spirit to oneness with God, but true practices of love and righteousness with attitudes to live and let live will. We do make mistakes, they are everywhere. If one realizes there is spirit/soul, that we have to live for it. Our attitude must change.

Moon in the Dark Night

I saw this vision of the moon and the space was filled with big and small stars. The whole space was filled with stars and I was touching the moon.

Loneliness

Here, I write about loneliness.

Loneliness is why I think people get married. It is an illusion. Some decent people who get married and fulfill their life purpose of living together, helping each other in every way and for those couples, they do not feel lonely. In family, there are several or few children and they should be best friends with each other. In very many families, there are daredevils who are selfish to the core. Earth is filled with people, still loneliness prevails. Battered and shattered homes, nursing homes are filled with old and weak people who are subject to abuse. Why? Because there is a lack of understanding, lack of love, lack of true presence of God. Because they do not understand what god is, life, purpose. Humanity surrendered to the power of darkness from the very beginning. It is continuing to do this with a far greater force. If there is love, there is unity. If there is unity, there is peace. All these facts are missing from our lives. Nobody can correct this. So, live, eat, fight, procreate, or not. Useless are the deeds of humans.

There is no one in the true sense of acting to guide humans. Religions are interested in collecting faithful and keeping power over them, pretending they have power over heavens and souls, life. Religions fight among themselves, pretending, they have the truth and others don't. To establish their truth, they kill others. To clean themselves of their sin, they sacrifice innocent animals. Humans have endured so much debt to each other, to the Creator and above all, the innocent animal kingdom. Until and unless we clean up our act and live for one another and other beings, loneliness, rejection, suffering and so forth will continue. People, nations, leaders, fools, unrighteous people, liars, and criminals all feel powerful. Vanity, vanity! The great leader conquered the maximum nations and plundered the riches of those nations. Finally, some infectious bacteria attacked him, over which he had no power to fight and conquer. At his bedside, recognizing his hour is coming, he called his faithful servant and told him, "Put both my arms hanging outside of the coffin and write, I conquered all, but I am leaving empty handed, carrying nothing." But one thing he gained is this wisdom even at the last hour. How many of us even think to get a glimpse of wisdom to live and have a good peaceful life with each other? If all humanity and creation can feel and understand, we are all part of each other and all creation is connected to the Creative Power and we should never act against each other, but rather work for harmony and peace. Then, the perfect humanity, creation, will live in the center of the powerhouse of the creative force.

It is a good idea to enter into communication with each other and grow spiritually and help each other by expressing that we are all in it together in the journey of life in the physical and spiritual. Rather, okay, I read. Big deal. We know it. Charity begins at home. If the home is a war zone, loneliness continues and spreads in the world. This is what we see today. Heal the world by doing the right thing, avoiding evil and harmful deeds.

HARMONIOUS PETALS   ROSE

Here, I write about pleasures.

How true this is: Ninety-nine percent of humanity is a victim of physical pleasures. It is like pouring water into a bottomless bowl. It never gets filled. Or like a desert, where you put water into it, it dries up in a second. We want to be full; we are thirsty. We become so blind, we do not realize what damage we are doing, how harmful this is, if not contained. Pleasures of the body, becoming powerful, gaining name, fame, eating, getting rich. To accomplish any or all the above, there is always some damage to other beings or our brothers or sisters or parents or other innocent beings. We feel lonely because we are not in tune with the divine. Well, it is not so easy to be always sitting and meditating, chanting the name of God. We are in the physical world. Animals have their herds. Birds fly together. In the physical, what we have is physical existence. We must go through what it intended and brought forth. So, it is, that every one of us is on a journey through this maze and must finally come out of the maze as learned souls/spirits.

The "Tree of Life" (The Great Kabbalah) teaches that the single spirit/soul divided and descended into the physical world and took the physical body to make the journey of ups/downs and ascend to the highest and unite as one spirit/soul. It is our task. We all must realize this and be kind and thoughtful towards each other and help. Take responsibility for our actions. Do not dwell on the fleeting pleasures of all that the physical can offer. Do not cause others to fall. We must manifest universal love. War and violence, doing selfish acts all are off the path of the journey towards the infinite. You do not need to read millions of books. Try to read our own "Book of Life," by opening ourselves to the higher level of light, which is continuously flowing. Allow it to flow and settle into our inner beings. We all have to take a good look at ourselves and turn back towards the goal, which should be our highest goal, our soul/spirit purpose.

Chapter 31

River of Life

Be an instrument and vessel for the River of Life. Let the river flow, do not put dirt in it or block the flow. Nothing comes so easily. We have to be frank and plain. We must never paint ourselves as something we are not. There is some force watching within us. God always knows. If we know, then, God knows. God walks through Creation. All creation. So, collectively we are connected to the one life force.

Here, I write about initiation.

Religions and groups all have some kind of ritual and initiate people. This is a pure outward act, and it has nothing to do with the true spiritual path. This is a process occurring within true seekers. Nothing outward will cause one to experience the God within. It is through the practice of righteousness, empathy, compassion, self-awareness of who we are and what is our inner goal. To get caught up in the drama of this world and feeling, "People get initiated into this particular way or that way and am sure to be enlightened." We can deceive ourselves and the whole world. But not the divine. It is pure, transparent.

Any contamination of deceit, crime, evil, selfishness, cruelty, self-glory, these are leading to paths of darkness. Not the light. Light, one cannot buy, it is accomplished by self-discipline, giving up all that enslaves the soul. We must dissolve all the clutter that no longer serves our soul's purpose. What serves is living a pure, love-filled, compassion- filled, honest and humble life. The one who knows who is initiated by their divine self, knows and loves to walk the path that is clear of powers of darkness. We are sure to face storms, violence, crucifixion, that could drag us down to the filth. Challenges are 100-fold on the path. Well, if we choose to seek the soul path, by the grace of the infinite light, struggle on, there is light in the darkness. And that light is only available for the soul who seeks to grow through physical existence. Without physical existence, we cannot make much progress. We have to swim against the violent stormy ocean. Happy are those souls who managed to cross the stormy ocean to the shore of the ocean of splendor, joy, love, where dwells the Heavenly Jerusalem (the Habitation of Peace—of the Highest). All initiates in all religions or true spiritual practitioners went through the fire of initiation. Clear away the clutter we love so dearly. Give up the ego which enslaves the human souls/spirit. Do not be satisfied with some or even lots of reading of Holy Books and visiting worship places. Rather, try to live a pure life of kindness, truthfulness, compassion, live and let live. I wish you all a happy true initiation in the soul sense within.

Harmonious Petals — Rose

Here, I write about how revolution is accomplished. The physical revolution is something all can participate in and make noise for a while, and it is accomplished. All over the world, that is happening and has happened. The leaders who can speak eloquently like Hitler, were among those doing this. But to accomplish the evolution of the soul, speeches will not help, gathering multitudes and marching will not help. To accomplish the soul's evolution is a silent recognition of the fact of the existence of God/soul/spirit. From the nothing existence

(Ain Soph Aur) comes all things in existence. That includes human spirits/souls. We can make spiritual progress when we recognize that we are spirit/soul, and we were sent to Earth to fulfill and learn what the Creator expected us to do. Learning to be mature souls/spirits and return to the spirit world and do the journey further according to the order of progression by the divine order and plan. Hence it is important that we practice love, empathy, compassion, righteousness, etc. We must expand our awareness of the self to the whole self, the God self. Our beliefs and faith must aid that. Shun crime, evil, harmfulness to others and other beings. As long as we justify doing the opposite of the truth, compassion, and love, unity, we make little or no progress towards the evolution of the spirit/ soul. The Holy Kabbalah teaches us about the evolution of the Soul. It descended and began the long journey through the "Tree of Life," learning, transforming, ascending into the Highest existence through transformation. Traveling through the Middle Pillar, which is balanced and transforming. As long as we can close our minds to the havoc we play in each other's life, where other beings are brutally our ascension will be harder.

Order and Disorder

Here, I write about order and disorder, chaos, etc.

Boy! This is a serious subject concerning only humans. The great majority of people do not even bother to think "What is order?" They are so entrenched in this chaotic existence, and it is next to their nature to live as they do. Can one imagine if all solar systems and all other cosmic bodies behaved in a chaotic manner, what would become of the physical existence? It would be a fiery cosmic soup where nothing else could exist. We believe we are superior animals with divine nature and potentials. Are we paying attention to it and practicing it? Maybe a few on Earth. They are called the Sages, Saints, and virtuous people, who live a balanced life wherein they are mindful of everything. They do not cause havoc, nor cause any sorrow or pain to other beings. They are respectful to all bodies in the Cosmos. I know this for sure, people who live in disorder, disharmony and do not live in peace and order and if they die of natural causes, they will be troubled and wandering souls, restless, seeking to put the things in order and wanting an opportunity to correct the wrong. Well, they had their time; they purposely did not do what they were supposed to do with their lives. Why do I say this? Because I was fortunate enough by the blessing of the Merciful Lord to experience such spirits/souls for years. So, I wish that people would set aside their ego or say goodbye to their pride and live in order, create order, leave behind order and harmony for those they leave behind. Let no one leave trash for the living. What a world, humans have created for others, other nations, homes, animals! Well, we pray continuously and follow all that our religions tell us to do. Well and good. We live in mess, selfishness, crime, and cause pain for all the inhabitants of the earth. Some very small minorities of people are living good and sane lives. That is only a minority. We are enslaving each other and brutally abusing and killing animals. Evil.

Take this writing as a short notice and warning for all humans, who believe in God/soul/spirit and those who do not believe in anything. Such people are sometimes far better than the so-called believers of God. The Atheist has discipline, character, respect, and causes no harm or problems for others. They are a moral law unto themselves. We have a lot of work ahead and a very short time. This hour is ours, not tomorrow. Our thoughts can create demons in the astral then, what our thoughtless living and participating in the continuum of the endless suffering would create? We really do not and cannot comprehend our potential and possibilities. We are here on the Earth to allow the God seed in us to grow with light, beauty and to spread it to the rest of the creation. It does not come easily. Live with the responsibility of our purpose as soul/spirit on the journey to gain knowledge and wisdom through living. The Earth is a growing and pruning ground. Pruning, we must do. We must recognize what needs to be pruned and what doesn't need to be pruned. We behave as if our life is only on the animal part of the food chain. This is only for physical existence. We are in this sense, on the top of the food chain. Because of our ability of brain power, we can subdue all the lower animal kingdoms. That is what we are doing. It is wrong. We must understand our divinity is hidden within us, and abstain from all selfish behavior, killing, evil, and supply our body with live food made with sunshine, air, water from the blessed Earth, which is all herbs and plants. This is the only way our soul will be enlightened to expand our consciousness to a higher realm. We must not abuse our procreative faculty for pleasure. Most animals do not do that. Are we not better than animals?

If we think we are superior, then we must act like that. Renounce all pretense, lies, falsehood and practice love, charity, empathy, and compassion towards all creation. With grateful hearts, we do the work assigned to us and this is how we praise the Lord of all. Follow the true light. See it for what it is. We cannot manipulate God with flowery words. The Power of God seeks our truthful, love-filled action in the physical. "Thou shall not kill" means, thou shall not kill one hundred percent. One who takes the life of any living being whether it man, or a beast or a bird, is violating God's law. We, humans, have created a great mess. Misguidance is the way of our existence. It fits into our way of living. We cannot see the truth of anything. Emotional killing. Don't think that animals have no emotion. We are blind and deaf and refuse to comprehend. Our many words of glory and praise from the mouth will be carried by the wind of darkness to the dark clouds and fall as rains of suffering to us and everyone else.

Be pure in heart. If we seek God, seek with pure heart, mind, and body. It will happen when we stop talking and engage in the act of living. We have populated the Earth with this two-legged animal, who has no love, no remorse and keeps violating the laws of the creator and making hell out of everything. Some people help with that. Because they are stupid, yet pretend they are wise. What a beautiful Earth, yet what we have now is fear, and terror of human evil, war, overpopulation, etc. Each life is a pearl in the rosary of the great journey. We must do good to ascend the spiritual ladder. This is what our great creative power (God) wants us to do. This is my understanding.

Male and Female

What I write about here is the fundamental subject. The foundation for physical humans and in turn, spiritual existence. Without the union of the two, no human would be on Earth. The Creator force caused this so that its creation and purpose will be fulfilled. That is one thing. With this power, two powers emerged side by side. The Good and noble and the Evil with its destructive power. The two entities. Male and female sometimes give promise to the form, the image. Some give promise to the essence, the soul factor. One who makes promises to the spirit/soul, survived and faced all challenges and came out victorious.

A strong tree growing upward and onward to the height of perfection with its branches in good shape and strong. The one who makes promises to the world of form is like a dam filled with poisonous substances that fill up and finally it bursts and causes great damage to all in its path. This is what is the case today for the majority of humankind. Millions of children live on the streets and are abused by humans with bleeding souls. So, if somebody did not keep to their promises, do not feel sad for them, catastrophe is averted by the providence to give us another chance. Be strong. Because of characterless humans, people have to test for who is the father of a baby. Countless children in their entire lives do not claim their entitlement and destroy the very essence of their soul's purpose. There are noble children who are the torch bearers and hope for some glimpse of God's light. Allow their light to shine. No one wants to bear the responsibility for their lives, and no one teaches us the implications of our actions.

The sun is always shining. Sometimes, the dark clouds obscure the light. It does not mean the sun stopped shining. That is also true with our spiritual journey. Our light within is always shining to guide us to heights of the infinite sun, the divine light. When each soul is created and the spark of the spirit of the infinite light has entered the soul and it inhabits the soul and the soul inhabits the body. This little spark is the key which will open the Palace of the King. It is embedded in every being, all entities, and it fills the cosmos. It is our inheritance, and no one will take it away, or prevent us from entering it. Challenges are one hundred-fold on the path. If we choose to seek the soul path, by the grace of the infinite light, struggle on, there is light, in the darkness. And that light is only available for the soul who seeks to grow through physical existence. Without physical existence, we cannot make much entering. But surely with our tendency to live so as to create the dark cloud that will obscure the light sometimes, we walk in the darkness and fall, fall, and finally, we realize that we created the dark cloud, they are worthless and if they stayed, they would be living in hell. Do not miss them for a second. A major event averted which would otherwise bring us into the pit of suffering. We are doing this to each other individually and collectively, seeking power, and all the other traps. When we seek for ourselves only, there is somebody else who falls victim to that. We spread hot ashes onto that being. Hence the Bible says, "Blessed are the peacemakers," we must knock; we must search, with a loving heart to inherit the Father's kingdom with ardent desire to make the journey and reach the doorsteps worthy of opening the door.

We have to remove all the clouds and darkness with light, with righteous living, truthful living.

As we walk the path, do not push others into the pit of suffering. This is an abomination from the person who says, "We are on the path." There is a saying, when one digs a grave for someone, dig one more for the person who lives for themselves. Be conscious of everything. Live with empathy. Without this characteristic, no human soul/spirit will enter the complete light, nor experience the light. It is the nature of the soul/spirit. We can speak and speak plenty. We can wake up a person who is deeply sleeping, but a person who pretends to be sleeping, that person cannot be awakened. We as humans have great potential to reach the highest dimension of spiritual heights. Like Enoch or Buddha, Mahavir Jain and so many. What they did, while living, they avoided the power of the dark cloud and hot ashes, and they loved all. They basked in the sunshine once they woke up as a soul/spirit. Listen to the cry of the helpless; heal the pain and suffering of the lower Kingdoms. Avoid everything that causes you to fall and do not cause others to fall. Be strong in the way of the righteous. Once we do all that, we do not have to worry whether the Palace of the King is open or not. We then have that peace that nobody can snatch away. This great responsibility is endowed to us by the Creator. Because we are superior beings, and we must live high above the clouds. Once we, by the force of circumstances, cause clouds to descend upon ourselves with our selfishness and all other vileness, we cause others also and many of us are doing that. Spirituality is not mere talking and rituals. It is an actual work for us to walk the path, through living. Father in Heaven is waiting for the children to return home safe and sound and do the training successfully and worthily. This is the journey and destiny of the soul. So, each one of us should be responsible for others. We are our brother's keeper!

We must cleanse all vileness from the very core of our existence. Let no one be troubled or have to suffer because of our deeds. Enough is enough, seekers of the path. Take the true torch of love, empathy, compassion, and truthfulness and make the journey while there is still time and light shining on us (while the day lasts). This is my wish for myself and all children, all beings. I am not bound by any dogmas. I, as a spirit and soul here for a long time, maybe eons, so I know the ways of darkness and turn to the road where the light shines. May we all cut the forest of darkness and say, I am on the path. Shalom: May shalom (peace and wholeness) prevail among humans. May all humans leave the path of darkness and evil. Good and evil cannot survive together. One has to die. Choose. Use your free will. Do not harm or kill others on the way. Whatever a person's decision, they will be accountable a hundred-fold.

Story

Today, I will write a little story.

Here it goes: In India, there lived a man who was a Pujari (priest), who went to temples each morning, after bathing, in the Holy River Ganges (double blessings). On the way to the temple, he always sees a prostitute's house and a beautiful lady escorting men and having a very marvelous time, according to him (the priest). But on the other hand, the prostitute looked at the priest seeing him going to the temple each day and felt so sad and felt desire for God and God's temple. Both died and departed to the soul/spirit world. Here comes the beauty. The angels in charge of the soul/spirit took the priest to the lower dimensions. Then this guy got so mad and told the Angel, "I spent my entire physical life, going to temples, practicing rituals and prayers." The Angels said, "You did all in appearance and your heart was with prostitutes and worldly things." Then the Angel carried the soul of the woman to a higher dimension. She said, "I lived a very low life, and I am not worthy of this honor." The Angels told her, "You did all that in the physical, but your heart was with the divine." The Priest even complained to the Angel, "This woman was a prostitute and lived a low life." The angel replied, "She did, but her heart was always with God."

What one can take from this is that religions, temples and churches, such groups are good and enable us to transform and cause us to be transparent in our inner life. We must never use these religions to gain power, glory, riches, fame, etc.

If that is our motto then, it is like holding a plastic flower that has no scent. So, when the Angel of wind and honeybees visits the flower and recognizes that this is a lifeless object, and it does not produce scent and honey. So, it is with each religion and group leader. Their followers all should be selfless, humble and have an inner transformation, peace. They should preach, propagate, and participate. It is the inner life, *not* the outer glory. Be on guard from the deceit of the dark forces who seek continuously, self-glory, pretense and misguiding the naive. We must learn to unravel our inner life. Our heart is the dwelling place of the Most High, which represents purity, love, empathy, justice, compassion, etc. If one beholds that, no matter whether he is a teacher, guru, preacher, or leader, well done. He is the embodiment of all that is good and loving. Self-examination, transformation must take place, before we utter the precious all-name of the Holy Oneness (God). Thou shall not take the name in vain. If all religions, groups, teachers, preachers, all practiced and guide the folks thus, can one imagine what the world would have been in the lower animal kingdom? Okay, Rose; stop it, we have no time to do all that, and we have time to play the game of speaking. The world is suffering. Earth is suffering, animals are brutally being abused and being killed by criminals. I went through the tube that is filled inside with sharp nails and I pushed through and came out. I was part of a wonderful group; my departed brother and my inner being made me who I am today, gave me the strength to write. Taste and see that love (Lord) is good and share the love.

Here, I write about exposing ourselves to wonderful nature .

We are all part of nature. If we can feel that and make a support system of unity, oneness, peace, empathy, compassion, and love for each other and the entire Earth, and all its inhabitants then, we will create a positive thought that turns into positive action. Fear, isolation, etc., will disappear. When we stop seeking for ourselves at other's cost of safety, then peace and tranquility will prevail, and nobody will think negatively. Know that if someone thinks negatively, somebody else is responsible for that being in the inner mode. So, we, as humans, must be aware of our conduct in terms of relationships with other beings. Live and let live. Let us practice a true sense of the right of all and of living for all. Let us practice as the sun does. The sun lights up all on the Earth. So, let us shed the shadow of darkness and shine like the sun for each other. Let everybody smile. Everybody wants to feel joyous and feel the joy of living. Allow this. This is the way of the spirit/soul/mystic who seeks the Path of God. Everything else is the power of darkness.

Listening to music is better than counseling for depression and stress. It soothes the spirit and soul. Here, I want to write something different. What awakens the soul/spirit and what are the symptoms one goes through when that happens? This is a general experience. Everybody experiences something similar. Here it goes.

First of all, once it happens, their inner world turns upside down. They will be hypersensitive towards all outer happenings and inner happenings. They will be highly protective of the voiceless animals and their suffering. They will be very empathetic towards all kinds of suffering. They love everybody. They hate cruel and selfish people. They hate war, violence, cruelty to each other or any living being. People frame them for the things they never dreamed of doing.

All people in their lives, one by one, betray them. Because the betrayers cannot stand awakened people, they emit a different vibration. They suffer depression due to all that is happening to them inside and in the outside world that is not harmonious. For them, the hill rises, they doubt about the existence of God, because of the cruelty and selfishness of the people. Ascension of the soul/spirit will be harder and harder. They experience the dark night of the soul. Every human being will eventually go through these things as they desire to leave the wider road and enter the narrow road. One lifetime is only a fragment of the entirety. Religious people go through the doctrine of the particular one. Spirituality is a kind of a preliminary approach to the awakening of the soul. A spiritual being is kind, sensitive, and truthful, tries to avoid clutter, tries to clean up and throw out what is not needed for a harmonious living for themselves and others. They have taken the

Journey ... if they are truly spiritual. They do not say they are spiritual, but they live spiritually. It is their private life between them and their God. To that person, surely one day, soul/spirit will awaken. With their little sailboat of life, they enter the stormy ocean and if the boat does not sink in the ocean, it will reach the Shore of the Divine Presence. All souls will go through this eventually. As the evolution of the soul progresses, one automatically becomes kind towards all creatures. They avoid all selfish and evil behavior. This is the calling of the Lord to give up the dark road and enter the road of light. Justice and peace will be the portion for those who truly seek the light of God for their souls. In their physical lives, nothing significant will happen. But they go through pruning and transformation. I think, some time ago I wrote something similar. This will enable us to examine our inner existence.

Here, I will write above love…

This is the foundation of all physical existence for humans or animals. But what is love? Not everyone knows how to love, maybe just a few in the world. And they bring forth good seeds and they will be pillars, which balance the unbalanced foundation of human existence. People's love is mostly skin deep and lasts a few hours, a month, or a few months. Then the playground will be a war zone, emotional abuse, shattered life. Useless offspring are made, which bring calamity in the world. Look at the world today: Whose fault is this?

The foundation of men and women who entered for the kill. Everybody goes to worship their god in some assigned buildings, not recognizing the fact that in their homes, hearts, and the whole creation, the Creator's love permeates. By the Creators love that was brought forth to all the inhabitants of the Earth including us, and the billions of galaxies and all that there is. When the two who might love meet, surely their world changes. We must learn to open the book of life and read and practice what the Creator wants of us while in the physical, to turn to the eternal journey of the soul. Blessed are those who live in harmony (which is very rare), for they will fulfill the purpose of creation in their little way. I will write about garments.

This is good teaching for all who seek the spiritual path. Why do we waste time wearing garments that represent something? Our garment is our physical body, and physical life must be used to prepare and walk the way of the spirit. We must not waste any more time with all this baggage. All that we do in the physical is baggage for the soul/spirit. How much are we paying attention to? We have to use the solvent of reason and purpose to remove everything that hinders our progress. Live with morality, courage, and justice with compassion, and practice empathy. Without all these present in our natures, our spiritual journey is in limbo. We have to erase many things written in our "Book of Life," rewrite things while we can. Pride, selfishness, ego etc., have no place for a person who is walking the spiritual path. Harmony, peace, justice, etc., should be its nature. Nothing else.

This is a terrifying story about human ignorance. I have written about this subject many times in the past. Humanity now and in the future. What happens to the children who never get to see their parents? This is a real tragedy for human souls/spirits in physical existence. Some of these children who never get to see their parents, they are great souls/spirits who entered this evil existence through a foolish male and a foolish female who involved themselves physically to gratify their animalistic nature. However, sometimes they try to prevent pregnancy, still sometimes a child results, and this happens generation after generation. So, the wildfire is set in motion with one person's actions and continues for many generations to come. Is anybody thinking? Are the religions thinking? No. They have no clue about the links leading to foster homes/abuse, homeless children, child labor, orphanages, child abuse, etc. Why? Scriptures, religions, what is their purpose? There are very few children who have parents, who enslave their parents, mooch on them till the end of their days. They punish their parents for bringing them to existence. Some foolish stupid parents imagine themselves to be wiser and allow their children to do the most vicious evils and feed them with riches and riches. Not realizing that they, too, are souls, they have to learn to overcome and ascend. Both kinds of parents are bound with these souls for eons to rot together and also this binding happens also to other good children and people. This is the intermingling of the good and evils. Nobody can comprehend this, except the awakened souls. For them, it is a painful affair. Because they realize they are one with the world and the world is one with them. So, all endure the struggles. In the process, the animal procreation, suffering, killing, war, violence, rape, murder, etc., happen. Of course, religions have figured out everything. Even heaven and its functions, the end of the world, and the eternal condemnation of souls/spirit. Scientists try to find other planets in our solar system or in our galaxy. But wherever we go, we go with our evil power, within no time that place also becomes uninhabitable. The messengers will be killed. They do not want to change, do not want to acknowledge their deeds. You put on the TV that it is all about God, about what God thinks? Speaks? Feels? Why can we not stop talking about God? Talk about the blessing that we are in this world and have the opportunity to transform the world for every living creature, wherein the author of all will be pleased and manifested through creation. In human history, there were many times when nations were wiped out, this is also in religious scriptures. God got mad and destroyed the people. Is anybody paying attention to what is happening and realize what our part in the Creation is?

During the Soul's aging and progress, we human beings which is Souls in the physical existence, do, go through, achieve, did not achieve, done, not done, that of good, evil, love, compassion or anything elseit is all stored in the Soul memory, nothing is lost, nothing is Not accounted for Fruition, it will come to pass either as blessings, suffering, peace, discord, disharmony or whatever. As a highest intelligent organism, the humans, we must be aware of what we are doing, whether our doing, living is contributing to peace, harmony, destruction, construction, coexistence of all under One Creator. One may ask, are we dividing, or unifying, causing to suffer?

We human have a lot to think, change and transform.

We are only a Minute [tiny particle] part in the whole panorama of the Creation. Our Blessed Earth, all inhabitants of the Earth. We are not the destructive Force brought here to overpopulate and destroy everything. It is time to think in the collective sense. We are not alone. Contribute for peace in the creation and our little environments. Do not live in chaos, do not leave chaos to the generations that follows. This is our Soul work/Spiritual work. Do all things correctly for the Soul journey. Anything missed out, will be forced to deal with in a different soul time, in a worst way. Do not walk blindly will fall and hurt. As inhabitants of the Earth, we human have done great damage to each other and rest of the creation. We do not think what we are doing.

Because we are not trained to do. From the inception human existence, all we thought was, body, its wants, and how to achieve, power which is in real sense No power at all. It is for the few ardent seekers of the Soul journey to live consciously recognizing the peaceful coexistence of the collective. One May waste hundreds of life times, reading holy writings those writings will be holy, when we live by those writing and pass it on to the next generation, then next. I do not know, why I write, nothing will change. As usual I wrote theses without any prejudice and no offence meant to anybody. Shalom Rose.

PART TWO

I receive countless times in my dreams, visions of books. This is the "Soul Book" that we open and write in the physical existence living as souls.

Soul Realization

This is an important and carnal subject for all humans. Many of us strive to get the best education, jobs, positions, etc. Very well and good. It is very important that we achieve these things physically to support our lives and stay afloat. Rather than suffer and be a burden for others or the Government (for some countries like the US that provide help). Other nations, if you do not have anything, you do not eat, and you suffer and die. Nobody cares. That is for the physical. But there is something beyond the physical, something we humans have to acquire that is self-realization/God-realization. This is solely, surely, slowly acquired by the spirit/soul. This is eternal and cannot be destroyed. This is part of the Creator. It is like an infant, boy, adolescent, young adult, mature adult and old person. Similarly, souls will have to experience and grow to know themselves for who they truly are, as part of the infinite. It will come to all. This is our path: Learning, acquiring the diploma and doing the work for the souls/spirit endowed by the Creator. Sages, saints, and all are doing it. It is an infinite process. It is long, it is hard. Through physical existence, all humans will achieve it, ardent desire, work, overcoming the many distractions and attractions. One step at a time. There is no free passage for anyone. We have to earn our rights through living. Light is shining but in the soul level, most of us are blind. But when we remove the clay from our eyes, we see the light, the road. May the infinite light shine on all those who seek the way.

The Bible says: "God formed man from the clay and breathed into his nostrils and he became a living being." Once we stop breathing, we are proclaimed dead physically. Not in the breath, which will return to its sources and it is God's Breath. Of Course, with it, we carry all the impressions of our lives lived as soul/spirit memory. So, let us strive to create good and joyous memories for our soul/spirit.

Seekers of the spiritual path: Read and pay attention to what I am trying to tell you. In human existence, very few people understand what matters in the journey of the souls through the physical journey.

Some people understood, so, some of them went into caves, others retired from the worldly life and spent a life of devotion, love and lived out their lives. They are called the sages, saints, and true travelers of the path. You likely cannot recognize them. They may be sweepers or cleaners, dwelling on the street as beggars, or holding some meaningless job. Nothing is visible about them. But they are giants in the order of progression on the spiritual path. They are aware of the millions of organisms working in our bodies to keep us alive. We must pay attention to what we eat, do, drink, with whom and how we mate, etc. Every time men and women engage in sexual relations, billions of spermatozoa are allowed to die. When we eat, billions of bacteria—good and bad—are at work to keep us alive. When we drink excessively, our precious livers work to keep us alive by detoxifying the poison from our system. Along with the kidneys, the heart, brains, the muscles, lungs, blood, etc., billions of organisms are at work continuously trying to keep us humans and animals alive. When we take drugs or alcohol, we damage our brain cells, liver cells and finally, they will not be able to function properly. Humans were not taught to respect their bodies and minds. Overall, they indulge in what gives them pleasure of the senses. Our great forefathers failed; religions failed. They had some faith, beliefs, etc., "Do that and you are saved." About the anatomy of the soul/spirit, they have no clue. About the anatomy of the body, they have some. Still, even if they know these things, they live for pleasure and finally die. What happened to the souls/spirit? Well, if they earned something through living, they get a little diploma, it is very useful. This is part of the "Book of Life." Here, I love to mention two people in my life. One is my daughter. She is very kind, helpful, gentle to the little creatures, honest, does not seek out praise. Very smart, very wise, and quiet. She lives in her little world peacefully. If anyone tries to rock her world, can one imagine how awful it is, how evil it would be? Another person is my nephew, who is very kind. He is in his early thirties, married and working. If he sees some people suffering, he will even take his shirt and give it to that person. He has been married for the last ten years. His wife has pain, and it is constant, so every night after putting the child to sleep, he massages her to make her comfortable. There is some true love in their marriage and all their lives. He can experience the joy and sorrows of others. So, the infinite God shines on him continuously. I am happy these two people are part of my life.

What I aim at is, we must cherish all life. We must not ambush anyone's peace. Once one is spiritually awakened, no one has to tell such people not to harm any being either mentally, emotionally, or any way. If one can have an animal farm and kill the pigs or any living creatures and just enjoy that saying, "Oh, I love meat, pig, etc." Once one is awakened, all things will change. Also, if you expect someone to forgive you, it is up to that person. If the living spirit of God is active in that person, he will forgive. It does not mean they will not feel the mental/emotional agony. If people acknowledge their inheritance as God's manifestation in the physical, when one knows one has harmed somebody emotionally or otherwise, feel remorse and go and apologize. This way, we can take comfort in that, "I truly felt remorse for my action and before God; I did what I could at the given moment." Ego has no place in the soul journey. Eloquent speech has no place on the spiritual journey. There is no man or woman; there are people, animals, and the Earth. Love all, respect all and live, let live. First, transform internally and walk with God. God is "not out there" in somewhere in the building or a faraway country. Our heart is the dwelling place of the divine. All hearts. There are two forces at work: good/God and evil. Recognize to whom we are giving salutation and worship.

Trials

The infinite God has infinite time. Here, I have to mention the teaching that came down to me. Even if people are bad, their souls are like stars and follow the path of light. So, nothing will be destroyed. All go through trials, corrections, and finally, union with the whole. I do not like mentioning this. By mentioning this, I am trying to say, nothing will be lost nor is there eternal suffering for the soul. But this is our one lifetime. Change one's ways, attitude, and try your best to experience the God within and within all Creation.

One body, and the one body's organs. What happened to humanity? What is ruling humanity? Here I love to quote what Yeshua said, "When one finger hurts, the other finger cannot say, you keep hurting, we are fine." That is exactly what is happening in homes (most homes), villages, nations, and Earthly existence. We are shattering each other, killing, and abusing everyone without any remorse. A time will come when I will stop writing. Because it does not go anywhere. The majority of humans are like a pot with a hole in the bottom. It is all about them, no one else exists. Nations destroy other nations. Fools and evil powermongers are in high places. They have collected some pennies and they think they are untouchable. The powers of money, hormones, self-deception, power, lust are theirs. They are preying on other people, nations, and animals, etc. Earth is being mutilated for its hidden wealth. Stupid overpopulation, evil production of animal farms. There is only fear and terror. Noble teaching remains in the books they read. Who are they fooling? The approximate life span of a human is, for the majority, seventy or seventy-five and they die, and they die as if they never lived. They lived as if they would never die. If people do believe there is life for the soul/ spirit after physical death and if they are convinced about it, they will live differently. They preach, have an idea, a shadow, a myth, and act as if it is a reality. Boy, if people abstained from all these hormone-based, lust-based, power-based ways of living and transformed themselves, contained themselves, subdued their lower natures and practiced "live and let live". Even if there was no God, no life after physical death, still we have this supreme quality of comprehension of the consequences of our actions, and ability to predict the future, and many millions of ideas from that. Only humans have its full spectrum. Why can we not stop evil and do a job wherein peace and harmony are present for all creation?

People declare Jihad on others, what is Jihad? It is—in one sense— overcoming themselves and their lower nature. Not going and declaring war on others and converting everybody to their religion. It is a huge evil error they are trying to perform. Suppose if one manages to convert one person or several persons into their faith physically, internally they remain faithful and convinced of what they have is their way, then what good it is to declare Jihad on anybody? They fail to control and conquer themselves, so, it is easy to conquer others. History shows this very clearly. Ignorance and evil is the nature of men. They have to recognize their innate nature, fight, and ascend. I am really stupid to be writing all this. Because I am also human, stupidity is the way of men. When will our world be sane? Do not worry, war, violence, and destruction are the sign of the end of time.

Here, I will write about the universe. It is alive and well. Is Earth not part of the universe? Are humans and all other life forms not also part of the universe? How many millions of stars and planets are in the universe? Are all these stars and planets moving and working in harmony with the universal law? Of course, they are! There are two worlds simultaneously: the spiritual existence of all that is and the physical existence of all. What exists in the physical has a spiritual existence with the infinite God force. We say infinite because *nobody* can fathom the infinite God force. If anybody claims to and speaks of it, they created an infinite into finite form, and then it is not infinite in that sense. However, the true infinite is not working on the whims of the little man. In cosmic existence, we are only a very tiny speck. We are making so much noise, making such outrageous claims and have so many attitudes. This will not affect the universal law and its creation or dissolution of matter into energy (return to the spiritual existence). Humans will bring about the annihilation of all that is on the earth with our evil. All creatures and humans will die. The deathless will return to its infinite existence, to be manifested again in some form. Earth will be barren; still, it will finish its course in the universal order. You see, our sun is a living existence and finally, it will burn out and become a dead star and it will explode into and create new stars. We observe many shining in the sky, they must have been dead millions of years ago, due to the distance and time it takes the light to travel, yet we still see them as living. So, let us not assume that the end of the world is coming. Our human existence will be ended by us. We are stuck with many evil desires, killing each other, and hurting everyone and everything, we practice deceit, dishonesty. We are overwhelmed and we are lost in a sea of problems. We do not use our talent for honesty, empathy, self-restraint, love and so on. So, this is what we have since inhabiting the earth, overpopulation, crime, violence, etc. Other inhabitants of the blessed Earth are suffering so much at our hands. Whosoever speaks of God/spirit must try to transform and abstain from doing anything harmful to anyone in existence. If one knows a person is evil, correct him or do not support his evil. Whosoever is good and honest, support them and multiply goodness. Teach teenagers to respect and love all creatures. There is a storm going on within me seeing so many evils among humans, and still, they take the name of God. That is an abomination, and who am I to speak? I am not perfect. Nobody is perfect. But we must collectively love and abstain from selfishness and seek peace for each other and the rest of the world. War is not the answer. Wisdom, love, and empathy are the way of life.

Books

My soulful thought for today is about the masters of all time, to invite all of us to close the books of many words written by somebody and that is derived from somebody, and the list goes on back and back to thousands of years. No solution in sight, no light in sight. It is rather a pity. It is time that we open our book of nature, open ourselves to the magnificent creatures, the cloud, the sunrise, the sunset, the dark clouds that bring forth rain, the birds that take flight into the air and soar into the sky and again scoop down to the seashore to get its food. The deserts, the mountain, the snow-filled forest, the golden leaves of the autumn, the animals in the forest, the innocent babies, the life forms in the ocean, the meandering rivers from the mountain through the hills, valleys, to the plains, then to the ocean, All singing the glory of the Creator in its own way and functioning and fulfilling its task in destiny. Wonderful are the ways of the Lord.

On the other side of the coin, men and women fight each other, go to war, seek the destruction of nations, perform robbery, cheating, raping, and pillaging, tell lies, do evils in action with full strength on and through other humans. From this chaos, they are here and there, people who live, act kindly, cherish all lives, experience the splendor of the infinite Creation in all its majesty, know the joys, sorrows, of living, the struggle, the path, the ascension. In the middle of the chaos, one can experience the balloon effect, provided our hearts are pure, filled with love for all creation, and we desire to experience the joy of living by allowing all to be joyous in their living. If there is any selfishness, cruelty, intent to harm any beings either physically or emotionally, that person will never experience this balloon effect. When we are in love with infinite, we will feel the balloon effect—maybe for a second, a minute, or hours, days, depending on the experiencer and his/her innate soul quality. It will not come easily. We must be willing to take the narrow path that leads to the harshest mountain climb and finally, when we are on the top of one of the hills, we feel the balloon effect. The elation, the ecstasy, blessings to all.

There is a saying: It is in giving that one receives. This is very true physically. In the spiritual, what one receives from on high must be practiced through living. By our transformation from within, it will manifest through action in a very profound way, and this becomes a great sharing for the proper candidate. About spiritual experiences, if one shares with anybody and everybody for flattery, or even pure joy of sharing with someone, sharing with those who have no clue of what they are sharing, we are bound to lose it. Everything is so delicate, and it must be balanced and practiced for our ascension. See, however much we share our thoughts and experiences with someone who has not yet realized or is convinced about their spirituality/divine nature, etc., they will never change. Until they get a call to change from on high. Or they have a set of belief systems, and they are quite content and convinced if one says anything different to that person there will not be any change in that person. So, that is why saints, sages and noble souls, who are in tune with universal love, retire from the noisy world, recognizing the fact that we can move mountains, but human hearts cannot do this until they get the call. Hence one must never disclose sacred encounters to all. But unfortunately, we do occasionally need to prove a point or to suggest that what is going on in the world is not the right way. We lost something so wonderful in the process. Well, we meant no harm to anybody, but to see harmony, peace, safety, and love for all.

Tree of Life

Here, I mention something very profound and essential for a human's soul journey through physical existence. From this, one can realize there are two worlds that exist simultaneously: The inner world and the outer world, the spiritual world and the physical world. With careful observation, we can realize this. Like in the biology lab where people keep skeletons or internal organs to explain to students the anatomy of the physical body, similarly, the diagram of the tree of life is an analogy of the anatomy of the spirit/souls for the westerners. For the eastern religions, they have their beautiful teachings. In the mystical sense, all are the same. The language differs. Christians must never feel that the tree of life (Kabbalah) is something outside of their faith. The Christ principle presides in the center of the tree (the heart of all existence). It is the principle with which humans must live and interact with God's Creation to allow all to exist and fulfill their task in physical existence. We must consult with our inner guide (Christ presence) in all we do, think, and feel, in all our interactions. If any of these are going to cause any destruction or suffering to anyone, emotionally or physically, abstain from it. That being is a creation of the infinite, so allow its course to complete. With all the glory and desires of the physical world and its loud music of "me, me, mine," the inner voice sometimes (for most of the people, all the time) is forced to shut up. Inner voice and Satan in its full strength devours that soul for a long chain of life/death/life/death until the soul learns its lessons and breaks free of that force. The tempter—this, too, is created by the same God force. People love to eat cakes, pleasurable food, have sex, seek power, glory, egoistic existence, and I tell you that these are the attributes of the dark power. When we are entrenched in all these, we are doing great service to the dark power. Of course, we go to worship places, sing songs, bow our heads to the idols, etc. We must ask ourselves where is our heart and affection in terms of physical life? Where is it in terms of the connectedness of all that is. Are we living and applying higher consciousness to all our decisions, or we are allowing falsehood and injustice to prevail, and innocent beings are put in harm's way to justify our convenience? We must learn to judge for ourselves what is always present in our heart. It is a good and noble judge. Also, the evil judge inspires us to do the opposite. Watch and pray ceaselessly with our actions, so that we may not fall short before our judge within

Here, I write about spiritual masters and their power and responsibility. You see, if you give a precious gift to an animal, a virtuous human, a seeker of life/spirit and also a person who does not believe in anything but himself, and he has physical accomplishments of every sort and he lacks nothing, a beggar who seeks only his one meal who has no interest in anything. So, the precious gift may not have any value for anyone except those who understand what this means. Only they will cherish that gift. So, nothing should be given to just anybody and everybody. It is how it is.

We are all going through in our own phase in the long journey of the soul and are maturing slowly. First, when I sit to write, there is a downloading taking place within me. What I am writing is not meant to offend anybody. I am not expecting anyone to agree with what I am writing. But it would be human and good if everyone who receives this message shared their opinion. We are, as spirits, all on a journey, paths that may appear to be different, but the destination is the same for all. Occasional comments would help each of us to recognize where we are in our inner thought patterns.

I heard a prominent preacher speaking that this Earth will be destroyed, and Yeshua will make a new Earth and we all will have a new body and live with Yeshua on the Earth. What is wrong with this Earth? Earth did no crime. We are full of everything. It is not Earth's fault. We all have a spirit body. This spirit body will survive the physical body's death. In the true sense, there is no death. We are souls/spirits having a physical body and experiences. It is the will of God that created spirits/souls and the physical body. It is through this Earth living that we learn to fall, rise, and ascend as a spirit. This is undoubtedly true, I know. Why can we not be simple/honest/righteous, with empathy and love? Teach children at a very young age to be good, honest, that the gift of speech must never be used for lying. Then, when one becomes a teen, what they go through is the tempter enters their physical world and they will guard themselves against falling into a so-called love that is not love. We all did that once or twice. Actually, very few people know what love is and how to love another human being. This is the state of affairs. This is how the power of the physical manipulates the spirit to stay in bondage until understanding comes. Then the journey of the spirit/soul begins.

Do you know how trainers train their dogs to be rescue dogs, or helping dogs, or any service dogs? Well, the untrained dog is our physical fleshly life, but once we train our minds, bodies, and physical existence to transform for the soul/spirit purpose, then the spirit will guide the rest of our physical existence for transformation to ascension. Once trained, a dog will guide its master. Think about what I am saying. It needs recognition of the fact that humans have the potential of reaching the God head through living. That is the plan of the God force. It is like a child thrown into the sea to learn the swimming that swims ashore. This is the physical world and its many-colored faces, wants, etc. We must choose, and we are choosing.

Silence vs. Noise

Here, I will write about silence and noise.

If one notices, someone can be quiet and the same someone can be very noisy when the storm surges inside. Some old and wise people seek solitude, and they commune with the stillness of existence. These kinds of people are very rare; these few are the blessed ones who understand the world of the physical and beyond. They understand the symphony of Creation, the rise and fall of creation. The stillness/ the nothing (The Ain). The masters gave this name to the master's reachable existence called the infinite God/existence. No human will ever reach this place of existence—if it does, it will be after billions of deaths/lives and transformations into the purest form. This is the place of no return, oneness with the infinite.

From this existence, all spiritual worlds, and the physical world and all the noises and silences come into being. This includes all the billions of stars and our Earth. I am not going into all these details; it is not in my power to do it. However, we, as superior creations on the Earth among the animals, must recognize our responsibility and place in creation. We have this supreme talent to comprehend and do everything to fulfill our purpose in creation, to participate in the creation, helping and being kind to all moving things, raising all lower beings into a place of peace and rest in the very core of their existence. The Karmic Storm from the ocean of life is surging due to our irresponsible living. Humans forgot our inheritance in Creation. We think of ourselves as flesh, mind, ego: This is solely occupying our human existence. We create havoc for each other and the rest of the creation. At least, people who take the name of God understand what God is, the purpose of our living is beyond the physical and this creates stillness in all souls. If one shakes a tree, all its branches and leaves will shake. Do not be pretenders. We are all participants in the great work of bringing about the ascension of all physical creation. Nobody is alone. Dogmas will take humans souls to the very next level of the physical but no higher. But love, empathy, compassion, and righteousness will take us far up the ladder of the spiritual existence. It is work, the inner transformation, in turn, transforms the outer.

When one debates about God, asking: "What is the nature of God?" From that perspective speak, act, live, cause to live. Stillness will come to the one who speaks of God properly and the one who hears. Miracles will happen. Work to unravel all knots of dark powers. God and Satan cannot dwell together. We must never mislead ourselves for praise and glory. God is nowhere near that person's heart.

My soulful thought for today is about being true in the physical and in the spiritual sense.

When we look out for others and their wellbeing, heaven will look out for the wellbeing of our soul and in turn, our physical as well. However, we cannot compare our material wealth with heavenly wealth. One is perishable and the other is imperishable. For the materialistic, it is all about wealth and power, no matter who they hurt or kill in the process. This is the situation for the majority of humans. Here, I have to mention something, when I write it probably looks very negative. It is only on the surface. The sun is always shining; however, the clouds obscure the sunlight. Once the clouds pass, the sunlight will be ever brighter. So, please look for the brightness as you all are seekers of the spiritual path. You see, Earth is an arid desert for spiritual seekers, if you want to get water in the desert; you have to dig very deep. This is the case with souls who want to walk the path towards the light. The many desires, cravings, people with their ignorant living and action, the suffering of the women, children, and animals—all these become a huge, huge mountain for the seekers to climb. They are little ants, before a giant elephant. The elephant will crush little ants as he walks the path. Examine yourself and realize what I am saying. This applies to the one whose soul's eyes and ears open. I do not like to speak of these things, but I have to tell this to prove what I am saying. Here it goes, "The destiny of the Soul is determined by its journey through the physical." Small teachings came down. But the meaning you can realize. These are the direct experiences that made me who I am. Because of that, I feel I have to express what I was given somewhere. Blessings to you all and may the Infinite Light Guide all those who seek the path, and The Mighty Light and Love will be their strength to stand the Storm that rages around them while they are in the Physical.

Beliefs

My soulful thought for today is about how the whole of humanity should open their inner eyes (souls) and read what I am writing here. This is what I truly know from my heart: One creation, one Creator, one tree of life—knowledge of good and evil and from it proceeds all physical creation, all solar systems, galaxies, planets, including our blessed Earth and all its inhabitants.

On top of the scale of animal existence, we are human beings with great potential to do the work of maintaining and keeping the living organism of the physical Earth. If that is the case, why are religions divided? Why are so many faiths, so many beliefs, all fighting to establish one faith over others? Have we gone mad and are thus incapable of really doing what is right? The right that is the unification of all that is into oneness? People put so many things into pretending their beliefs are from the mouth of God and they fight over that. I am right, you are wrong, etc. I think we are all wrong. We have to allow the river of love, light, and wisdom to flow uninterrupted. Due to our faith, dogmas, and selfishness, all is fragmented. Let all creations rejoice that all are here physically for only one purpose of being in the physical world. Spirit/souls visiting the Earth for a while return to the soul/spirit world. They visit Earth again according to the divine order of progression. So, we all have to stop acting as if we are here to rule and subdue all others and act like an evil king who has lost his head and feet. This is exactly what is happening to the mighty rulers of the world. How many rulers came, caused war, and havoc and where are they now? People even think of their name as something so bad. But the saints, the sages, we lovingly think of their names and feel drawn towards them. What did they do? They practiced love, empathy, and wisdom so that they still live on in our hearts? It is my prayer that humans recognize our God potential and stop feeling like inflated balloons with huge egos, and live. Rather, stay on the ground, participating with the rest, feeling loved, shared, cared for—and let no one suffer. This way, we will do good with our physical existence and in turn, God's purpose will be fulfilled.

A new Earth is established, where love will rule (God is love) all will partake of the honey of wisdom, and the milk of understanding. We all enter and dwell in Yerushalayim (the habitation of peace), paradise. What we have been experiencing for the last four thousand years is paradise lost and that is due to the selfishness of man.

My soulful thought for today is about the true teaching for humanity, and whether they follow the divine law or not. What I write here is so very true. Human arrogance is ascendant all over the Earth. Every creation is on its path, this magnetism of living on the Earth is too much for these souls. The amount of pleasure, power, glory, the lower nature of the soul, the animal soul, causes most to forget our higher potential. Good is a heavenly affair. Evil belongs to the lower nature. Animals have no sin. Why? Because they live in the present. They do not scheme. With our higher mind, all we do is scheming to seek pleasure, subdue other beings, destroy others and we tell ourselves, "Who cares what will happen after death?" Well, they think they can get away with it. No way.

The whole universe, the physical and spiritual belongs to God force, a time will come when the soul will be made to realize its failures and it will be forced to correct them. Happy are those who really seek peace in their hearts for themselves and others. Because they may avoid the penalty or, if they have to, it will be bearable. One second in the soul life of suffering can feel like one thousand years of living in the physical. The point is, we have to contain ourselves. All religions and groups must unite in the perfect bond of peace and love, teach all humans to be careful and loving to each other and to the rest of the creation. Let no one suffer mentally or physically. Stop the abuse of procreative, God-given talent, trading it recklessly for the choice to abuse procreative pleasure. It is there, use it carefully. Reduce overpopulation by abstaining from misusing it. Men and women, I ask you to live in harmony and educate children to be noble, caring and respecting of all life forms. Eat for living and do not live for eating and pleasure. This is the only way we can make any progress. The other way results in prolonged Hellish living for the soul. All souls/spirits are part of the divine. Hence, I feel and believe there is going to be a purging each soul will go through and transformation through overcoming evil. The divine spirit is ever-present in each of us and in the rest of creation. Only humans have to work and get access to it by loving and being gentle to all creation, living with honesty and righteousness. Also, meditate and sing with groups, stay awake and pray to Jesus. If one practices it, one will feel the "rising from within" effect. One will have no cares in the world. They are in love with their lover, the divine, in effect.

Saint Teresa of Avila and so many saints, and sages experience this Holy Spirit effect. Learn to experience stillness through meditation and desire for peace and love. We must open the channel and allow the good to flow. It does not always have to be agreeable. We all perceive things differently. This is the gift and beauty of a human being. We must be as transparent as a clean crystal at our soul level.

My soulful thought for today is about the destiny of the soul. Spirits/souls are born from the womb of the divine. Through the union between a man and a woman, we entered the physical body and physical existence. However, the spirit/soul brings with itself the memories of the source of its existence. Even if one's destiny is to go through suffering either by disease or any other way, we cannot stand watching other beings suffer. That goes for animals as well. Instead of watching their suffering, one must nonetheless try to lessen the suffering of other beings. Not only that, but we must also never be an instrument for others' suffering whether mental, emotional, or physical. The truth is, we are all over the place, causing havoc for others, other beings, and nations. See, our souls/spirits existence is comparable to a caterpillar inside a cocoon: our soul/spirit is wrapped in many layers of matter. It has to break free of each one by one, a little at a time, to break free and fly and soar into the sky, or even fly to the branch of the tree to make a nest again. So, we need a religion, faith etc., to realize the life of the soul and its binding and connection. Once we realize and break out of these entanglements, we as souls/spirits must take flight and experience the freedom of the soul, freedom from all that is binding. Our soul wing will be comprised of wisdom, love, empathy, compassion, love, unity. If one misses that target, all such misses, we go back to the cocoon again. You see, we humans are not mere animals, so there is always an inquiry going on within for most of us. We begin in the physical by accumulating things, and not satisfied with that, get lots of sex, not satisfied; you do more of what you want. Eating lots of pleasurable food will not leave you satisfied. Take all the toxins of drugs; you will not be satisfied, there will still be something missing. Finally, some of us find an answer in union with the divine, maybe a little. That is the first step. Souls/spirits are not bound by time, space, dogmas, or any religions. Soul/spirit is like a gas, like oxygen in a canister. Once the canister opens, the gas escapes. This is what happens at physical death. If the canister is contaminated, then the gas will also be contaminated. We have to go through the process of removing the contamination. I am not saying some theory, dogma, this is my spirit speaking within me, and I use my hand to write.

Every woman and man who ever existed in human history was once a child, then a teen. Once one becomes a teen, the world and all its power takes over that being. God creates spirits/souls and Lucifer is involved with physical existence as if he is its creator. But Lucifer is under the domain of the infinite God. Lucifer would like to keep the physical world and its glory for himself. So, he amplifies in the humans and animals this powerful sexual desire, which starts from teenage-hood and continues for countless numbers of soul years, until we purge it for God's purpose. This is an instrument with which God spirit manifests. Animals have seasons; humans have all seasons, every hour, if possible. They are drowned in the magic of the physical. I do not have to go any further. With this, humans create these monsters in the astral and go down to earth and back to astral, down to earth and so forth, making no progress. This reveals an untold amount of suffering of women, children, and animals. What ignorance! Humans live only for the pleasure of the senses. Through which astral entities are created and they, in turn, rule human hearts. When we kill, do anything evil, the lower astral entities take great pride in this and enjoy nourishment from our doing, eating, spilling seed. Humans have entered this network of crime and evil and through this, we created lower astral entities.

To clean them, we have to think purely, lovingly, kindly, the desire for absolute light, God presence. It is a difficult job. We have no place to go, to hide, or to revive, because the storm of evil is ever-present in our inner and outer environments. Well, with one little step at a time, we will slowly but surely ascend according to the infinite purpose. We have to reduce the population by the love of God and by abstaining. Teach children not to trash their sexuality. Do not allow animals to be bred for our pleasure. Do not ever abuse a dog, horse, or other animals. Stop hunting. They, too, have to have sex to procreate a baby and we go and hunt them recklessly for pleasure. Just imagine how cruel we are. As if they have no life. They breathe the same life-breath as we do. We have the superior quality, which God has given us not for trashing but for utilizing it for peaceful co-existence with all that is.

Religions, parents, government: No one teaches us anything. That is why each one of us has to know ourselves. There is a saying, "Know Thyself." If we do that, we will know God is in us. Things will change. Do not ever destroy the spirit of a human being, a child, a woman, a man, or an animal. Until we clean our inner, any number of visits to worship places and all the noises of our prayers will remain as a dark vibration in those places. Let our hearts be the dwelling place of the Most High first. Speak less, live more for the love of all. For a while, I am here, and my hand will express what my spirit wants. It may not be pleasing to anyone. Please forgive me, if I offend your pride.

While intellectually one may understand, what is the use of understanding anything if one cannot put it into practice in daily life and living? Oh, my goodness, many people are campaigning for God, God, God … where is God? Is this campaign only in the mouths of humans, and God is begging people to praise him, praise me, so that God can expand like a balloon with ego? No way, friends. The God force brought all things into existence and its presence is hidden in all creation, all universes. Connect with all creations, cherish them, let all come into being and manifest their beauty, and purpose and return to its sources. Let us come to know the music of the spheres, the symphony of creation. The rivers, lakes, deserts, oceans, trees in the forests, the birds flying, the animals running. We must rise above and experience the wonders of creation and enjoy the joy of living, experiencing, and moving on. What is in us is deathless. From Lucifer, we inherited all destructive things, the lowest ego nature, with its out-of-control lust, lies, selfishness, pretensions, and vileness. So, what we have is overpopulation, disrespect for all others, treating each other as mere objects for pleasure. With that lower ego nature, we tell ourselves that animals and all creation are for us to destroy and indulge ourselves in, bringing fear to animals, and destruction of nature. Violence, war, rape, etc.

If we consider ourselves as humans, we must live differently, experiencing God and the perfection in God's creation and purpose. This is the only thing we can do. Animals live in the moment. Luciferic nature should be subdued to the maximum if we are to save creation and have some peace. Vibration is some huge energy, which can be good or evil. In some places you visit you can experience this. Either it is good or evil. We have this tremendous capacity. We are not using our God-given potential; rather, we are using the Luciferic potential for slavery. We can make such destructive weapons, trillions of spending for destruction, yet if we spent only one eighth of that amount, if we could use the rest of the money to eradicate poverty and bring peace and unity, oneness for all on the Earth. For that to happen, we must convince ourselves, knowing that we are here for a short while and we are here to fulfill God's soul purpose of learning, knowing, and ascending. All religions must participate in educating people not to overpopulate, not to kill any life forms. Women are not some feelingless commodities for men's pleasure. Male-female is the foundation of physical creation. This act must be used for its proper purpose only. Everyone makes mistakes but it is high time to abstain from them, from killing animals. We must get busy educating our children and everyone else. Our behavior has become out of control and the Messiah has to come. The Messiah came and it dwells among us, within us. Feel, experience it. They say war, violence, natural disasters, etc., are signs of the Messiah's coming. It has been this way since in advent of man on the Earth into physical creation. People are crying about global warming. Maybe it is warming and if so, it is due to overpopulation, animal farming, deforestation, etc. We are not doing anything to change this. We are so helpless. We created these huge, monumental problems for ourselves and the rest of the creation.

Wisdom of the Sages

Firstly, I am thankful to God that sage's wisdom has come to me. A few years ago, a very good soul who knew me on the inner level, started sending this to me. Then, after a long time, I started sharing it with some of my group members and then I started sending to few more. So, we are today connected through the sage's wisdom. Their teaching speaks to my soul, and it is in complete harmony with my understanding. I am not saying it is in any way easy to live. Well, we have to try. One accomplishes nothing without effort. In the physical, you can give billions of dollars to someone, and he can be rich. But for soul progress you have to work and earn your place in the Father's home. It is not a matter of believing in God. It is a fact that without God, nothing would exist. Not even a grain of sand. When people say, God, they picture some tall figure with a long beard holding a long staff and wearing a white robe. On the lower planes, we can see such beings. They are pure beings who lived out their lives in the love of all, serving with absolute desire to serve, who have gone through all their trials and tribulations with a smile, recognizing that in order to ascend the ladder, hardships and trials are a key part of their physical existence. They choose that. They did not come to walk on the plains, but rather to climb the mountain of the Lord. As they climb, they assist the paralyzed, help the crippled to stand, heal the brokenhearted, bring smiles to the sad and crying, etc. The God force is infinite and eternal, it has no form, it creates forms and all forms have their being in the infinite formless. It is the artist, and all forms are its artwork. We are under the rulership of the infinite one. Our choices, actions, thoughts, relationships with the rest of creations will color whether we are beautifying divine artwork or tarnishing it. We all do it. But we are given time again and again as souls to remove whatever tarnish we have caused. We will all finally (one at a time) return to the author of the novel of creation. We must honestly and sincerely recognize the God factor within each of us and the rest of Creation. Worldly glamour has only one purpose, and that is to enslave the soul and prevent its ascension.

How much do we express our gratitude to each other, God, and the rest of the creation? How much are we thankful to the one who wiped all tears, how much are we thankful to the person who gave a glass of water when someone was thirsty? Or said a word of comfort in their time of distress? We have a lot to learn, undo, and walk (not talk). I am thankful to my niece when she was sixteen, that she had the wisdom to write a long letter when someone acted inhumanely. I am thankful to all people who have said or done good for me. I am thankful to my brother. I am thankful above all to my Heavenly parents who walked with me even when I walked in the valley of the shadow of death.

My soulful thought for today is about money. Without money, in the modern world, one cannot live a minute. The demands of the world and society require it. The key thing is to acquire money through the right means. Not by causing suffering to anybody or any being. Money should not rule people. People should rule money. If you have money, spend it on real needs and not for luxuries. Do not show off with money. If one has excess, it should be used for alleviating the poverty and suffering of other humans and animals. Every able-bodied person must work for their daily living. We should make sure that after our passing, the money we leave behind is given to the needy and suffering. Some evil children/ people kill others or parents to get their money. This is happening all over our world. Wise are they who take precautions so that evil will have no power. Humans have a lot of work to do to cause the ascension of our soul and spirit. Not talking about it but doing it. The eternal spirit is trapped in the physical, fleshly world. It is like a bird with its wings cut off and put in a cage. Even TV preachers who say, "Send money to us and receive the Lord." How ego-filled is their way of talking? The Lord is not in their command. It is for every human to realize that God dwells in their hearts already. The Bible says to the seventy-two, "When you go to a town, carry nothing, say shalom to the first family you meet, and if they are of godly nature, they will receive you and you may dwell with them until you leave." There is so much to think, act, live before we come to realize the purpose of our existence. We have been created with the good and evil nature in our hearts. It is up to us to decide who will be our Master and Lord and discover what leads to Godly living, or Evil living. Choosing the way to travel.

Life, living, creating, dissolving, etc., is part of the soul's experience in the physical. Physical existence does not stand independent of spiritual existence. There is an interconnected existence of both. Let no one think that one can have one without the other. There are huge spheres within its many spheres, and all are spinning. From the center, souls are created and sent into the outer sphere to make the sacred journey of the soul. So, do not strive to create some kind of "good" image of oneself, which could crumble like dry bread. Live with the pure desire to ascend by learning and overcoming. The image people create and desire to be acknowledged by is idol worship and it is all images and no substance. Let no one waste their time talking and convincing others how wonderful they are. Convince the God within and live. There is a saying, "Without God's knowledge, not even a hair on one's head falls." What does it mean? There is a recording going on at the soul level, of what is in our inner life, outer life. What we create is manifested in the inner spheres. Let us imagine our soul life as a book that God gave to us. We have to write our story in it. If it is wrongly written, rewrite it. Play it in the garden of life, which is the dwelling place of God force. Wisdom must come to assist us if we are humble.

The wise sages say that everything is alive, people with a clairvoyant ability sense millions of things in their environments, which the fifth sense capacity of people cannot experience such as emotions, which are the gift given to soul/spirit by the Creator to live in the physical world. Through these faculties, man gains wisdom, learns to abstain from many evils that otherwise one could inflict pains on other beings. We all know how we feel, but we seldom think of others' feelings, and when we hurt others. An empath can know how others feel, an awakened soul knows how others feel, but not a self-centered human. The physical man who refuses to tune into these faculties lives below the animal level. Humans are not supposed to live this way. We are above the animal. But we use our five sense faculties to create weapons, guns, and other killing equipment to subdue and kill other beings. A man will rape a woman, a child, a boy, but not if he could feel if that was done to him, how that person feels. Because feeling for others is totally shut down in themselves. If you watch the animal herds, for example, elephants, see how the herds move together, how the herds protect their infants. How they travel together, supporting each other, the mother figure will be the guiding force and the herd follows the Matriarch. What is going on with humans? Where is safety for infants? Mothers, themselves, are ready to dispose of their infants, surely not every mother, but many. I am not going into details about this. In some beliefs system, people were sacrificing perfectly healthy animals, birds, etc. And they brought the God aspect down to the dirt. For their sin, what do animals have to do with that? People were even sacrificing babies, captured slaves or defeated people in battle. First of all, if they could experience the feelings of fear in animals or humans, they would not do that. All these memories are in the subconscious minds of the collective. We do not want to face the reality of love, truth, empathy, compassion, but instead, live a dreamy life and just do whatever. God force is life, living, and feeling. The evil force is selfishness, no feeling, no empathy. Do not take my word for it. Be still and explore the subconscious memories of the collective. Do not curse me for bringing forth the doings of humans.

Trust

Here, I write about faith and trust. They are more or less the same. A little baby has one hundred per cent trust in their mother. That is instinctual; the soul/spirit is born with it. As they fall, the mother will always be there to pick the baby up. They will help them to walk, and the mother's hand will be always there to grab them if they fall. Her arms will always be a soft place to fall. As they grow stage by stage, through their environment they develop knowledge of who to trust, and not to trust. They learn this because they experience betrayal in many situations with many people. If the mother does not allow the baby to be independent, they will be a grown tree with all the physical functions but no soul growth. Not only will it not grow, but it also gets stunted emotionally at the baby level. So, the precious mother allows the babies to fall, rise, experience many good things, bad things, learn to distinguish right from wrong. Then they will be a contributing member of physical society and the soul will be growing in its journey to fulfilling its purpose. Parents first, then school, then company, and society, in general, will always play a role in the development of the soul or the underdevelopment of the soul. Well, there is a price to pay for everything. Nothing is free in God's universe. Some establishments of faith tie souls to a place of limbo. A maze is created, and they are allowed to enter it without being shown the way out or, no exit is visible to these stuck souls. It is not permanent. The divine plan is not what man carved out for the rest of humanity. They have no power over God's plan. They may speak of God's plan but without much awareness. I will give two examples to recognize soul/spirit that are underdeveloped or in limbo. These people can beat dogs, horses, and any animal, they beat the crap out of it. They have no problem in doing this. They can even advertise how smart they are to hunt a bear and show off. Farm animals and chickens are killed for a good meal. There is no feeling in them. They are sleeping souls. These souls have no problems killing, raping, and otherwise abusing humans and animals. They talk of God, and with the same mouth, they lie, deceive, cheat. These are all learning tools. I am not saying anything against it. When a boy and girl fall in love, often one will cheat on the other causing loss of faith and trust. Next time, they will be very careful about trusting the opposite sex. When the trials mount beyond our ability to bear, we lose faith/trust in God and man as well. These are passing moments in the soul's journey. We will rise. If an awakened soul sees an animal or human suffering, such a person goes through the same suffering. Sometimes, the ones they see suffering are beyond their physical reach to render help. But they can feel. See, once souls awaken, they see a different world, they feel awful about the road they traveled and regret it. They will do everything possible consciously to live by the call of the spirit life. Then ensues the dark night of the soul with challenges, trials, betrayals by trusted ones, huge injustice, witnessing the killing of animals, rape, violence, they may be framed by people who are called their own. To maintain balance in this circumstance is a task, and you may even doubt the existence of God force itself. All of this takes place on the physical, but an awakened soul cannot go back to the old ways. Job, in the Old Testament, experienced this. All sages, saints, and all high order spirits experience this. Again, this is the way to the growth of the soul/spirit.

HARMONIOUS PETALS

ROSE

My soulful thought for today is that I shall write about breathing... or the breath of life.

First of all, I am trying to express how to navigate souls/spirits into awareness of the breath of all breath. That is the infinite God force from which all comes into existence. We think it is not teaching us, we are here and God is up there in a faraway galaxy. Of course, I believe there is an inaccessible region in the cosmos and that region is so vast or dense beyond the spiritual dimensions, and of the physical creation, nobody knows the totality of it all. Scientists so far have discovered only a tiny fragment of the physical world. So, without understanding the mighty existence of God force, man speaks so much and understands so little. What we can understand is our physical Earth and humans and other beings. Who knows how many more plants and creatures remain to be discovered? What I am trying to say is that physical and spiritual creation is the field of the Lord. Through its breath, all living beings and creatures came into the field and danced for a while and returned to their source. So, if we allow anybody/beings intentionally to stop a being's breath and it is killed, we are violating the law of creation. I know from the advent of humanity, we have done many wrong things, considering only ourselves. The perpetual unbreakable links of steel were created, and we are part of that link. We have ears and we do not hear; we have eyes and we do not see; we only see and hear what suits us and adds to our pleasures. We, too, will be joined one day with the killed or destroyed ones. The physical destiny of all the creatures is the same. But for humans, because of our superior gifts of many faculties, we will have to face as spirit and soul all the side effects of our actions during the soul journey. When I write, things come to my mind; I express it in a raw form. It may not be pleasing to everybody. I feel I am part of the world, and the world is part of me and it is just my desire to let all live according to the Creator's plan and die when their time comes. We may think: "What is spirituality, how can we achieve it?" People go to worship places, then come out and kill others, declare war, and do all sorts of things. What are they thinking?

My soulful thought for today is how to observe nature. We, too, are part of nature. Learn to observe the workings of our inner being. Is it in harmony with the laws of love, creation, and creator? People on the spiritual path (as they claim to be) have the greatest responsibility in their own lives and for the lives around them. They must recognize the gift of all working of the brain, mind, heart, and life in general. All these faculties must work in harmony to bring peace to their own environments and around it. Avoid evil, falsehood, lies, pretense, be a vehicle for peace, love, empathy, and harmony. Do not waste your God-given time and life with empty talk about God while not living by the word of God. Be part of the great work of unification of the great God force ever-present in the creation. Let us be the contributors of peace and well-being for all, rather than self-seekers, no matter who will be harmed in the process. People who do not want to live by the law of God: It is better if they do not talk of God to others. We have preachers everywhere. What is the world today? Is anybody safe, secure here? No animal will harm us, but humans will. Where is our ability as humans? With our thoughts, we create Sheddim (evil spirits/forces) in the lower astral. If one knows that, stop creating them. We created the Hell regions, astral regions with Sheddim (evil force) and which are devouring human/souls with lust, rape, killing animals, violence, disrespect for each other and God's creation. Oh, we read scriptures, holy writings; we sacrifice to God, God's creatures, yet human conditions grow worse and worse. All religious groups must first understand and teach humanity what life is and to live with decency, righteousness, empathy, etc. No matter whether there is Heaven or not. We have one beautiful Earth, and we are in it together. We must support each other. If one is destroyed, another will be automatically destroyed with time. So, take the garments off, garments of falsehood and evil, and live plain, simple, honest, lives. Many people who live with huge selfishness, jealousy, evil-filled hearts, yet still, insist on receiving the Lord every day. So, they talk of God, and they know it all. Is God gone from them once they receive? What a myth. Why do we deceive ourselves, and try to deceive God? That can never happen. How can people take the name of God, and receive God, when their inner self is filled with blackness? We all have this blackness, only the degree of it changes. Observe nature in yourself and in the entire creation. Rejoice in the blessed ability we have and use it to the glory of love and light.

Comparison

My soulful thought for today is about comparisons. In physical existence, humans make plenty of comparisons. Animals do not compare anything with anything else. This comparison is not good, because there is no end to it. People who are content with whatever they have are the richest in the world. They may be street sweepers or janitors. All the chaos going on among humans is because we are never satisfied. Rich men want more. In the spiritual realm, comparisons will never work. The higher the spirit travels in one's life, the humblest will be the spirit in the flesh. So, do not judge people by their garments. A sweeper may be a high order spirit in the inner life. Some people demand respect and honor because they feel their inadequacy, so they dominate others. Those souls are lost who feel great by putting others down. They may be putting a saint in the lowest level physically.

Humans have not yet resolved most problems in spite of the tremendous progress humans have made in the physical. What progress? People destroy their health with bad habits, then invent medicines to treat them. They invented weapons so that they can kill each other and go to war. Millions of others suffer more. Humans are mostly among the earthbound spirits while living and after they shed their bodies. Because they live in the five-sense world and live for "me, mine, my need, my fame, my accomplishments, let all suffer for my glory." Religions have divided us even more. I am not saying anything is wrong with religions. If religions are practiced for true spiritual awareness for all beings and (humans) unity, the love should be practiced for the wellbeing of all souls. We must abstain from "I have the truth and you do not." That is where religion has caused war for thousands of years. People go and kill other humans. What do they understand about the soul/spirit? They kill a body; the soul/spirit departs from the killed body. This soul/spirit will never die; it is part of the Creator. The idea of killing will not work in the realm of life, which is the God force. If one would look into human history, emperors, rulers, kings, religions have all killed millions and millions of humans and other beings. Are they wise who understand life, physical death, and live for harmony and peace and leave? Leave no legacy for our souls and leave no legacy for others by not performing our tasks and duty while able and alive? Live with wisdom and justice. Read the book of your own life, correct whatever mistakes one finds there, rewrite whatever one can, so that when we are ready to shed the garments of flesh, which is our physical body, our precious soul should not have a memory of lots of unfinished business, and a residue of the darkness and pains we caused to each other, and other beings. Let our soul/spirit soar.

If the soul wing is tied to too many burdens of our evil and not good deeds, it will not travel very far into the spiritual realm, rather it will be plunged down to the mire of physical existence in a worse way. So, we must read our book of nature, inner nature, keep a good record, so that when the book of life opens when we enter the spirit world, we may be able to read about ourselves and not be ashamed. In the soul world, everything will be made visible and naked. We cannot fool ourselves there in that state of existence. Here, we play the game of life, we present ourselves with excuses due to our inner inadequacy, but our cleverness will not be able to use those stories in that plane of existence. Let us all clean our slates, live with honesty, love, empathy, compassion and be kind to all beings. Our soul/spirit will soar the expanse of the infinite God world. There will be no stopping, no ending. Joy will follow that soul who lives a life of love.

HARMONIOUS PETALS   **ROSE**

What I write here relates to all of us (that means, ninety nine percent of people). Instead of connecting with the soul/spirit of each other, we see the frame, the ability to convince the other, the flattery, the pretense. We all have fallen and still fall prey, because of the carnal nature of physical attraction. Well, we suffer, we fall, we rise, it is meant to be. We are not born wise but gain wisdom and understanding through the soul's journey, through physical existence. The creator willed it to be this way for creation.

Now, I want to write something away from this theme. In our group we discussed the father who had two sons and called them to work in the vineyard. One hesitated to go, but finally went, the other son said "okay, I will go", but he did not go. Who are these two sons and who is this father? The father is Jehovah, and the sons are the Pharisees and the Sadducees. One is the priest group and the other is the political group. The brothers are very powerful. They hold onto their power at any cost. They have such an attachment to their power. The tax collectors, the harlots, are the ordinary people living and getting by under the pressures of this upper class. These poor people have no power. They are humble. Their hearts are not as stubborn as those of the powerful people. Yeshua recognized these powermongers and their power over these poor people. So, this is what is happening today in our midst as well. People wear garments of God, but their heart is far from Him. These poor people are the fertile soil where God's seed will grow without much effort. A soundly sleeping person, we can wake him up fast. One pretending to sleep, one cannot wake them up. The kingdom of God is within us. If our heart is the Kingdom, the King must dwell in our heart and must rule. Without a king, the kingdom would go into anarchy and chaos. We can see this for ourselves.

Jesus said, "My kingdom is not of the Earth." Jews waited for a physical king to come and rule them forever. What is in the physical will face death and decay. But what is inside? The soul/ spirit belongs to the Heavenly Kingdom. Jesus made us recognize that He belonged to the Kingdom of Heaven, though, physically, he was on earth. So, our soul/spirit is part of heaven. Otherwise, we have no need for Jesus or any High Order spirit to enter the physical to tell us that the way we are conducting business is not the way to the Kingdom of God but rather to the kingdom of Lucifer. Jesus says, "I have come for the one who repents, realizes, changes and transforms." Not for the one who sits on a throne and pretends to have the key to the Kingdom. The keys are given to each soul/spirit and are buried in the recesses of our being. We have to uncover them in physical life. Existence is like this, we have to peel layer after layer to uncover the precious key made of love, light, wisdom, empathy, compassion. With which we will open the gate of Heaven and enter, travel, higher, and higher, into the infinite world of the infinite God.

Then, there is a discussion about marriage. Who gets to receive Holy Communion? Everyone who receives with the intention of its full meaning, I think it is fine. But being part of the church, you can have no love or decency in your heart, go to Mass, receive communion, come out proudly. In the eyes of man and laws of the practicing church, they are members and entitled. God and every action in this regard is a matter of the heart.

Regarding the Pope, he understands and makes a decision as a human being. Before the mighty law of God, who is he to say or do this or that? He recognizes that we are all falling and rising and we must decide for ourselves with our free will what is right and what is wrong. He is clearly saying, though, that he is the head of this group called Catholics and he has no authority over God's kingdom. How many people have extra-marital affairs and are still practicing Christians? How many people have many sexual relationships before getting married? This is all over the place. But once a religious person becomes spiritually awakened like some sages and saints, they are a law unto themselves. They do everything that is good for their souls/spirit. Nobody can inject spirituality into anyone. This will happen during the journey of the soul. What I feel, I write. If anybody feels offended, know that we have to make more progress. Still, something in us feels angry, and then human lower ego is in charge so one feels offended. We are all part of each other. We feel. It is natural. We have emotions of all sorts and levels.

HARMONIOUS PETALS

ROSE

If humans are truly spiritual, they look at stars, the heavens, and the oceans, the lives within them, the sky and the birds, the precious Earth and all inhabitants in it. No, we do not have time to pay attention to anything. We are busy with our plans and agendas. Well, we go to worship places made of bricks and stone and say prayers. Well, we humans are in it for a long ride. As souls, we have millions of years of the soul journey. We cannot love God without the love for the entire creation. We are pickers and choosers. As long as we do not feel empathy for the little brothers and sisters of the lower kingdom, so long as we can take guns and shoot, go to war, and physically or emotionally kill humans or animals, when we abuse our physical temple with all sorts of evil pleasures, we are not even starting to walk the path that leads to God. We are slaves to our tendencies, to our lower ego. It does not mean we will be cast to hell eternally. There are millions of levels of soul planes, we will choose one of those depending upon the purity of our hearts, to be back again in the physical and start all over again. Soul memories will come to play as we progress. Temple/ worship places are places where the communion of the saints occurs. What did it mean to be a saint? Those who struggle to walk the narrow path, for their own soul's sake? We experience many trials on the way, within and without. We must recognize the indwelling spirit within us, within all creation. God walks through creation. Pay attention. Ever since I can remember, I have been on trial. All I can do is my best, which I am trying to do. I am sure some of you are as well. May we all have the strength to climb the ever-higher ladder which suspends from infinity to life eternal.

Empathy

Humanity should realize that we are endowed with high spiritual capacity or non-spiritual capability by which we create astral entities. When we live in a selfless, loving, empathetic, compassionate way, we create angels, and they serve us in the soul/spirit life. If we are selfish, self-seekers, cruel in our life of action, thoughts, we create dark forces. While we are in the physical, they serve us. We are their Master. Once we have dropped the body and crossed over, they are our master. They say, "While alive, I made you rich, you did everything against love and light, and I supported you. Now, you will serve me." Humanity must change the way they think, act, and feel towards each other and all other beings if we are to have safe living and safe passage. Any amount of reading Holy Scriptures and religious discussions will not transform us unless we live for one another and the rest of the creation. Anybody thinking, what will a dog, horse, elephants, cow, chicken, or turkey go through when we abuse them, kill them? Can anyone know how many dark entities surround slaughterhouses, can one experience the fear of an animal that goes to the slaughterhouses? We are capable of doing better. An empath can feel all that. We are not slaves to anybody. We must create an environment where, first, man and woman share their living and homes with total love, harmony, and discipline, the children to be good citizens of the Earth by nature, and naturally, they will be good citizens of the heaven as well. This is what is terribly missing from the inception of human existence. We are proud of ourselves as superior beings, but at the most, we have been inferior beings from the time of our presence here on the earth. What is the use of technology, advancement in science and medicine, when our inner spirit is shackled with iron chains attached to the physical living of all sorts? Do you want to see what the difference is between an awakened being and a religious person? Interact with them. Read the writings of saints and sages of all religions, learn, and understand to absorb and transform, to be part of the spiritual progress for all the inhabitants of the Earth. Wipe their tears, remove their fears, and heal the emotional pains we have caused to all other beings. Practice goodness for the love of it, and for our own soul ascension. This Thanksgiving Day, how many millions of turkeys will be slaughtered? Why can't we give thanks for all the blessings from the temple of our hearts wherein dwells the spark of the infinite love/light and refuse to kill turkeys? For humans, it is all about physical pleasure of every sort. But when you are in love with your God spirit, that is the only way we feel happy and contended. We seldom recognize that and do it. Sorry if I offended anyone. We have free will, and we use it for good or evil.

HARMONIOUSPETALS   ROSE

My soulful thought for today is about the gatherings of the souls. So, let us all, all religions, groups, and individuals of good will and peace, let us repair the Olam (world). We humans disobeyed the Creator and have fragmented the Olam, and we have to repair it with our living. Some thoughts are emanating within me, so I will write. Just imagine a grand electric grid (which is the infinite one) and from this, current passes to all big poles, small poles, tiny poles, etc., far out into the spiritual and physical creation. In physical creation, that current is running through each of us. While the current is continually running, if we insert a bulb, it lights up. This is what happens with male-female relationships, a new life, new being. If you break the bulb, the light physically disappears, but it does not mean electricity is not passing. No bulb. This is what happens when some beings, whether animal or human, are killed. The essence of that being still exists. This is for true spiritual seekers. Be aware of what we are participating in or not paying attention to. We have traveled too far from the God force. In the west, a perfect light shines through Jesus. It is still shining in all hearts that live in love, purity, empathy, and compassion. In the east, the Great Buddha serves. And so forth.

The electric grid analogy fits perfectly into the tree of life of the ten sephiroth shine, bringing forth all wisdom and understanding. In the center, the great sunlight shines. I am not going into details. We will go into them later. We, as Israelites (who seek God) live in Israel (physical existence) and must strive to enter into Yerushalayim (the habitation of peace). If we do not make progress while in Israel, it will not occur after the death of the body. What we create for our souls while living will go with the soul to the place we have earned. There are many levels of spiritual existence. This is not for bookworms, debaters of God. This writing is for the genuine seekers on the path. I have no qualifications to write, but I write what flows through me. So, do not waste time talking about God, rather do the right thing. Love the life of the righteous. God's current is ever- flowing through our lives: experience it. Live, and let live!

There is no other way for humans to connect with God force, but they must do it through compassion, kindness, and empathy. No flowery praise and speeches about God suffice and satisfy the law and love of God, but action from the love of the heart. All creations and beings are the words of God made to manifest. So, we must act in accordance with the laws of God and free will. With free will comes the great power for darkness or great light. So, know who we are serving. Eventually, we all will learn to serve the light.

In the soul levels, there is light of many shades; there are many mansions, depending on the love and life we lived out. The people who lived their lives with selfishness, cruelty, corruption, killing, lies, deceit, abuse of animals and humans, irresponsible living, abandonment of others, cruelty to women, children, animals, their souls enter a house of complete darkness and their souls' slumber in the greatest torment. They are sleeping, it appears, but they are going through the suffering they inflicted on other beings. Nobody can wake them up. They are in great torment. Eventually, high-order spirits descend into these realms and wake them up. So, we may think we can fool the creative law and the Lord. No. God is in control of its law, even though on the physical level we may play at being victorious and successful. We cover-up our evil deeds with good speech. And in doing that, we are betraying the very God force within. The repercussion of that will be great and unavoidable. Watch and pray. Say goodbye to your old friend, deceit. All religions, groups, and people must join and stop animal suffering, overproduction of humans, and abuse of sexual power. Protect the Earth from destruction with all activities of humans. We are turning this beautiful earth into an arid, depleted land where no life will exist eventually if this continues. We must stop talking about God and do the work God has entrusted to our soul when they were sent out to the Earth. May good sense and good attitude prevail in all that we do.

Chapter 11

Changes

Here, I will write about changes. Changes are happening all the time, on the inner level and outer level. We even move from one place to another physically, relocating from one place to the other. Are there true teachers readily available? I wonder. Who is a teacher, one who understands the Creator, creation, and is working on all levels? In human history, real spiritual masters have always existed. What is their job but to spur the slumbering human spirit to awaken, or show the way? But it is for each one to do the actual work. There is no automatic transmission of spirituality or God/Heaven to students. People must be vigilant in following these so-called teachers. There are teachers who may have had some glimpse of the other world, and they immediately change their ordinary garment to put on orange garments as great beings and hold up their rosary beads, to sit on golden thrones, gather disciples and demand worship. They are false teachers. True teachers are the vehicle for God's love and light and they live out their lives expanding that love and light in all they do. Follow them. Universities cannot produce a spiritual teacher. The true teachers for good or evil are latent in each human. It is the parent's duty to awaken that spark in the child. Provided the parents know anything. In the absence of good parents, children, most of the time, follow evil teachers and this will guide the human being into the disaster of indulging in pleasures of the flesh, raping, abusing others, killing, etc. They are burdens on society and the Earth. There are children who follow the inner teacher, which is love and wisdom and they live a life of kindness and compassion. They seek safety for themselves and other beings. Recognize them for who they are. Look at their action from the heart. We all have a lot of flaws to reconcile, and we need to make changes in our lives, attitudes, discipline and so on to bring the world into a realm of peace. If the true teachers are not there for us in the flesh, there is great wisdom imparted through writings like proverbs, The Sermon on the Mount, The Dhammapada, and The Bhagavat Gita, etc. These are all similar teachings. These teachings tell us how to live with honesty, compassion, and love, and transform ourselves and ascend the ladder to eternal blissful existence.

See, the God force is universal and there is unity under one King. The disparaging of humans for whatever reasons will have no effect on God's love for its creation. It will have a big impact on our souls/spirits. In the garden of God, there are many flowers. The Earth is our garden where humans and animals must live out their lives without infringing on the right of all to exist. Seek harmony in all things. What have we humans created out of this beautiful creation of the Earth and its inhabitants? If one believes in God, then you need to show love and caring. If the opposite happens, there is no God-awareness in that person.

During this time on the Earth, we are heading towards the destruction of all here. If People were wiser, more loving, Godlier then the result would be different. We have to wake up to view things from the soul level, what we have created and where we are exactly. The extremely lowest ego rules! Because of that, those looking at the world from that perspective can look down on other people as inferior or treat animals as commodities for their abuse. Everything is part of one ecosystem. Once part of it goes, the other part also goes. Allow your free will to manifest in a good way to produce the fruits of peace, love, and unity, where God's presence is felt by all beings. Let no one suffer. May god's will and love be experienced by all!

Here, I write about Karma (western traditions call it sowing and reaping). When a person goes through suffering of all sorts, some would say they are paying for their doing or not doing. Well, that is true enough. However, if we stand by watching others go through suffering, and if we do not help a drowning being, whether human or animal, we are adding to our own sowing and when the time comes, sooner or later we will reap. Then we complain, no one is coming to help us, too bad. Humans are causing others to sow, reap, nobody is free from it. With our great blessings of wisdom, we must minimize this causing of others to sow, so that we too will be sowing less. Humans have flooded the Earth with suffering. Earth is soaked with the blood of all kinds of beings. When will it stop? When people realize God is present in all hearts and all beings and in Creation. When we decide to do anything besides love and compassion, we have already created a sowing effect for us. We add one more nail to our cross.

My soulful thought for today is about the teaching by Jesus: "To achieve the kingdom of God, give up the riches of this world." It is not necessary to give these riches up, but so long as one is attached to wealth, glory, power, selfishness and gaining wealth at the cost of other beings and their suffering, this accumulation of wealth will weigh down on each soul that lives that way. It will break the wings of the souls and such souls will pay dearly after the physical death.

One can see that rich people buy every sort of pleasure with money. They get intoxicated with this money, and such people (most of them) just do evil things to satisfy their senses. This is too bad. I see on TV, preachers who say: "Receive the Lord, believe in the Lord." They speak so loudly. Can we receive the Lord from the sky or some outer galaxies? Where is the Lord? The Lord is in every one of our hearts. Our hearts are the dwelling place of the Most High. We have to learn to experience within ourselves the richness of the faculties with which every human is born, which is love, compassion, righteousness, and so forth. When we fully engage in fleshly pleasures, killing and ambushing, causing suffering to any and all beings for our selfishness' sake, we produce poverty for our souls. When we go to worship places, we must see to it that our God within is fully realized and if we can do that, our collective communion is worth it.

My soulful thought for today is about issues we all face. This blessed physical existence and the wonderful Earth are the fields of the Lord, where souls incarnate to do sowing and reaping. This is how we will grow and mature. But we must be willing partners in the process. Our souls/spirits are composed of potential evil (in the lower soul nature) and potential good (in the higher soul nature). When I say this, by sitting quiet and focusing inwards and go through all that happened in our lives so far in this current existence, I recognized we are a mixture of the higher and lower nature. In the physical, we use our lives to do good or bad. It all depends on the commander in chief, the indwelling soul/spirit. We cannot storm heaven for retribution or otherwise, but if we take the correct action to solve our problems, Heaven will help. At least we will have the satisfaction of trying to correct our wrongdoing. It is of paramount importance. So, as much as God seeks His people, it is important that they live a legacy-free life, so that our soul wings are not severed with a deliberately ego-filled life and living. We must collectively heal all wounds, heal the Earth, and protect the animal kingdom from human abuse.

Only with planning and prayers should children come to the world. We must not produce Shedim in the physical world to destroy the good souls, animals, etc. The whole Earth is now filled with these forces. The battle is raging. There is one Creator, but people say, "My Lord, your Lord, their Lord," and there is battle wherever there is discord, there dwell powerful entities, who belong to the Dark Zone, which humans created. It seems that the majority of us choose to live by the power of Lucifer. I know, I am not an authority on the spirituality of anything. But I must write what is in the common good of all and well-being. Is anybody thinking about the destruction of the nations and people and their suffering? How is all going to be healed? Overpopulation? Children on the streets all over the world? Ignorance is the way of human life.

My soulful thought for today is about our immense ability to create heaven or hell on the Earth or anything in between. It is absolutely true. Parents should help their children; beyond the mere bodily comfort they provide them. Anyway, since sages wrote about the creative power/word, from today onwards, I am going to take up the Hebrew letters one letter at a time to write a little about them . Today this inspiration came while I was having my walk, I wrote to a brother about Hebrew letters. Hebrew letters are Holy Creative letters. Sanskrit is the Most Ancient Holy Language and Hebrew, Aramaic; Greek, etc., are derived from the Ancient Sanskrit Holy Language. People may debate this: let them. I have no interest in debating anything. I see people are debating about God etc. wasting the hundreds of lifetimes (soul's lifetimes). Achieving nothing and not making any progress towards the ascension of the Soul. Please bear in mind that I do not know Hebrew. I only know the letters and their meanings that are essential to know. Yeshua is the embodiment of the complete twenty-two Letters of ITS meaning and Power. This is true for all the Avatars (The True Avatar). Even Jews do not pay any attention to these meanings, but this is not my problem. If anybody does not want to receive this writing on the letter and its meaning please let me know. I am fulfilling my life purpose with a few spirits like me.

Chapter 12

Spirit and Matter

My soulful thought for today is about spirit and matter. Spirit descends into matter (physical) then ascends to its dwelling place of Holiness to continue to partake in creation under the law of the ineffable power. There is no way around this. I am wondering, how many people read the true teachings of the sage's messages, how many think about this, how many take actions towards the ascension of the spirit within. Maybe small baby steps, now, as I said yesterday , I will write one letter of the Hebrew: The second letter is Beit, which means "House of the Cosmos." It also represents the Holy temple. In our physical body/ heart dwells the spirit, the spark of the divine. Hence, we have to keep our temple Holy and free of evil. Keep peace in the physical house, in our hearts, on the earth. There is much more. These are just some very important things about Beit. May we all strive to meet with our beloved in the realm of permanence, which is eternal in essence. We must start this while living right here while in the physical. Remove all pretending, obstacles, doubts, selfishness, self-serving, and practice love, empathy, compassion. Love all creation. Without all these attributes, no souls will take any steps towards the ascension. No amount of magic will work. Have hearts that seek love and God. Amen.

Humanity has gone mad. All we value is success, name, fame, losers, and winners. If somebody has to win, somebody has to lose. The losers are considered as something to be looked down on. What if the losers have a soul/spirit that is the highest order of spirit, and he does not need to parade his victory? Do any religious organizations really pay attention to what is happening on the Earth with humanity committing all this bloodshed, war, killing, animal farming (it is the gravest evil) and besides humanity practicing abuse of the procreative power, on top of this, the mediocre business of wasting time by debating about God and its function. The God force was, is, and will be here whether or not we debate or praise it. We are God's representative here to experience God's consciousness in ourselves and in all living forms. We must respect our reproductive ability and not trash it because this is the first abortion. And then follows the full abortion. It is as though humanity is traveling at the highest speed racing on the freeway and not recognizing that there is a collapsed bridge ahead, and there is a drop into an eternal canyon where all earlier speeders just disappeared, so will the following ones. Wise are those who take a detour somewhere and change course. Religions keep souls in bondage to their power. They have no power over a soul/spirit; truly, it belongs to the infinite Creator.

Wars for religions, nations, territories are all folly. Winning/ losing all is folly, abuse of physical bodies, whether of ours or others in any form or size is evil. We are creating a heavy burden on the indwelling spirit. While in the body, it is of paramount importance that we recognize that we are souls/spirits having this physical body as our tool to achieve spiritual heights. Knowledge will come to an honest, humble soul and that will be their driving force. It will be their strength. They may be a loser in the eye of the physical winners. They have to win over their lower selves, then they can say they won. They will recognize when it happens. Then they will not give a damn about success, glamour, trophies, in their eyes, these all will have no value. Do not seek praise from others. Seek praise from the spirit within. We must be content with what we are and learn to ascend the high mountain using the strength from within. There may be hikers on the way; they will surely support each other. A true traveler will recognize the other travelers going towards the high mountain. Such is the strength we need.

My soulful thought today is in the very absence of the true divine connection that shows up by human behavior, or maybe from the very inception of human existence. However, there are lots of God worshipers, talkers, echoing it on the Earth. However, these echoes do not cross the physical to spiritual but go down to the darkness. Why? Because these are empty praises and not from the heart that loves. Humans can use many languages by means of eyes, gestures, facial expressions, body movement, etc. This gift was given by the Creator to humankind only. Honestly, we have to think how we are using this ability for the ascension or descent of the spirit. What are we doing here with so much fighting? We are waiting for a miracle to happen, it will happen, provided we accept our part in creating miracles. Our Book of Life is full of not so good writings. We must erase all that and rewrite it. Breathe the freshness of divine air. Allow all inhabitants of the world to live. Let no one suffer injustice through our works. Say, "Enough is enough." Feed the soul/spirit with the food of love, peace, joy. Let everyone feel they, too, are part of the Infinite love/God and they have a right to exist. Then we will see the living God, living among us, within us. God's purpose is then fulfilled. May we all seek wisdom, love, light, so that the earth will be the habitation of peace for the soul/spirit of all creatures.

Humans have this attitude of self-righteousness, even thinking that we are God. The infinite power manifest to us, we will say, you are wrong, and we have the truth. We are here to enjoy life, gather power, even conquer heaven and the God force itself. Humans are that ignorant. Our souls consist of two parts: A part belongs to the light of God and a part that belongs to darkness, attachment to the physical, animalistic nature. When we give such weight to animalistic existence, we fall far below the animal levels. We claim to be made in the image of God. It all depends on God, the dark power or the power of light. We have made this wonderful Earth into a slaughterhouse for humans and animals. We are busy using procreative power to produce humans and animals. Then we kill them, abuse them, practicing brutality all the way. Children are born even if we take precautions. Animals do not do that. Millions of children are born to be homeless and suffer abuse of all kinds. Surely, we are playing God, but not in a good way.

There are probably many gods; the Jewish God, Christian Gods (because there many denominations with claims of being with God and the rest of the world will be cast into hell or left behind). I have no authority to say what is true or false. The ones making such claims either know what they are talking about, or they do not. Maybe these are entities that hold power in the lower regions, and they inspire people to worship them. If there is the only one mighty force called God who created all physical and spiritual worlds, then we all are under the rulership of one creator and one creation. If one believes in one creator, then there is no single one who can claim to be God's people. Every soul/spirit came from one source.

Humans are at the highest level in God's ecosystem. We have a great responsibility. We know what is right, wrong, we love, hate, kill, make war, commit violence. Physically, we exist in the lower regions, the physical, and the moment we realize we are on the wrong path and serving the power of the dark force, we must run for the light, which is absolute love to receive the light. I certainly do not feel good about all the suffering of children, women, humans, above all the dear little animals, who are being farmed and abused, killed, and eaten. Suffering is their way of life. As long as we serve the power of the dark forces and act and live life like that, we are making very little progress to walk the way of the light/God.

We all know there is a mountain called Everest. We have the map, and we know where it is. When we reach the place, we can then take steps towards it, reach the foothills, and then ascend. Similarly, all mystical Holy Scriptures should be our soul/spirit map, showing the way to reach the mountain of the Lord. Every esoteric teaching of all spirituality is the same. The path requires selflessness, love, self-awareness, Overcoming the lower nature. The fundamentalist side of all religions reached for power, and all make false promises and trap souls. If anybody wants to have peace on the Earth and in Creation, work to bring peace. Gain wisdom, empathy, compassion. In the Kabbalistic Way, travel the Middle Path. It is a mystical path of love to ascend from the lower to higher, step by step with wisdom, knowledge and the desire for love, light, ascension.

Here, I write about the companion of the soul/spirit journey. What is in my heart? So, here goes the gathering of two like spirits.

I do not have any selfish interest either. I wish for a better world for all creation. That includes humans, animals of all sorts, who are in the air, water, and land. We are the most sophisticated animals currently on the planet Earth. Probably in earth's history, there were, before civilization we know about, far more evolved spiritual ways of living and maybe they were myths. Like Atlantis, Sumerian, Aryans, etc. But now, they are sort of mythology and perhaps twenty thousand years from now, we will also be mythology and if some human civilization remains then, they will have terrible stories to tell their children, if they are better off than us.

What are we doing here? Why have we become so low (beneath animals) in our thinking, actions, why do we create weapons, why do we go to war, why do we abuse and kill helpless animals? We have become lustful/flesh-eating robots without feeling. Not all, there are many who are practicing kindness to all. Why are we raping the Earth this way? Why all these religions claiming they have the truth and other religions do not and fight to establish their way? Are they practicing peace, love, empathy? Is anybody thinking, what has gone wrong with the physical earth by humans? People are waiting for deliverance. Nothing is going to happen like that, except destruction, until we change. If humans continue this way, the Earth will be desolate and charred where hardly anything will inhabit it. Controversies about the right to bear arms, not to bear them, the right to life, no right to life, rich versus poor, etc. We have all the rights in the physical sense. Does anybody realize when we fight for all these physical rights what is happening to the indwelling spirits/souls? Many people, in any practical sense, do not even believe they have souls/spirits. They may talk and make noise about God/souls/spirits. Action proves how they are living to remain null, nonexistent. Every parent's responsibility is to raise their child to be morally accountable. If they are failing to do this, they will be karmically connected to that child's soul until both have learned and are ready to ascend. It may take thousands of soul years.

Pray for peace for the world.

Of course, we complain, cry, weep for all that is happening to the blessed Earth and all the inhabitants including humans by humans. You see God's voice is a kind of wind and whispers in the human heart and life. But the evil voice is like thunder and lightning. Of course, we hear the louder and clearer voice and follow that. What is this evil voice? It is nothing other than the me, the mighty me, my desire, my wealth, my comfort, my pleasures, and my kingdom, me and mine?

Harmonious Petals

Rose

All we humans are full of it. I will tell you something, see, the pythons, large snakes, they crawl onto the largest animals like elephants, humans, lions, cows, etc., and simply crush their bones and choke them and kill them. Not that they want to eat. It is simply their nature. They are the embodiment of the most powerful evil. It is amazing they exist. Of course, they do not think they are doing any evil. They do not have such comprehension. They do not know any better. We who are human, created with mighty powers of recognition of good and evil, can feel the pain and suffering of ourselves and others, we can feel compassion, we can imagine the future, imagine the consequences of our actions. What are we doing with that? On the Earth, we are the mighty killers of humans and animals alike. We have created sophisticated weapons of mass destruction of all kinds that can deplete the Earth completely of any life. We have to ask ourselves this question, are we better than the ignorant pythons? When we ask this question, honestly, we feel offended, and we are ready to kill the one who points it out. Well, sadly, this is nothing other than self- righteousness and self-importance. It is high time we addressed global issues and local issues. Start from each home to the religious thrones to the street. Religious empires have great power, and it is time they come down from their thrones to the level of creation and teach humanity to abstain from everything that will bring annihilation of creation on the Earth. Understand the Creator and its purpose of creation. We think that all will be destroyed and the righteous will fly in the clouds, but indeed this is wishful thinking.

My soulful thought for today is about atheists and their take on life . The fact is, even if they are atheists, even if they don't acknowledge the existence of souls/spirits; they do exist in atheists as well. In the long chain of the soul's existence, they will come to know themselves as souls/ spirits. People, who believe in God/soul/spirit, should be playing their parts in accordance with the law of creation. They do not understand the anatomy of the spirits/ souls. Hence their dogmas evolved that created the Atheists. Everybody is responsible for everybody else's fall or rise. Spiritual people must be examples for others, showing how to manage our relationships with each other and the rest of creation, Recognizing the fact that all are part of creation under one Creator. When we pick and choose what to believe, what is right, wrong or justify our actions and lives just to suit our convenience, we are causing a stir in others, and they would rather walk away from this kind of faith. We are very smart, very intelligent, with the potential for great things and one day, we can be the inheritors of the Fathers/Mothers' Kingdom provided we recognize our responsibility and work for our ascension and cause others not to stumble. Rather, we must help the weak, the unfortunate, the hungry, and the little creatures that look to us for support. We must give up all selfishness and self-serving behaviors. We inflict pain and emotional, physical, and other kinds of suffering on other beings, people, nations and try to justify ourselves for doing it. Before the law of God, we will be held accountable. Our intelligence will blow up in our faces before the judge of compassion and equality of all spirits/ souls. We will be our own judges for our own deeds because the Great Judge dwells dormant within every part of creation. In the afterlife, our souls will take the road to whatever level we have made for ourselves by living on the physical. No one will have to say, "Go this way or that way." We will surely go where we should, that is the law of the divine. It will never make a mistake in judging.

Here, I write about humans' fundamental problems. Discord between people for whatever reasons! People cause trouble for others and beings due to their ignorance, selfishness, and characterless behavior. The accuser will, in turn, be the accused by human law (not all the time). It happened that during yesterday's discussion , we were talking about people who hold control over others, have money, power, etc. How women were controlled by men and simply say, "You can leave now," and the woman goes. There is nothing glorious about it. This I wrote many times, this is the fundamental cause for the problems that, today, humanity is facing, the battle between the sexes for power. No one is safe today; every physical body is the pleasure house for another, maybe a child male or female, man and man, women and many women, many men. No sanctity for anybody. Not even animals. Everybody seeks power over others. Most importantly, the religions do this. What vanity! In a nutshell, they may hold power so that they may destroy the bodies of other beings and animals. However, no one holds a spirit/soul captive. They may choose to torture, kill, or abuse anybody, but the soul/spirit is boundless and cannot be killed.

Humans must try to gain wisdom through love, empathy, and compassion. Nobody can make room in heaven/spiritual plains for another soul/spirit. Each will gain a place with God force according to their living, realizing, transforming, while in the physical. This is the purpose of God's creation for all. We all can help each other or hurt each other or delay the progress of ascension. Those who surrender their souls and spirits to the King of the Earth, which is the physical existence and all its wants and more wants made a vow to The Great Cesar. We have to live right in the physical and learn to control ourselves and we have to walk the narrow path. All will do this eventually, as eternity has eternal time. We cannot ask why we are here. We are here and we have to do everything to commune with our spirits/souls. Consummate the divine marriage of the flesh and spirit. Ego has no place before the spirit. It has its place with the fleshly King. Know who we are serving.

My soulful thought for today is about our divine potential. According to all the scriptures of the world, we humans were created with such great divine potential. However, with the glamour of the physical with its bodily demands for pleasures, causing pain in others, trapping the lower nature, we humans plunged into darkness and create more darkness for ourselves and for all creation. One might talk for whole days about God, God's wonders, reading scriptures of holy writing and chanting, yet, however we think, truly we must know where our heart is, and our state of mind and the purity of our hearts and thoughts. Once we can sort out and remove this powerful darkness from the human heart, and establish righteousness and love for all creation, wonders will happen. Until then, we mimic and mutter about God. We have to earn these possibilities until they are achieved, they will remain distant. Light is ever-dwelling in our hearts and creation. But it is wrapped in many layers of physical clothing of wants, desires, selfishness and so forth. As long as we remain stuck in the "me and my world" we will not achieve our task as humans, which is union with the divine while in the physical. If that does not happen while we are in the physical, it is not going to happen after we leave our great physical body.

My soulful thought for today is about beliefs. Let's all accept the facts in a nutshell. People are keeping their tongues busy, talking about God, miracles, and so on. We all have to participate in bringing miracles into this Earth, by recognizing the fact that by our hands, humans, animals and the blessed Earth as a whole are being raped and violated, destroyed, blood spilled, and endless physical and emotional sufferings are being caused. Here and there, there are good people. But the majority are white-washed tombs. They swallow blood and vomit, poisons to kill everything. Of course, they are serving God, but which God? When they can take the name of God and commit such evils, crimes, rape and abuse humans, (treat them as commodities), what God are they serving? Do they not have feelings, or are they just flesh only? Is it that the divine spirit is not dwelling in their hearts? The fools who made such evil and created rules by it to put in the scriptures and say "This is the Word of God"—they are truly agents of Satan. Also, any woman behaving this way and dumps a good man is equally the servant of Evil. No excuses. Humans kill other humans, animals, and disrespect here, nobody feels safe here on the Earth.

Of course, we are created in the image of God. If we claim to be that we must act like that. If one wants to inherit the wealth of the father's kingdom, we must work for his kingdom, each proving their worth. Robbers and criminals will have to change their ways, clean up what they have soiled, make amends, and do the right thing to be that image we claim. There is no bloodline claim at the soul level. That only happens in stories of thoughtless humans. Boy, what is waiting for their souls? The soul/spirit line is God force DNA, we as souls have to work for it. Every able-bodied person must live for their physical well-being, spiritual well-being and their children should be taught to be members of civil society, and society of the soul/spirit family of the divine force/love. God is deathless, souls/spirits are deathless. If one worships the God force. We must worship life everlasting.

Soul Travel

Countless times, I have written like this. You see, in the world, there are many people who travel the earth, the sun, and nature. When I think of all these things, my blood boils with seeing all that is happening on the earth. Who is going to heal the wounds humans are creating? The God force is not partial, it takes no side. The majority of humans are spiritually bankrupt. They feel satisfied with the mediocre, spending time reading, discussing, wasting time as their accomplishments. They accomplished nothing before the divine law and justice. Their legacy will play with them, before them, a hundred soul times. This is how the God force law works. Every pain, every tear of humans, animals alike will reach the throne of God and it will shower down upon all those who are responsible for this Earthly mess.

People who have brought their animal nature under control do travel to close regions of the spiritual world by grace. Some people develop this skill through their God-nature. They are bringing in more spiritual reality than any ancients. The problem is that the religious authorities claim to have it all, so, there can be no more revelation. That is the trap ancients brought to humanity. Because of this trap, people cannot even trust their own blessings; instead, they follow the set of rules given long before. Rules can only apply to the physical only. Nobody on Earth will ever map the physical world or the spiritual world. It is eternally being created, dissolving, appearing again, and ultimately disappearing into the infinite Creation. So, let us humble ourselves, do our best recognizing, we are (the spirits/souls) sent here by the will of the Creator to learn, gain mastery over the wildness, which is like a forest where many dangers, traps, mysteries, corruption, overpowering lust, drugs, and all other substances are hidden, above all, thinking that, "this is it," that destroys everybody else and everyone on the Earth for the pleasure of the body.

This bodily existence should be used to travel the trails in the forest of darkness, to hike into the mountain of the Lord. Every writing and scripture should be our staff to release ourselves (souls) from bondage and allow the soul wings to fly or give strength and support to our legs (spiritual legs) to hike the high mountain. This soul journey will never end. I am here and now it is done. It does not end, because if you reach one ridge, there awaits the next. So, if someone says, you do this, do that, your Kingdom is established, they are misleading you. No one dictates this to anyone in any way, we have to earn our soul journey through physical existence. If one misuses physical existence for evil, selfishness, that life is lost even before the journey begins.

Everyone is participating in the ascension or stagnation of soul/spirit existence, selflessness, compassion, love, overcoming the slavery of lust and all stimulants in the way. These forces will retard ascension. Say no to killing, war, violence, discipline your children, instruct them in their responsibilities and the purpose of existence. Even if you are not a good human being, do not destroy others. The river of life is ever flowing through all creatures and creation. If you do not have the love or an understanding of sex and its purpose, then it is better if you do not engage in it. But spirit is ever ready and flesh is ever weak. So, desire spiritual freedom, and eventually, we will be successful in eternal time. Do not misuse any physical moving body of an animal, child, or human for your pleasure. The abuser's journey will be the hardest because each creature has a body for their living/being. If one destroys that, by emotionally killing, by abuse, they are crippled even to the bone. The abuser will never make any progress. The one who causes such suffering will endure millions of times more than they caused. There is no easy way out of our responsibility. This is what is flowing through me right now. Perceptions of the spiritual world and psychic world do not sit well among most of the Earthbound/ physical people. The abuser will never make any progress.

Chapter 14

Men and Women

This is why I write: Humanity is in peril. Everything starts with a man and woman. Folly is the way of humanity.

My soulful thought for today is about harmony. I was not planning to write anymore. However, someone said, "Write." So, I write. Our Creator handed to humans a perfect Earth with all its inhabitants and beauty with harmony and with one accord. We are the stewards of the Earth and what do we do? We make total discordance and disharmony. It has gone beyond anyone's control. This misery will continue to expand, and pain and suffering will be the cup we drink from. That is the case, and it starts in our homes. Our Divine Mother wants us to be compassionate and heal the suffering of all her children. That means all creation. Let us play the symphony of creation with one accord. Not with discord. Then it will not be music, rather it will be noise nobody can stand. That is what we have on the Earth. Creation on Earth by humans is playing a symphony with notes of fear, killing, suffering, war, violence. All of us must stop and think, what is the point of all of this? We will not take anything material with us, rather the etheric body with all the memories of our physical existence, as a result of that life we have created in the physical, either, love, compassion, unity or the Great Discord.

My Soulful thought for today is about artists of all kinds and their work. Wonderful, indeed! The artist or poet can see things and experience what no other person can experience. I would like to draw your attention to the universal artist. The Creator who created the cosmos, all the galaxies, planets, suns, and stars, etc. All the earth and all the wonderful inhabitants of the Earth, including us, the thinking, conscious beings. What a gift we have as the animals of the Earth. Humans can not only experience the wonders of all that is on the Earth and in the sky and beyond, and with our spiritual capacity, we can sojourn the spiritual world as well. However, the majority of humans lost themselves completely and did everything to destroy the blessed artwork of the great artist. Imagine, you go into a garden and see a rosebud, you grab it and smell it once, maybe, a beautiful smell, and then you crush and destroy it. Or you see a beautiful woman or a man, just have the fleshly desire with them for a moment and walk away, or commit rape, or abuse. But then what is happening to your indwelling spirit? No one thinks. Similarly, maybe you see a deer prancing in the meadow, you take a gun and shoot it and you are having fun hunting it. We are keepers in the garden of God. Are we keeping the garden so that it is good and beautiful, or we are trashing everything? What the religions are doing, with their dogmas, separations, doctrines, and promises and trapping souls in the matter? Once they shed their bodies and move into the spiritual dimension, then they will have the shock of their soul lives. I am most certain that this is what people who do not practice love, unity, and peace will discover. Any religion may cease to exist in due course, maybe 100 years or a thousand years. Have a blessed day in the garden of your life. Experience, feel and love the beauty of all life that moves. Be humble and gentle.

My soulful thought for today will be about our thoughts. The storms rage from inside and outside. That is why Kabbalah teaches to stay on the middle pillar, which is balanced. If one goes to one side or the other, it loses its balance. For us alone, the Kabbalah, and all spiritual practices and religions exist. In spite of all this, humans have lost all balance and control. Each one of us has to take responsibility to make sure that the tree is not shaken due to our actions or thoughts. Everything is alive and creates motion, storm for the rest. If everyone were conscious of others' vulnerability to our action or inaction, the tree would not violently shake. In the last four to five thousand years of this current civilization, there have been many religions, spiritualities, sages, masters and prophets have come and gone. Yet what has happened to us? Have we made some progress collectively or individually? There are so many wars; there is so much violent mistreatment of creations. Some justify this by saying it is the end time. End time for what? We, individually or collectively take no steps wherein we make sure that no one is harmed or violated. Innocents are always the victims of evil. Humans are so self-absorbed in our glory; we give no thought to our inaction or action, which creates storms in others. Then we justify that by saying each one of us creates our own storm. Of course, we do, because we are all on the "Tree of Life," if a storm comes, an individual leaf cannot say, I close myself and do not feel it. That is probably why the true sages left the noises of the world retired to some lonely place where no one will infringe on their peace. It is time we take a long, hard look at our lives to see how much we participate in the peace and well-being of other humans or other beings. How much we shook the inner chamber of their sanctuary. Correct the wrongs, wipe the tears. Participate in collective peace. Nobody will then be taken by inner thoughts and in turn to the actions that will bring disaster to oneself and others. We all are in it together and we must participate in the peaceful continuum of all that is.

I do not know the why and how of anything. All that I know is that we should be the catalyst for change for the better, as humans were a catalyst for change for the worst suffering for all creation. When you get to send out your thoughts and prayers to all corners of the Earth, for all creations, their safety, well-being, and the joy of living, let the sorrows be ended. May all evil actions be transformed into the experience of God's love! The reason I write was because I saw the breaking news: Thousands of dolphins and whales were slaughtered ruthlessly on some island by people for hunting trips. The ocean water was filled with blood, as far as the eye could see. I was desperate. The power that brought me into existence has been making me experience all that is going so wrong. We crucify each other and the rest of the creation. This is our story. I am for love and peace. This is how I love the Creator through loving creation.

Friends: Let us read and absorb and live according to the law of love. This is what all esoteric/mystical/true religious practices for the spirits/souls teach us. This is the only thing we should focus on while we have the gift of physical living. Here, I am reminded of a story I heard when I was a small girl.

Once upon a time, there lived a King, a righteous King (manifestation of the divine embodiment in the physical). The land was prosperous, everything grew well, people were happy, loved one another. Animals were loved and taken care of like children of God. There was joy in those days. No one knew sorrows, tears. The King of the underworld (Lucifer) dressed, and transformed to look like a sage and came to this righteous King and the King with his noble heart welcomed this sage. He enjoyed the hospitality and was finally ready to depart. The righteous King told the sage, you can ask three blessings (boon) and the King will give them. So, this devil in disguise (as a sage) asked three blessings and the King agreed. Then, this sage grew like the sky and he asked the three blessings, the first was the Heaven, the second was the earth, and I do not remember the third. But with one measure, he measured the heaven, with a second the Earth, and there was no place for the third, so the righteous King sat in the lotus position and bowed, and the evil sage put his feet on the head of the righteous King, and he pushed him into the world below (into the unknown). People still believe that one day, the righteous King will return to rule them.

Is it somewhat familiar? This is the story of each, and every soul/ spirit descended onto the Earth. Lucifer rises, reaches with his ego, and captures everything, dwells, and rules. The divine spark has been pushed down and put to sleep. It must awaken one day to give and experience love, empathy, compassion, sharing with all that is. Then we all will rejoice in the presence of the God within us, within all. All creatures will be happy with the return of the King. We will say goodbye to lust, selfishness, lower ego, and its multiplicity of glamourous colors that have brought all suffering to all creatures and cast out the noble King. So, let us prepare for the noble King's return.

Where are we, as human beings, created in the image of God? Where are we going? Who is responsible for these conditions? Humans alone are responsible for all the chaos experienced by humans, animals, and the Earth as a whole. Are we not endowed with all God's qualities like the ability to love, create, destroy, experience joy, sorrow, pain, suffering? We may ask what we have done with these faculties. Well, we crucified them, and did it well. We, as souls, came or were sent out to exist as animals in the animal kingdom. We choose to live like animals, so we went down below the animal level. The truth hurts. This is what it is. Instead of us living in the image of God, we created God in our image and justify everything we do. We go to war, rape, violate others, produce children who have to live on street corners, indulge in drugs and do all kinds of violence, destroy other's peace and sanity for our selfishness' sake.

What is God? Well, we will never be able to answer this question in the full sense, until we navigate through all the physical worlds in billions of galaxies of the physical world, then the spiritual world of many dimensions beyond anyone's comprehension. One may ask, when did all this start? Since, if there was a beginning, there should be an end. How many times has it all began and ended? How many times will the spiritual physical world occur? If we can answer these questions, we will understand God's almighty power. This is to say nobody is going to understand the infinite. If finite beings like us could understand this, the very infinite become finite, and it will not be infinite. All that we can do is be loving, gentle, caring to all on the Earth, love creation, so that we may love the Creator. Without loving Creation, no one can love the Creator. Justifications for overpopulation, going to war, killing any being, these do not love the Creator. We must not seek our convenience and pleasure. Our concern should be our neighbor. Let the earth be our worship place and dwelling places of all that is on the earth, air, and water. We are abusing our speech to say millions of words to praise God. God sent us to do the work, accomplish transformation leading to ascension for the soul through living. While I am writing, I am asking these questions to myself, recognizing my part, the failed part, the loved part, etc. We have work to do as gifted creatures of the earth.

What a beautiful way the true sages have been advising us. This is the way of the Lord. Relating and connecting with all creation that includes people for their well-being and harmonious ways to live and relate to others. Humanity created families; even animals have their ways of keeping their families and raising their children. Like birds create their nests and lay eggs, chickens take care of their chicks until they can be free and fly away and create their own nests. Humans create their nests some which, very few, last a lifetime in peace, a few last a lifetime not in peace but in chaotic existence. But the majority create their nests made of balloons and they pop that very day or a few days later. They make war between men and women; have no rules for their children who become menaces in society. For them, they have no boundaries, but anarchy and chaos. This is human society today. This all started from a little nest made of loose ends. No solid foundation. Character, understanding, empathy, caring for other beings that entered and united with one another to form a nest, no nest can survive if one burns the tree. Most of the nests are being burnt, because their tree of life and tree of the knowledge of good and evil are on fire and all within them. No amount of preaching of God will help, except the realization of what we are doing, which pours cool waters of love, empathy, the compassion that must be put into this tree of life and of knowledge of good and evil. Then we can save this tree. We must examine ourselves to see how much we care for and have nourished this little tree of ours. Most of us can say, very little or none. This is what humanity is doing. We are in a world of action. We must act whereby we nourish the tree so that it can grow into infinity. When we do not try to gain knowledge and wisdom by our living, we waste our lives and others as well. Every day is a day to examine our relations with each other in the nest, and all nests in the tree, that includes all beings. People of God/spirituality, live with love, decency, and character and they recognize their God witness within them. We do not have to try to convince others—we are spiritual or not. We must be in harmony with the divine within. Talk less and live for healing and repairing the limbs and branches of our own tree and in the collective. Let no one live in fear of evildoers. If all humanity practiced the law of the creator, what a world we would be living in! We must correct our mistakes before we depart with the heavy burden of trash bags on the shoulders of our souls. If we do not, the soul's wings will have been cut and the soul will be Earthbound. I am not talking nonsense.

Harmonious Petals   Rose

These finer bodies are part of the soul's existence. Once we depart, our soul remembers the effect of these bodies, whether what we did to others or what had been done to us by them. For these reasons, morality, self-disciple, character, self-restraint, God, Heaven, and hell are there. One believes it or not about God, heaven, purgatory, but these are real for the soul. The soul seed is planted with all its aspects in the physical body. If we ignore these things within ourselves or in other beings, we are in for a great rude awakening in the soul level of existence. Blessed are those beings that live with restraint and live in balance and try not to violate them within ourselves or others. They will climb the mountain of the Lord and see the light of God. I myself do not know and wonder why I write all these things. Maybe it will come into use in some of our oldest age when we are ready to say goodbye to these misguided physical existences. Stay awake and pray. This is what happens when we are aware of these finer bodies in us and all beings.

Hearts

Friends in spirit: Today, I will talk about our hearts. This is the reality of our existence.

Everywhere we go, and even when we go inside to get away, still the noise of the outside world triumphs most of the time. There is no getting away. Especially, this happens to the most sensitive people like me. You see, God put the first humans on this Earth where total harmony existed. All creatures, lands, and nature lived in harmony. Lions and deer were drinking from the same stream. Humans are the representatives of the divine force but once we focused on flesh and pleasures, we brought this Earth and all inhabitants to this level of suffering. We will have to correct our mistake and re-establish God's order in all things. This is the plan and responsibility of humans. But we have gotten lost in a tangle of debate and dogma.

I think in our times (the great sages, of course, passed on to their divine home with the Father), these were genuine teachers, who wished only good for all Creations and creatures. I occasionally watch a glimpse of a TV show. I will not watch more than a few seconds. What they are showing, are these fools? Throwing away money for booze, women (foolish women) show off with their skin, planes, boats, ships, they are on the top of the world. I pray, these fools' hearts may be changed, and the money is used for starving children and all creatures. They are carcasses in the soul sense. Well, their time will come, the tables will turn. There is a story of the rich and poor brothers. It is the same with preachers and God-debaters. What is their private life, home life? The God within them must be ashamed of them. Why are humans with all these abilities doing a disservice to our own Creator. It is the silent witness to all our deeds, thoughts, action.

Just for a moment, close your eyes and imagine: The blessed earth is the field of the Lord and we all from humans to animals to plants big and small alike, we can hear the voice of the Lord saying, "I am." The light we see, the sound we hear we are also hearing and seeing with our souls. In return, we say, "I am so and so," all of us, humans, males, females, and animals, plants big or small. These little voices of "I am" echoes back like tiny flashpoints to the great I. So, realize from that "I" came trillions of I's. From one divine spark, all sparks came into being, of different sizes and forms. When the forms are dissolved, the multicolored I's will return to One I, the universal I. Be mindful of that. Experience the pain and suffering we are causing to each other, the voiceless brothers, and sisters (animals). You love your Creator first and then your neighbor. We are not applying this truth to our daily lives. We are causing suffering to neighbors, man, and animals. We love our ego-driven everything, we even use God' name to achieve that. Some very few humans are great souls. They are sages, saints, and true teachers, who speak selflessly for the well-being of all in the soul sense and all other senses.

What I am about to write, I am sure most of the people will not take it well, at least, those who are not sincere in their core existence. The ardent and sincere people will listen and examine themselves and make necessary changes in themselves to experience the Prince, God within them. When we pray, Lord, come to my heart and dwell, God does not come from another galaxy or solar system or from a foreign land. We, in Creation, are the dwelling place of God's spirit. What happens with humans? Is it that we are so overcrowded with billions of cluttered things, possessions and desires of all sizes and forms? By doing so, we corner the spark and put more clutter over them. What is obscured cannot shine. So, we are plunged into darkness and darkness will take us for a good long ride. This is our selfishness, making us live without peace, amusing us with all glamour of pleasures of the mind, body, and so on. So that we pay no attention to other beings' suffering and we inflict suffering on others. Above all, we are engaged in harming any creatures, not ourselves, emotionally or otherwise. God's nature for us is love, light, wisdom and all goodness. We can and must exercise all these blessings so that the blessed force can be active in our hearts and guide us to the Holy mountain. The Bible says, "Not everyone who says, Lord, Lord, Lord, will enter the Kingdom of God, but those who do the will of my Father in Heaven."

Our will is not God's will. By God's will and love, the worlds seen and unseen came into manifestation. We have to be participants in the continuum of all that. Do not mess with; abuse the psyche of this Creation nor the psyche of any being either small or big. We cannot get in tune with God's light in any other way, but by pure loving, living, caring, sharing, helping, being kind and caring to all, because all are the vehicle of the indwelling of the divine. When a river starts from the mountains it is clear, clean, and pristine. As it meanders from the mountain to the hills, valleys, and plains, it gathers much dirt and debris on the way. This is the story of the spirit/soul. We must remove all our habits, which might have tarnished our flow of the God light. Desire God light, work for it, transform yourselves, and then you will see the wonder of the infinite light shining within us. Desire to shine on all creation. Because this is the only way we can experience true joy. As long as we are stuck in "I and me," there is no hope for us.

Love, hate, anger, fear, and lust: All these emotions belong to animal nature. We as souls/spirits came on a journey through this animal kingdom to experience, and practice patience, love, and the rest for our soul's growth. It is the will of the absolute that we do. We cannot identify our nature with animal nature or go down below the animal level. If we do, we are not practicing our higher nature (God's nature).

I would like to stress something. Yesterday, in Church, someone stood up and was talking about single mothers and their needs. True, we have to help them. No single person can become a father or mother. It takes the two getting together. It is not some kind of accident: They did what their impulse said to do, with no thought of yesterday, no thought of tomorrow, no thought of whom they are involved with, and completely no thought of the implications of their actions. Poor children, I feel terrible for them. Humans were given talents in whatever number: Ten, five, three, two, one—however many. As father said, "We each and every soul/spirit are endowed with some talents. It is God's plan that we, as souls, use them for the well-being of our spirits and ascension of the Divine aspects." We are not doing that, if you look at the birds, animals in the ocean, the bears and so forth. Except for dogs, I believe. How much trouble birds take to build their nests, then once their nest is ready, they lay eggs and wait for the babies to hatch, find food, feed the little ones until they fly away with their strong wings. Similarly, some of the animals in the ocean travel thousands of miles to some safe place to deliver their babies. Yet, human with so many talents bring babies to barren environments where there are no parents, or there is just one parent and no love. We offer them nothing for their soul's growth. The money or materials they get from others is just to help their physical body grow. When they grow a little bit, they do the same thing. Where are the God-given talents in all of this? Nobody can say anything about this to anyone anymore. If we do, we are interfering with their rights. What about the rights of the child? The religious authorities and all other authorities stand against it. And these children are tragedies for all civilization. Killing, rape, violence, cruelty, and selfishness are all derived from abusing the God-given talent of our procreative power. Those who do this are wasting their talents uselessly. Weak, very weak, we are. Indeed, in our deepest reality, we are superior and made in the image of God, but if that is so, we must live accordingly.

Who has the ear to hear what Jesus said or for that matter what anyone else said? If we hear something useful and good for our souls, it may be contrary to preconceived dogmas, and ideas. Also, we do not chew at all what we hear. We are filled with our physical, fleshly pleasures and all that goes with them. We worship the almighty God of food and all other riches of the world. God, well, we praise him with words. We are okay then; God is satisfied with the volume of our praises. Soon, as I write, it will be Thanksgiving. Millions upon millions of turkeys and animals will be slaughtered for us to give thanks. Those same poor animals miss the opportunity to give thanks to their creator because some humans want their flesh. Instead of eating a stomach-full of flesh, sweets etc., why not instead eat a humble meal or fast and give thanks for life, all creatures and plants and the creation as a whole. Reflect that if one of these is missing, our life would not exist, because God and all creation are interconnected. One will not survive without the other. Do humans take time to realize anything? I realize my faults, my early life, living now, and the changes that I am making to a better tune with the soul plan. I am not there yet, but I am sincere in my thinking. Who cares what I think, right? No one has to. Then we must not waste our time talking about God. All Creation has life, and life came from the one light/one life. Seek unity with everything. Otherwise, our lives will be like the house built on sand, the waves come, wind comes, it will fly hither, thither and it is gone by the waves or wind. Live and pray genuinely. All of what we are doing, including me, is not right before the Creator. From the one light, all sparks came, and then all sparks will return to the one light/ love.

My soulful thought today is I give thanks to all the human angels who risk their lives to save, help, and protect the beings whether humans or animals. They are God's love and compassion in action. At this time, may we all appreciate the beauty, friendship, companionships of these angels and spirits/messengers of God force who work untiringly to enable the earth and all its inhabitants to continue to exist, in spite of the ignorant living of humans, who care for nothing! I wish all religions, all people, could participate in peaceful co-existence with all that is. Let us all live carefully, responsibly recognizing the fact that our actions or non-actions has its pros and cons in the physical and on the soul level! We must praise God through our action. Creator loves all its creation. All life forms long for its life. We humans can distinguish right from wrong, love, hate, selfishness, selflessness, and so on. So, let us live as the Creator intended for us to live, for higher purposes. Not lower purposes. All these apply to one and all, especially those who believe there is a Creator and creation, and we have eternal life as souls. There are many levels of spiritual planes, and we will enter into one of those after our current physical living, dying physically to enter there.

Consider this writing is a blessing for all who receive it. We live like sheep lost in the wilderness. These wisdom teachings should be used as tools to direct our souls from the darkness to light. While living, we must feel love, light, wisdom. If not, we lose the key to the eternal home, due to our erratic living. Of course, we can still go to worship places and do the reading, follow rituals, etc.

There are "ten" virgins, there are "ten" commandments, there are "ten" Sephiroth in the tree of life as Kabbalah's teaching, (and one unmentionable) one as well. Amazingly, sages write about the world consisting of two kinds of lodges, and there is yet a third one, which in Kabbalah is called AIN , it has no quality but itself. I understood this by drawing the tree of life under some invisible force's inspiration. I do not wish to go into that now. Let me write about what these "ten" virgins are. Virginity is a quality, which human beings, either men or women recognize. In the physical, one can be raped, or forced to have sex, but that man or woman can still be virgin in essence, because their heart is not yet contaminated with lust or such acts from others. Therefore, they fall into the category of virgins. But some choose to stay physically virgins, but if they have all the desire for sex and are overpowered by lust, that person is not a virgin in essence. Physically, that person is. So, this can be like the story of the five virgins with oil, and the other five without oil. What is oil? The quality of the soul, which in essence is a God quality. For it is love (God, manifestation) and empathy, compassion, kindness, truthfulness (animals will not lie, though people do). To lie is a total betrayal of the God essence. So, the Virgin's hearts are filled with oil, (when the groom enters, the heart lightens), such beings will enjoy the presence of God everlasting. The other five who have no oil, are the talkers with microphones, on the airways, they speak with their mouth, but their hearts are void of anything good, filled with evil. They are mean, cruel, they kill, rape, abuse emotionally or otherwise, they seek praise, they stand wearing fine garments and preach God as if God is their handmade toy. Sorry, are the affairs of their hearts. This Earth is filled with such virgins. The other five virgins do exist here, and because of that, there is still light flickering in this world.

White lodge, black lodge (duality). White lodge—what is the purpose of a lodge, it is a place to take shelter, live (in the white lodge, goodness is the shelter). In the black lodge, evil is the shelter. What is this shelter? Our hearts are the dwelling place of God, that force. Christ's presence. (El Shaddai).

The black lodge is a dwelling place of evil. So, those who have no love, but for themselves, who seek the blood of others, lies, evils, selfishness, robbers of light. We all have that in us. Once we overcome good and evil, we enter eternal permanence (which is the primordial existence), which nobody is going to understand. Right now, we can only try to be like the five virgins with oil, or in other words, enter the white lodge. If we can accomplish that, we have accomplished something worthwhile for our soul/spirit. The sages thinking and my thinking go hand in hand. I think the Sages' spirit is inspiring me. I thought of the story of the virgins with oil, and without oil. They had me write about black and white lodges. They are similar in essence.

I can feel the sages desire for peace and God-centered existence for all God's creation. Over the thousands of years of human existence, there were countless, truly good prophets, sages, saints, and people with the intention of harmony and peace; they have come and gone. Some of the scriptures are from them, some are their writing, speaking. We read and discuss them. This is our spiritual practice. Some do not even do that. Due to our pride, arrogance, selfishness, we created this massive suffering and the destruction of the creation. All these started from the very beginning, when a man and a woman, once they enter physical life, chaos, and desolation arose and from the chaos, emerged their offspring who are the reflection of their environment. What do we do about things like that? Nothing! Maybe we pray the Messiah will come. Or most religions believe that some high order spirit will incarnate and put all things into order. To do that, we humans must be the conduit. We should be like the five virgins with oil. Then the Messiah can ignite the lamp. Why did God give us all these powers, such capacity? Why have the majority of humans joined the five virgins who do not have oil in their lamps? We completely drown ourselves in the Malkuthian existence, where flesh, pride and selfishness rule. We are slaves to our ego (the lower ego). Hence, we can have pride, walk with chins up, look down on others, and destroy everything in our paths for our benefit. We have no regard for anybody, or other creation. Even if the Messiah came today, what will they find, and how will you answer when they ask the question: "I gave ten, five, three, two, one, etc., talents. What did you do with it?" These talents are our quality, ability, character, etc. If we do not put them into use for the well-being and coexistence with all in harmony and peace, we have gained or gathered nothing. We are like clay pots, and they will be shattered, will be blown away by the wind of darkness to the abyss with similar ones.

So, we must make changes in the little world (first, our home), then our village, then our country, then the world. A child must be raised by two parents, not by the village. Nowadays, villages are trying to raise someone's children, in the form of foster homes, orphanages, and so on. People with such an idea should be aware. Billions of children are on the street, doing child labor, enduring unending suffering. Ignorance is bliss. There will be a time to account for all this on the soul level if there is a power that created and rules.

The institution—it is our higher mind (God's mind) to those who possess or have the ability to perceive, they perceive the inner, the outer, the exterior and interior. The person who is completely engrossed in the gross earthly existence understands only gross matters, which are perishable in essence. Such gross matters include our bodies, which we struggle to maintain at all costs. Well, it's only a matter of time before they discover that they were on a quest, which will have them imprisoned for long periods of the soul's existence time.

Anyway, let us look at what is going on with humans? What is the difference between humans and animals? The animals do all that we human do, have sex to procreate, look after babies, find food for them, etc. They have fewer capacities than humans. They are emotional (yet definitely not like humans). They are driven by instinct. Their capacity to feel the pain of others is probably nonexistent. They care for their pack and their babies very well. They protect their babies. They have no agenda, no preconceptions, but they do not think of God, nor contemplate what the afterlife would be like. What are the consequences of their actions? Some of them eat leaves, others eat other animals, not from their kind (mostly, ninety percent of the time). They have no sin. They live, they fight others for territory, get killed, they die. Their minds are as transparent as water. They, too, have a place in the spiritual planes of God... not as man does. They are directly guided by divine entities (angels). After they die, their souls go a place of grassy meadows, and they prance in the sheer joy of spirit living. The spiritual world is full of archetypical existence based on the physical plane. There is no killing in their spiritual land, air, or in the water. That is the beauty of it. Do not ask me how I know. Now, I write what I feel. That is it.

Because this plain of being's existence has no body, what they have is energy/lights. Humans existed in the higher planes (as souls) and we are born by the Creator's plan to be some man or woman. When those two are united physically, there comes an entity called a human child with the potential to reach the highest plane of God's world. So, we have concentrations of emotions like being capable of love, hate, preconceptions, revenge, protection, schemes, meditative life, and so on. All these we have to develop slowly and surely. If we do not develop them, we will have wasted our lives as souls. Why do we have to fight for God? God is the creator of everything, billions of galaxies, millions of different kinds of life, different organisms. Everything! If God is all-powerful and controls everything, why in the world did we decide to fight to establish our way of faith? Because those who do this have no faith in God, they have no power over their impulses. They have some stupid idea of God. Because of that, they decide to kill others to establish their religions, their territories, and they divide everything (break it away from unity). They even think they have divided God. Really, they think this. For the survival of our individual existence as souls in the body, we must think rightly, establish peace and order, starting with our homes. If there is no love and connection in our little homes, we are playing in the field of deception. Such people are imitators of something. They are not truthful. They are untrustworthy, deceivers of the very love that brought them to this world. They are dishonest.

Chapter 16

Dimensions

My soulful thought for today is about the higher realms, higher beings and so on. These things are quite out of sight for all of us. We pray to saints (and obviously they lived like any of us), but they took the narrow road, overcame the power of their lower natures, faced all the challenges of the dark powers and regions and when they finally left their bodies, rose to higher realms and were willing to guide those in humanity who are ready to take the road they traversed. Are we willing? We pray, give us this, give us that. We must pray for strength, wisdom, and understanding, these are talents which will enable us as souls to walk the narrow path that leads to the mountain of the Lord.

Here, I would like to mention some vision dreams from three days ago. Dreams are good learning tools for all souls on the earth and the souls lost in the regions of darkness. Here goes. Two ladies and I were standing somewhere. One is an empath, but still, she looks down on other religions, animals are of no concern, etc. But this is okay, most people are doing this. The other lady is the opposite of what is good. I do not need to elaborate here. So, both wrote their thesis (exam papers). The one who is an empath wrote a brief paper with good things in it, confident that she will pass. The no good one wrote countless pages for her thesis, all useless, full of purposeless words and no substance. She knew she wrote it all wrong and felt bad about it, so I told her to rewrite it. We came into existence from purest realms, but when we live as humans on the Earth, everything we do, or think, whether lovingly, cruelly, kindly, or not, we are writing on our soul's slate. In the beginning, it was blank. So, with our living, we write on it, some good, some not so good, some evil. Only the good and perfect is accepted by the perfect God force, so, we need to rewrite our books again and again until they are perfected before the ineffable. No excuses will work. Praise is of no importance. We are here to learn, write our soul thesis, defend it, and ascend. This is the learning for all of us. Wise are those who comprehend the purpose of our physical existence as souls and live for love, harmony living, unity, oneness with all.

If one trusts somebody due to their impressive talk and interactions with them, if they are fake and insincere, they are bound to create victims who trusted them. There are such victims all over the world. It is like a sea of victims. What's up with us as humans? We were endowed with super capacities of mind and emotions; we are capable of love and empathy. If we do not practice those virtues and live like robots, we are bound to create victims, suffering for everyone who crosses our path. The Bible says, "To whom much is given, and much is demanded." These are the soul qualities given to man alone to develop and practice for the well-being and unity of all creation. Religions did not teach humanity, forefathers to fathers. They did not teach their children how to be decent and practice character. They are slaves to their animalistic existence. This is how sowing and reaping works. Ancients call it karma. We interact with one another to create karma. Until it is all cleared and balanced, we meet this life repeatedly. The people who preach about sowing and reaping usually do not practice what they preach. Hence, we have this overpopulation, suffering of every sort. Who is going to protect others and practice God's love? Maybe the animals will. Humans, most of them, are incapable of doing anything good in the order of God's love.

We check our temperature to see whether we have a fever. In the same way, we can realize whether we are in tune with divine order or not, because God gave us these talents, called the God within. Before we act selfishly and cause others to stumble and suffer, we must learn to check with the inner guide. Then we will not be in error. No one has taught us. We are indoctrinated to the contrary somewhat. The news told me that three hundred people were killed in Egypt. Is that not stupid and evil? We are busy doing God's work indeed!

Are we sincere in our quest for spiritual manna, and do we know how to acquire it? Well, a few saints (people) here and there are convinced about the existence of souls/spirits, God force, the divine heritage, etc., and they strive during the long and arduous journey of souls through physical existence. They climb the rugged mountains, they clear the thorns, thistles, bushes, with their axes, act on their desire and love for their souls/spirits existence with eternal and desire to participate in the continuum of Creations with eternal force. Most people only do all the outward activities and there is no change in their inner lives, their environments. They do nothing for their soul's ascension, and not only that, but they also create huge darkness in their inner life of the soul/spirit. Such people are cruel, only living for their own sake. They kill, destroy other beings and people. In their soul level, they abandon everything that is harmonious. They leave behind an evil legacy for the living. They are not prepared for their winter (the afterlife) during which their souls are frozen in its existence. There is no sun of spirit shining on them. People think nobody will know what they have done, what they have failed to do. These people do not recognize God's Holy Spirit within them and gently guiding them. They ignore the little voice, and they hear the voice of the dark power.

In the afterlife, our sense of feeling of joy, sorrows, pain, and pleasure is far stronger. But there is no place to escape from these feelings. This is the law of the Lord. "This is the day of the Lord." Listen to the voice crying out in the wilderness saying to turn aside from doing evil. Prepare for the winter. Do not wait for tomorrow. Tomorrow is not in our control. We all walk the valley of death or darkness during the sojourn. A time must come when we must turn away from the path we walked and say goodbye to the tempter, say "welcome" to the Lord of love, and light. Then we shall consider ourselves as called to receive the master's teaching. It is sincere in its content. There is no deception here. There is no desire for power. Nobody is preparing humanity for the spirit/soul's journey, and how to make it. No religions are doing it, either. Be sensitive to all life forms. Be careful not to misuse procreative power. Do not live a life full of deception. Do not leave a bad legacy of any kind to the living whether human or any other kind.

What we carry with our souls are our actions: The wrongs, right, selfishness, kindness, empathy. All achievements relating to riches or poverty will have no effect. But it will have an effect, if these talents were used for love, peace, harmony, and unity with all. I would like to write something about spiritual awakening and what will happen to that person who experiences a spiritual awakening. I wrote about this before. Once that happens to a particular person, they will absolutely become an empath, they will cherish all life, causing no harm to any in creation mentally, emotionally, or physically. That person seeks unity with all that is. That person has overcome their ego-driven life. The lower nature will have no power over them. They seek justice. That person will never use their speech to lie or misguide anyone. They stand against bloodshed. This person never stands for any abuse of any form, to any flesh, either humans or beasts. They seek no acknowledgment or praise from anybody. They speak against war, violence, crime, selfishness, and all other evils happening in the lower kingdom (animal kingdom). They recognize the right of all to existence. They see the Creator's love in all creation. They rise above dogmas and religions; they are free spirits bound by no power of the lower nature. They cleanse their soul/spirit. They are guided by their divine love within them. Once that awakening happens, people will, one at a time, leave them because they see no common ground with most others. They will feel lonely. But they go inside themselves and enter their own world most of the time. It all comes at a great price. That is why, the Bible says, "You must love your God with all your heart." That means one must seek their soul/spirit. Take good care of the dwelling place of the spirit. Feed the body with live food. Clean food. Always think kindly. Always be true to our light within with pure thought/action.

Harmonious Petals — Rose

These people are climbers of the rugged mountains, removing the thistles, thorns, and bushes with their axes, while axes are their desire for spiritual ascension. They recognize that their spirit/soul entered the animal kingdom with physical bodies with the highest potential for returning to the spiritual dimensions. I do not think we have any other choice. We must experience the thunder of silence. Allow the divine spirit to rise within and shine. Know we are in this glamour world to seek God in a true sense. We have to make no compromises. Live, love, let live. Let no one suffer because of our selfishness. Our abilities are vast, and we must use them to expand our consciousness. This is our life, our journey. Do not hinder others. They, too, are here to learn and to ascend. We are in the world of action, not the world of talk. Seek the guidance of the Holy Spirit within. First, desire to know and turn from all that is hindering the experience. Know that we have been selfish and cruel. We created these problems for ourselves and the rest of creation. We must heal these wounds. Help will come from on high with the love of God. Let us join the human angels and all high order spirits to bring about harmony. Live every moment with conscious and awareness of God in all.

The dark night of the soul: I wrote about climbing the rugged mountain. It is difficult to keep going sometimes when one's strength within has been depleted due to the forces of darkness. The true spiritual journey is arduous, and travelers are few. Eventually, we will all make this journey. Eternal parents are not in a hurry for us to take the high road, we are given all these beautiful talents, we abuse them, misuse them, and we will account for our use of them. People who think of souls/spirits/infinite God and its existence know we came with these powers of love, and we are responsible to return to its dwelling. For the true seekers, this is their life. They struggle in the middle of the stormy ocean of physical living, the demands, the lower mind, the upper mind, and the useless forces that are willing to destroy every good step we are able to take on the upward journey. Well, keep going! We may fall but will have the satisfaction that the infinite love will be there when we fall and when we rise. There is no cakewalk in the spiritual walk. It is hard. We have to develop love for the Creator, entire creation, with one love, one light.

It is like there is a holy river that starts from the high mountain ranges of the Himalaya. We are countless, people from all walks of life and from different parts of the world of colors and races. Also, we are kind to our animals and birds. Humans on this journey may carry some containers according to their liking; each container is different in size, colors, etc. After reaching the summit of the mountain, we then decide to go the Ganges where it starts, drink some, and fill our vessels and start to climb back to our physical destination. We all drink the water we carry in our containers, the same water, though our containers are all different looking, but what is in the containers is the same water from the Ganges. In appearance, it's different, but the water is the same and is from the same source. Keep this water pure. Live with character, morals, discipline, and be sensitive to all life forms. We may have to sacrifice some or many pleasures to keep the life force of all, which comes from the holy and mighty creator who waits for all to do well and return home with a heart full of love and joy of living. Know that I am nothing. Do not care for what I am saying. Care for what your inner guide says. If you are a true seeker of God, you will care for what I am writing.

Today, I write about our whole creation run by the mighty power grid we may call the almighty God force. The entire visible and invisible worlds, unknown, and known whether forms or formless exist by the will of the absolute. Without this power, no light bulb will light. If all the little people think they are self-made and they do not need anybody, that they themselves are the powerhouse, they boost their egos and live and feel proud of themselves and look down on other people or beings. Spiritually, they are little or small, they are a wasteland, a barren land where no love of God exists, and they are doomed in the soul sense. Animals do not feel proud. They connect with their herd types, are together and naturally maintain their herd order. Humans, the superior animals, with all the talents and potential for humility, pride, love, hate, empathy, goodness, righteousness, charity, and so forth. These are good qualities of God. But humans choosing evil, pride, selfishness are the lower quality that belongs to the animal kingdom. These, we humans, exercised very well, in spite of all the teachings, the appearance of the sages, saints, etc. We, humans are connected to both these kingdoms, one of which is the lower kingdom, the fleshly animal kingdom, and the other is the spiritual kingdom. Each person has to recognize that we are souls; we have to work to acquire love, empathy, compassion, humility, recognizing the interconnectedness of all that is.

Over eternal time, human souls are bound to enter the kingdom of the ineffable one and do the journey of the eternal order of progression, just as all saints and sages and all high order spirits did. If we have willing hearts, we are ready to acknowledge the fact that our pride will take our souls directly to shadow and we will see no light of God, until we realize our vanity. Never will any seeker of God feel pride. Pride is the embodiment of all that is vanity, chaos. We all have to look within and see where we are at this time. What are we doing with our talents? Are we using them to enlighten or bring darkness to our souls and others? We have a great responsibility to acquire everything through the desire for the good and noble with our lives, because we are nothing without God force. Know that we cannot survive without others. Respect and cherish all. The voice in the wilderness is crying out loud to all of us as souls saying seek the road that leads to eternal joy. Leave the life of pride leading to destruction and suffering of other beings.

My soulful thought for today is about how we can see the human world for what it is, see the work of those whose allegiance is not the soul, their pretense, loud speech about God, the building temples, their world is collapsing on its own, they rebuild, and it collapses again. This is what is happening to people of all faiths, religions, even with no religious connection. They are so immersed in this lower nature and gaining supplies if they do not come easily, they take them by force. So, what we have is a worldwide mess of immense proportions. If there was a physical body for the soul, hell, or lower regions of the astral would have been overfilled with these souls. See the creative God forces, which nobody can fathom. Nobody can grasp its power and mind. So, the little people created God in their own image and prescribe some formula of faith. Devotees are content. They attend worship places, fulfill certain acts, are contented and happy to be uplifted to the heavens to be with their God.

But being "with it" (awake to the spiritual path) is a different story altogether. Those on the mystical path of all religions, the mystics who decided to take the narrow path with blessings of the almighty God— they subdue their lower nature and its power. They built their inner temple, which is the dwelling place of the spark of the divine within. In recognition of this, they took a different approach. First, they respected all life. They kill no beings, they cause no emotional pain, which will affect their peace of mind and in turn cause a stir in the soul/spirit journey. This is happening to humans and other beings. Some invisible force brought me to this place of existence. I am forced to speak. I may be wrong but if so, then what is right? We all have to take a new approach to the work of spiritual awakening. It is as old as time and space in human history. In this physical existence, we have to realize why we do what we do.

Traffic and collisions of all kinds are happening in the physical plane for all beings, due to humans worshiping their stomach and sex. To please the stomach-mind, they have to kill all beings in the air, water, and farm animals. Boy, oh, boy, these souls will never enter the God domain until they feel the pain and suffering they are causing to other beings. They do not even feel that animals have life. A second problem is the abuse of the procreative talents God uses to procreate and keep creation alive and going, growing. From this evil attachment, nobody is safe, even little babies. It is painful to acknowledge, but this is the world we have. Religions and government and each of us are failing each other. It makes no sense. Of course, there are good people everywhere. But they are very much a minority. There is absolute beauty everywhere. We have no time to marvel at the creation and enjoy the beauty. We go to war, shed blood, and cause suffering to all other beings and each other. Does anybody really think animals have no fear, no emotions and so on? They are wrong. They (some people) do not have fear, or emotion maybe, but it does not mean other people or other beings do not. Thought creates Shedim (oppressive Spirits), in the lower plane, then, what would be the effect of all these actions of, selfish living, killing, working with the lower against the spiritual plan. As long we are covered with our skin, we have tongues to lie, minds to do all, we might think we are covered. Such people think nobody will see who they really are. Wrong. We see (the God within sees).

Unless all humanity takes a 180-degree turn and puts spirituality right, use of physicality, turn back to following the spirit's purpose in the true sense, life will be troublesome for all creation on the Earth. We have to learn to live gently, truthfully, accepting we all emerged from one source, and our spirits/souls return to that source. Learn to think for ourselves, know we have hidden treasures of the Most High within us. They are hidden; it is our purpose in physical existence to excavate those treasures through compassionate living and dying. There is a vast ocean, an infinite ocean on which we have to sail and enjoy the sailing. But if we remain stuck with our ego-centered living and killing, we will not even reach the periphery of the shore, before that, we will be sent back to deplorable conditions for the soul, because instead of preparing a strong boat and sailing with loving kindness selflessly, we have created rusty iron rollers, which cannot be moved. If one is seeking God, seek the path of the righteous, the mystic path. One does not have to go anywhere. One can do it within. Burn the demons within ourselves. Empty our hearts, so that God can fill our hearts and lives with love, beauty, honesty, and sunlight.

Physical Death

This is a deep subject indeed, an unavoidable subject. I tell you, this is the process given to physical creation, all of it, by the Creator. Even stars, including our sun, the planets—all will die. Of course, it may take millions and millions of years. But for humans, the story is a little different. We are conscious and animated with the highest ability of comprehension. There is something tangible we behold in us, which is from on high. That is what is animating the bodies of all beings. We say the spirit/soul has no death. There are people capable of occasionally seeing departed saints, and they realize, though these saints are physically dead, they are very much alive. The physical body is something soul/spirit borrows when it has decided to visit the Earth through physical birth. A man and woman come to interact, and a soul/spirit enters the womb and for a period a body is building in the womb. This goes for all beings. They all have a purpose for coming to earth for their soul experience and the growth of the soul. So, for us humans, it is of paramount importance that we allow our soul/ spirit to go through experiences, which will allow them to fulfill their task of physical existence. They must not fail. When humans are born, they have two aspects, which are the physical and spiritual and there is a conflict between the two minds. Choose life and ascension or life and descent. Death is not for the soul, but only for the body. Now the question is, what did we do with the time we were given in the physical? Did we learn to love? Did we grow soulfully or did we get stuck in the magical kingdom of vanity, killing, evil? If we practice love, we build strong wings for the soul bird and in the indwelling spirit to soar in the expanse of the God's universe and to further expand its learning, transforming and so on. Look within and see where we are. We are conscious beings and must live and act for the soul/spirit's sake.

HARMONIOUSPETALS ROSE

Yes, I have been convinced that evil is far more powerful than good in the physical planes and the lowest regions of the invisible planes. Because there is a coming and going taking place from Earth to lower planes, then from the lower to Earth. This is a lack of any awareness of the God force, love, empathy, compassion, lack of realization that all beings have their place in Creation and the right to their existence.

From the inception of human existence, we have been faced with natural disasters like floods and famines. Human lives were lost, and many started to believe there is some entity waiting up in the sky somewhere and causing all these troubles. So, they started to sacrifice babies to please these gods, or perhaps prisoners who were captured in the fight, and then they turned to animals. When one decides to shed blood, there is an evil entity that emerges from these selfish actions. And that has been multiplied many million-folds. We kill each other, we kill other beings. We are causing a dark cloud of entities who are hovering over the earth, around and within each of us. Religion's duty was to practice morality and love, instead, one after the other got busy collecting followers and they are careless of the souls who are being lost in the process of living, killing, abusing the procreative power, with lack of love and unity.

Religions only last as long as they have followers. History repeats itself. Now, so many religions are legends. It is not any better today, and not going to be any better tomorrow, until they practice the noble teachings. "Thou shall not kill" means, "Thou shall not kill," period. No exaggeration, no justification. All life is dear to the spirit-filled beholder and the Creator. Only humans can eliminate these problems because we created them. From one candle, we light another, from the other, we light the next, so let some of us at least light candles of love, peace, and unity with divinity and spread the light to all corners of the earth. Take the path of the mystic if you are serious about God, abstaining from all that can cause evil. Travel the middle path of the tree of life, so that we can—or at least our future generation will—have the earth God intended for all creation.

A Peaceful Heart is like a deep calm pool where the presence of God dwells, and one can commune with the divine. So, "Blessed are the peacemakers," Jesus says and all other great teachings also. What we do is read, discuss, dissect, and talk about the many versions of God's plans and ideas. Instead of doing what the teachings say. This has been going on forever. One thing for sure, the goal of creation/people is to realize God. To realize soul, spirit. If this is the reality, then there is a lot that needs to be changed in the way humans conduct their business in the home, outside of the home, in the world at large. If one is not participating in the peace process, they have no clue about God, soul, and spirit. Action speaks loudest. People with higher consciousness act and live—that is their life. The ones who live on the Nefesh level (low animal soul level) are like phony politicians speaking words and more words. Maybe this is how all should be. It is really sad for the higher souls that they have no voice in the face of tyrants and their deceit.

HARMONIOUS PETALS

ROSE

It is very hard to find true teachers who are from the upper world. To learn about the upper world, we have to desire with humble hearts and put aside the power of Nefesh. This is the powerhouse of the animal kingdom. We have to learn to control our animal nature so it will be like a trained horse. Once we control the power of the Nefesh, the higher power will slowly step in to help. For which we need good teachers, good noble writing of masters and sages. If you find a teacher, listen to their advice. A teacher can only tell his or her idea of God, heaven etc. Then we must find our way to travel or hike up the mountain of the soul to find out for ourselves. This process is all the inner working of the humble soul, I say humble because it is very essential that we humble ourselves. If one is sitting on the ground, they have no place to fall, but if one is sitting on the top of the material world with overstuffed Nefesh power, he cannot enter the other higher planes, because Nefesh rules here in the material plane. It is the ruler. It leaves no room to rise. So, the seekers of love/God must practice humility, love, empathy, compassion, etc. Do not speak of those qualities but live with these qualities.

Be willing to learn even from the ants. You can gain wisdom by looking at them, their hard work, and their struggle to live. Everything in creation is part of us and a learning/interacting tool for our ascension. Do not look down on any being. Do not harm any being either emotionally or physically. Those who do will never enter the heart of God until they have cleaned and made connection from the Higher soul level (Neshamah) with our loving, kind, compassionate living. We give power to Neshama and to spirit. There are countless layers to peel off to go higher up. Let us not be the frog in the well. We must come out of confinement and leap towards the eternal ocean of God/mercy/love. This is our journey back home.

The Earth is a classroom for the soul/spirit of all beings, human brothers and sisters. Nature is our teaching tool. Humbly let us take the help of the companionship of all that is on the Earth. Love and respect them. The people who go to war, kill physically or emotionally trouble anybody, there is no divinity in them. They are the cause of suffering. Darkness (the dark power) rules them, and in the process, all suffer. Because all living being from low to high levels register emotions, feel pain. If our actions cause others to suffer, stumble, we are agents of the dark power. So, if we know we have to follow the love/light, we must leave this path of the powerhouse of the Nefesh.

Friends in spirit, I will write about life, the giver of life, the giver of all life. This is what I am saying. No amount of justification suffices to justify taking the life of a human or any of our little brothers and sisters (animals). Only the giver can take, and at the given time. Humans have no authority to take any life of any being. Humans have to retrain our spirituality to live on the earth under the domain of the one who brought all things into existence. From the throne of God force flows the river of life. We are immersed in it. At the death of a being, something escapes from the being. Nobody can capture it. Nobody will ever fathom it. It is the life force departed from that living being, no matter who or what.

Life is Holy. All life is precious to the particular being. Humans never learned to respect life in its full meaning. We put our Nefesh and its power first. We become slaves to this powerful Master. "It" commands, we act. The little Neshama cries out in the wilderness to this Nefesh. It ignores the cry. This is the story of our existence in the physical. The spiritual path is the path of the mystic. Mystics live and act like any ordinary human, but they are giants in the spiritual path, and they put their Nefesh on a leash. It will not control these humans. But the spirit of God controls the Nefesh. It will absolutely be like a trained pit bull. Once the pit bull is trained, it becomes a servant for its master. This is animal nature that we must train. Without this, there is no hope for a human to ascend the ladder which the great masters and mystics climbed.

Our words have no ability to bring change. But our changed choices become the voice for liberation and path for others. It will not happen overnight, but we must desire it. There is a saying, we take one step towards God force and it will take two steps towards us, so the mystics say. All masters of the divine law say, to seek love, unity in all that is because all creation belongs to the creator force/power. If you love God, you love all. War is not our choice, in that case, killing is not our choice, and selfishness is not our choice. Emotional or any physical abuse of any being or creature is not what we choose. If we are genuinely on the path, then our choice must lead to the eternal glory of Father/Mother. May the light shine in the darkness (to the entire face of the earth). Children must be trained. Humans must change their ways, clean, and clear the debris. May the light shine in the darkness!

My soulful thought for today is about a beautiful soul abiding in the heart. This is the true inner teacher who speaks to you, not from writings by somebody, that you memorize, vomit it up to someone else.

These writings are not all knowledgeable. You get information from books, nothing more. One has to acquire knowledge of spirit through correct practices of truth, justice, recognizing the right, wrong, etc. These are the genuine heart treasures for the true seekers. To reach the mountain's precipice, first, one has to reach the foothills, then climb on, and carry on climbing. What a task for the body, for the spirit! This is the true living in this world for the soul, for those who realize it. Jesus says, I am here in the world, but not part of it. What a drag. What pressure from all around? But carry on, if you can, and if we are successful, one day we can stand on the top of the mountain of the soul and feel relieved that we did that, and the sun will shine on the soul. The steps are the inner cleaning, desiring to climb, taking the step, helping others on the venture. Do not push others who are struggling to climb. Walk while alive. The dead cannot walk. Keep alive the life of the soul in each of us. May the sun shine on all who seek to walk the mountain during the dark night of the soul/spirit living.

One has written, and it is very interesting, we are wretched, we are poor. We choose to be wretched and poor because we do not recognize the richness of the God-force. The God-force is the power that created all spirits and souls from its richness. We are endowed with the ability to have all that the divine has, but we must desire it. We must work for it. In the physical, one can rob, cheat, and kill to acquire the wealth of the physical. One may not even have to work at all. We are all involved in these physical dramas that will endanger our progress towards achieving the spiritual treasures waiting for us. If we do all these evil things to satisfy our animal nature, we are depriving the spiritual nature. In substance, all humans are spiritual in nature. We do not acknowledge this.

It is like we are children going to amusement parks for our souls. First, we enter the physical plane. We have to grow soulfully, spiritually. We are so fascinated with all the fun rides, pleasures, corruption, selfishness to acquire things, killing for pleasures, and lies. We may talk plenty of Gods, but God runs from that heart. Our heart must show God's- love by truly living with compassion, love, truthfulness, no killing of any beings, no causing any suffering. This is what a heart with God in it does. They are mystics. Religious prescriptions will not take anyone to God. It is the righteous who are compassionate, loving and living, desiring to finish the journey according to the desire of the spirit/soul to be united with one who is in all. God seeks no word that comes out of the talkers. God desires only a truthful, loving heart and the words that come out of the heart with love. Each one of us will walk our way alone to God, through the practice of the teaching of the Lord, masters, sages, and mystics. This job is ours alone. Religions have misguided souls and it will continue. There is no excuse for the pain and suffering we are causing to each other and creation. We should be the stewards to work and maintain the garden of God. We are causing havoc. No one has character, there is no love. It would be good if these dishonest people, cruel people, loveless people, do not take the name of the divine. The divine is pure in essence and in substance. Do not trouble or endanger the good in this world by the support of evil. We must change our ways, heal the sick, help the fallen to rise, soothe broken spirits. Stop causing suffering to children, animals, or any human who wants to live in peace. Make an iron fence around the good, so that evil will never penetrate. We have done so much damage to this creation and to each other. All good in this world is collateral for evil. Good cannot survive. The good has been pushed off the cliff. Human masqueraders of many colors think this is what the physical earth is for. Be genuine in essence and leave the dark ways behind. One does not have to please anyone or show anyone, but their own God within. It lies in the arid desert of our deceitful existence, waiting for a drop of true love-filled, compassion-filled action. Yes, action through living.

Is there any teacher who speaks directly to human hearts sincerely for the transformation of human existence? No, I do not think so. There were great masters who spoke, lived, and went into the eternal realms. People are immersed in all false writings and religious prescriptions. What is the current state of human affairs? This kind of evil is happening under our noses. Goodness has no voice. People do not teach their children what is good, what is character? The parents do not have much to teach, really. But even if they know, they do not discipline their children to be the good citizens of the Earth and citizens of the spiritual world. Why else do we have this super ability of comprehension, wisdom, love, hate, anger? They must all be used for the well-being of all creation and the protection of good. Hate evil, love good; create barriers where evil cannot penetrate. But at this time, it is an impossible task to protect and maintain good. Because the majority are misguided selfish children turning into adults and following the same path of the glamour of the two-legged being.

After all the work of religions, faith, spirituality, millions of noble writings, still, what is on the Earth? The good suffering at the hands of evil, I really feel lost in the face of these cruel ones, who are killing, committing crimes, making war, creating violence, telling lies, falsehoods, and characterless living as pretend-humans, powerful in their projection. Surely there are good and noble people also. We must take a good look at creation with all beings in mind. Allow every being to live in their own little worlds. These religions must teach people to abstain from hurting or doing harm to any being. We must strive for a co-existence of all beings. No one will do this. We are overwhelmed by the self-righteous. Boy, can one imagine, if there were no death and the way people live now. Despite the termination of life and certainty of death, still they give not a damn about the way they rule. There is no mass migration of souls into earth per se. Still, one human at a time manifests on the earth, so one human at a time departs with their soul-baggage full of trash or treasures collected as soul memories. This is the destiny of the soul. The Book of Life is opened, revealed, felt and the soul then plunges into darkness or flies into light and love. What choice we are making.

Good is the principle of the God-force. If we practice goodness, we feel liberated, elated, and no drug can provide this joy. To experience this joy, our hearts must be empty of all that is not good, with physical creation came good and evil. We go through, suffer the lack of peace and joy that only goodness can provide. The evil force also provides proud and overweening egos. It cannot last that way unless, to keep up, we continue to do evil, otherwise they hit rock bottom and are lost. In the long run, they will be lost anyhow. God will not allow this to continue forever. The not- God realized people can do harm, abuse, lie, cheat, and speak louder about all Godly stuff. A good godly person will abstain from harming any creatures whether humans or any other, because the giver of life force is embedded in all creation. The animating ones, the superior animals have potentials to become angels and coworkers for God. We must be aware of our potential and act accordingly, so that creation is kept and maintained in such a way, as if God was standing before us like a person. We must always be truthful and just, kind, empathetic and so on. God force is always assisting us with our ability to recognize what is good, what is harmful to the soul/spirit.

If we continue to ignore assistance, truly we are fallen creatures. Experience the suffering of others as if they were in our hands, suffering of all forms. Use all the faculties as the talents God-force endowed to us, so that we can experience ourselves and understand what others/beings are. So, be sensitive to everything. Respect all life. If one feels one is following the path of God, then observe the inner temperature with which one lives. There is too much God talk and not enough transformation. God and Evil both act through our talents. One is the opposite to the other. One cannot serve God and Mammon. So, we must use the talents for joy, peace, harmony for all beings. If one suffers, the spirit of God suffers. Tikkum Olam (repairing/healing the world). Instead of speaking, somewhere along the way one has to start. Something must be broken; only then does it need repair. We know it is broken within all of us and the entire physical creation has been broken by us. If we can start doing this within ourselves first then in the world, the miracle of manifestation of the Messiah will occur.

The cosmos is filled with entities, angels, demons, spirits and so forth (they are invisible to the naked eyes). Some were created at the beginning of creation as workers for the Creator. Some are spirits of departed humans and animals. Similarly, millions of entities (microbes, bacteria of good and bad), are also very much part of our body. They are all working together to keep us in shape. Also, when men expel sperm, are you aware of millions of little tadpoles rushing to one destination. They will not survive outside the body for long. If they do not reach their destination, they die. So, nothing is as simple as people think it is. We are living in total ignorance. This is a touchy subject. Oh, nobody wants to talk about it. If humans learn to cherish every being: themselves, others, their emotions, feelings, how each body works, how all long for peace and harmony within themselves, this world could have been a paradise. Now, we are waiting for the Messiah to come and fix our issues. The Messiah is always knocking at the door of hearts to enter and rule. Be aware of head to toe, in and out, how it all functions. What is our part in the game of life, death and what are the repercussions, consequences?

I cannot say it often enough: Humanity's talents were given by the Creator. Use them to repair the little inner world of ours first. Then the outer world (Tikkun Olam). If you do all sorts of reading of scriptures and there has been no transformation, pity is the state affairs of that person. The seed fell on the waste, arid soil. Do not waste any more time. No one knows the hour when we are asked to pack the bag of memory, pains, sorrows, love, hate and return to the spirit world. Let us be participants in life and let all live. Be mindful of the inner and the outer of all. We are all in it together. Our actions affect others in a good way or bad way, because we all in creation have a common ancestry. It is our Creator. Be mindful of all beings in the sky, on the earth, and water. This, only mystics can feel fully, and do. We all have to be mystics in the long journey of the soul. We will desire to do this with compassion, love, truthfulness. It will come easily at some point.

Importance of Practice

This is of paramount importance for our soul/spiritual awareness and ascending. We read, read, and read some more. Spirituality is not intellectual absorption and talk. If one cares for and recognizes the soul/ spirit and its purpose. We must live by the words we read from the masters. No amount or rituals or reading will take the souls to the high mountain of the Lord, but only the practice of love for loving sake. Through loving creation, we love the Creator. Millions of souls' time is wasted with our overly clever attitudes. Live righteously, respect all life. Wish safety and protection for all life. Pleasures of body, the mind will fail and the consequences we will finally take to the grave and beyond. But love, justice, peace, harmony, when we take our body to the grave, thanks to them, the soul will fly high to the realm of heavenward. One may think, too bad, all these pleasures of the world are so inviting and how one will miss them. Well, if one believes in soul/spirit/God, it is a different story. To that being, one has to pay attention to what is good for the soul/spirit. So be the doers of what is good while in the physical. That is why we are here, to experience in action by overcoming the many pitfalls of the physical. Eat the soul food through loving, honest, kind, emphatic physical action. Nothing is small, or big. We are all different manifestations of the one God force. Learn, live, and let live. I know, we are used to performing some rituals, reading, and muttering words, thinking they will open the gates of Heaven. No. We have to cut every weed, every rock, overcome every hurdle thrown at us by our fellow humans. We must be mindful of what we are doing to other beings in order for us to be on top and shine as victorious on the physical level. Do not be so confident. Those high up will hit the ground if one drags another human or other being down. This is the law of Creation.

My soulful thought for today is about how to meditate or pray from the bottom of the heart.

I put some water, say about a glass and a half of water, on the stove to boil to make my morning tea. I went to do something else and suddenly, I remembered I put the water on to boil. I then went to look at it, and the water was gone. Not a drop of water was in the pot. Where did it go, why is it not visible? Does it cease to be? No. The water evaporated and is still in the atmosphere. I am trying to prove something here. From the ocean of God, the souls/spirits rain down into the Earth and manifested as living beings, whether as animals or humans. When the time comes, those bodies die or are killed, no matter what the container was. That is the physical body, and something disappears from our view before our physical eyes. Do you think it ceases to be? No. It rises from the vessel that held it and will reappear into some vessel, which is worthy of it to be held again for the time being.

God and its creation will never cease to be. Forms may change. The essence will never change. With living as we have, souls fell into the mire of filthy pots, clean pots, and so on. If one is aware of anything, clean the pot with righteous living, kind living, compassionate living, and desire to be one with the pure water of life, whatever is healthy for the soul. Give up what will cause the water of life to be poisoned. "After the death of the body, the soul returns to the ether." No matter whether it is human or animals. There are levels of etheric existence. Prepare a place, a good place to enter. Humanity is living in cruelty, selfishly; this is due to being unsure of or unaware of the soul/ spirit. Okay, they speak of God; do outward practices of some sort. A human on the spiritual path who is convinced about it will live a life of purity, honesty, kindness, and will be compassionate and abstain from polluting the water of life, which flows from the Creator to creation. The Messiah is living and calling to each one of us to practice love and kindness. Do not take the life of animals or humans, do not torture mentally or emotionally. We are all invading each other's sanctuary of the Most High, which is our hearts. So, accept the connectedness of all. Live for the soul/spirit with the purity of heart.

I am sending out loving thoughts, for safety and peaceful living for all creatures. We show no respect for other bodies, other beings, we are ready to indulge in everything at any cost. Who falls victim, does not matter? Humans must be awakened to the love and light of God. Keep the heart free from corruption of all kinds, then what was revealed to the ancients, which we read as words of God, will be revealed to us more as well.

Prepare the way with the purity of heart and living.

There is no other way to enter the light. Everything else will cause us to enter the dark cloud to be rain again as chaos in the physical.

Allow other beings to live in peace. All suffering beings are crying out in my heart. I do not have the answer. I am that I am in all, I am present. I am the little ant and have no ability to change anything. God is calling to all; we are not hearing. We are busy talking about God. What is the color of someone's skin, what kind of hair? and they often forget the real question and how to answer the question.

HARMONIOUS PETALS ROSE

Spirituality is that we recognize we are not the body, and we are soul/spirit indwelling in the body. And that our physical lives and our body must serve to accomplish the goal for which the soul incarnated into the physical. Recognize the goals the soul has and how to accomplish them. That is why religions came into existence, to make humanity aware that we are soul/spirit. Physicality and Spirituality run parallel. Somewhere on the way, one must bend/merge and serve the other, whether it will be spiritual and everlasting or physical and does not last long, because the physical will cease to be and, in the indweller, which is the soul/spirit gathers the lower actions from living the earth-bound human existence. Here comes the choice for each of those here on the earth to do the job of the divine or do the job of the physical master (Lucifer). We need the soul/spirit to live on the earth and or in the spirit world of many dimensions, or to live in lower dimensions. The saints, sages, the mystics choose the path of the light world, though they may be rich, poor, beggars, merchants, or a sweeper of the office buildings. They live for something so vast and great. Others, too, live and gather for themselves, the opposite of light. Maybe these are all just a joke, live, die, and cease to be. If we live and recognize the eternal existence of the spirit, we have a long way to go and do a lot along the way. We must abstain from many things considered normal. Recognizing the one creator that we all belong to and all creatures are on their own mission willed by the absolute. To interfere in their lives is detrimental to humans and all other life forms. Be sensitive about how one lives. Ask, what is present in your deeds, selfishness, or selflessness?

Harmonious Petals   Rose

I wrote of the importance of self-inner transformation and ascension for the soul. The people on the path, we have no other way but to do the journey of transformation. We have to, to allow the light to enter and stay. This can only happen when our heart is filled with love, compassion, and unity with all creation. I cannot ignore this. There is no other way of entering into God's Kingdom.

HARMONIOUSPETALS   ROSE

Seekers of God and its path should read this, what all the ancient sages and masters said. In one whose God-consciousness is awakened; their world will turn upside down. They see everything differently. They connect with the whole creation. They become empathic, and they are filled with compassion. They want to see the world differently, but it will not happen. They are few and their voice will be silenced or ignored. It was like that for many of the great teachers that came and went. Some are killed, others escaped. Yesterday in the church, you believe in Jesus as our Messiah, and live and practicing his teaching. If there is a change, it has to take place on the Earth. We must practice what the prophets, sages, saints said and all God's people lived for.

The "Tree of Life," is the greatest gift for mankind. It is an analogy, a diagram in how it looks, but profound teaching is imparted through the analogy of the "Tree of Life." It is all about descending from above, experiencing, transforming, and ascending back to the source. It is all concerned with the spirit. God's presence is passively acting in humans, but the power of darkness is very active. This applies to all humans. God gave us such talents/the faculties that we must use for the common good and the well-being of all. The Father says, the wealth, recognition, having a respected name and fame all will vanish with physical death. True, these qualities will cause humans to be vain and that vanity will go down to the grave with the body. What will ascend with the spirit/soul? We have to ask whether we worked for the higher, spiritual nature or the vainglory of the physical. Only we, each of us, can know this.

Humans talk about lots of attributes of God, Son of God, the lineage, the virgin birth, and so on. We cannot flatter God. God was, is, and will be. "Ehyeh Asher Ehyeh" It is complete, it has no beginning and no end. No one will ever comprehend its magnitude. We have to see what Jesus said. It is our duty who believes in Jesus, to follow his footsteps, leave behind what is causing us to stumble. In human history, there were so many said to have been born of virgins, even born on December twenty-fifth, who died, or were killed. It is not important, what is important is his teaching. All creation came from one spiritual DNA, and we do not have to force ourselves to submit to some major hierarchy that apparently never really existed. Jesus came from infinite existence, saw how humanity had fallen, the suffering, and knew how to elevate the fallen. That was, and is, his purpose. Unless we do what he said, and follow in his footsteps, and live actively for the purpose of the spirit, we are wasting our lives, causing pain and suffering to all creatures and to each other. Our world is burning with evil committed by our human hands. The population is exploding. Animals are produced in very cruel conditions without any thought that they, too, have life. Does God care what we eat? If God does care, what do we do? So, gain wisdom and love, practice empathy and compassion, this is our task and the way to our salvation.

Yes, if we believe in soul/spirit/union with divine/God, we have to purify our inner lives and help others to do the same. At least do not cause them to be impure. It is possible, not only is it possible but we are continually doing it from the inception of time, which started with men and women. We can purify the water which runs through contamination or is contaminated by outside substances using filtration, reverse osmosis, or distillation. So, we can drink clean water for our thirst. But the water of life/consciousness of life flows from the infinite waters/infinite consciousness. It flows from the Creator to creation to bring forth all physical creation/life, including us.

Except humans, everything else follows their cycles, directly controlled by the invisible angels, invisible force. For humans, we have this supercomputer brain, so we have to always choose or not choose. Some people are in their infancy in their soul level, and they do not think of soul/spirit. They live like devouring monsters, just live for pleasure, and are involved in crime. The good people struggling to live a path of peace and soul/spirit ascension often fall prey to these monsters. They are cruel. They have to enter and spin the wheel of life for eons of soul time. Nobody is interested in purifying their inner life. Most of us are playing dress-up and pretending. Behold, the spirit is being crucified by our own ignorance. We have no right to do this; there is no justification for it. We must practice universal love and empathy towards all creation because all is within the love of creation by the Creator. However, how much we may connect with the glories of the world, are we aware we will be pulled out from the very root by the power and law of creation? Unless we become like the (holy) child, pure in heart, and allow no one to become impure in their hearts either. Creation is suffering, due to humanity. God is calling each one of us to partake in purifying what we made impure. We kill those who speak the truth for a change. They say, "What is the truth?" Maybe your truth is not my truth. So, we are fragmented with billions of falsified truths. There is no unity, no safety. I ache for my soul, my environment, the whole earth and all the poor creatures in it and all those who strive to keep their heads up above the stormy waters.

Harmonious Petals   Rose

Today, I will write about the desire to bring awareness to the masses, using many analogies. God is speaking through us. Creation is the symphony of God, and it is our duty is to practice and play in the orchestra with one accord. We, the highest intelligent creatures, decided to play each in our own orchestra with our own mind and whims. So, we created horrific sounds vibrating on the Earth, and in the lower nether worlds. It has gone completely out of control. We have no choice but to join the symphony of creation as part of the orchestra and play harmoniously so that we can hear and follow the conductor (which is the Creator alone) and the music will be a melody of love, wisdom, empathy, compassion. Such a symphony will bring new earth, a new life, one life with all life breathing the perfume of peace and joy.

My soulful thought for today is about free will. The choices each of us have to make in order to live on the Earth and in turn, preparing the right place in the spirit world are done with free will. Yes, nothing is going to be accomplished here or hereafter without effort. Too bad, we have to make the effort, choices. You see, it is as if we will eat a cake without knowing how the cake is made, what are the ingredients, maybe doing this one time is okay, but if we know how to make the cake, we can make it even better, even healthier. That was during the soul's childhood time. Parents provide, but once we are able and capable, we must earn our physical and spiritual conditions. Our Heavenly Father has given us all the talents to live well or live in evil. In the physical, dark forces are working to challenge us every step that we take. The great tempter. If we can direct this power with our will power to do good for our souls, and in order to do good for others as well, that is using our free will properly. We are taking one step at a time for our ascension on the ladder. Well, the ladder goes from the highest heaven to the deepest existence in the darkest regions of creation. By the will of the absolute, we can direct our souls back to the path of ascension on the ladder. The Father's heart and holy place is always open to its creation.

Look at the little butterfly, the stages it goes through as it transforms into a beautiful butterfly. Look at the animal kingdom, how they struggle to live each day. Why are we humans with all our talents and faculties acting like we are crippled and incapable? Because we directed our God's Love and energy to satisfy our animalistic nature and we put out or dimmed our light within. So, we fall prey to the entities who serve the Lord of Darkness. So, we have no unity starting from home to the village, to the nations, and the ends of the Earth. We kill, maim, torture, and are unable to feel empathy, so there is chaos. In chaotic regions of the astral, when back on earth men and women do what they do for lust's sake, by force. When lost souls enter the unprepared womb, what is the result? Children who look like humans but bear no qualities of humanity. Humans are potential angels who will take part of the great work in creation.

Yes, we humans traveled from our Father's home and entered the densest/darkest places for the spirit/soul. Humanity is living wretched and gruesome lives because we lost all our connection to the one light, the purest in essence, with love, and unity in purpose. We entered this ego-driven life, where no one but me exists. The whole creation is a battlefield for us, because of us. Earth is soaked with the blood of humans, animals, abortion. There are broken souls/spirits everywhere. They proclaim the mystery of God because somebody wrote it. Are we trying to understand what the mystery is? We may not fully ever comprehend God and God's love, but partially, we will if we can give up selfishness, crime, and killing. Treat everybody as God's creatures, desire to live a life with the higher purpose of returning back to Father's home. It may take millions of soul years, but we must realize this is what our higher spirit wants so we must take the steps, by weeding out all that will bind us to the lowest nature of existence. We must climb the rugged mountain with our axe (which is love for all, desire for purity, unity with all that is). Humility is paramount in the spiritual path. Do not look down on any creatures as our ego desires us to do.

If one has their heart and mind free, then they will realize what I am saying. It is the state of being our own being from within. This is the quality with which we all should conduct our lives in this physical world. We separated from each other. We separate Creation and God in our way of viewing things. So, we have landscapes of war, ignorance, violence, division. God is there, I am here. Can you imagine what it would be like if we all realized the fact that everything in creation is the offspring of the Creator? Religious division and all other divisions have no place in the mystic's heart, a saint's heart, a sage's heart. Truly, we have to come to this state of existence wherein we realize the face of God in a blade of grass, in birds, dogs, or humans. We will be forced to make this journey in due course. We hold on to our theories, of me, them, and the rest. These divisions will continue until we reach absolute perfection. From the one light was born trillions of sparks. This is true. Our job is to gain wisdom, and through wisdom overcome many of the things that divide creation. This is my way of taking Creator/ creation. I read the very book of my own existence, I read the Creation in Action. Very few unique books came in my way before this, which is a testimony to my awareness. I read them and am content with it.

Billions of minds, billions of ways, and opinions, are we ever going to meet in the one point from which all points emerged? Yes, in the eternal order of progression, we as souls have eternity at our disposal. So much has happened, will happen. Send out love, desiring safety for all creatures and children. A house divided will not stand. Unity is what we must seek in truth, justice, compassion, and love. Until and unless we have dissolved the music of discord, dark clouds of clouds of pain will shower upon all creation coming from humans. If one reads the teaching of any religion, it is written for transformation. If we read and forget it, it is better we do not read it. Souls will experience all divisions and not so good thoughts; action and living will be experienced by us as one, who are aware of a much more heightened state of existence. We will reap what we sowed here. It is our inheritance. Seek unity and peace wherever we can. So that when we are ready to truly leave, we will realize we did our best and did not deceive, kill, or do any harm to any being. A tomorrow filled with bright light wherein darkness should have no place.

My soulful thought for today is the desire to educate humanity that we have no future here. Our future as souls lies with Adonai (the Limitless existence of the ineffable one). This fact we cannot touch, but if we are awakened, we can experience it. We amass money and riches for ourselves and for generations to come. And the generation becomes spiritually impotent and bankrupt in the spiritual sense. They plunder riches, which they have not earned, and, in the process, they put their soul into an eternal furnace. We are all on a chase, not realizing ahead of us there is a bridge that connects the physical to the spiritual and it has collapsed and there is a vast drop where they have to spend time only to realize the time was wasted.

Life is a precious gift, and the majority of humans squander it. This is the fruit of our actions when we live without thought for others, showing no kindness, no love for anyone. If God is our destination, we have to realize many things and make a detour. We have to earn our living using correct means; also, we have to earn a place with God with our desire and work. We do so many things with our physical bodies to ourselves and others/beings. Our soul carries the burden to the nether world to experience all we have done or failed to do. I wish peace and harmony to all creation, wisdom, and empathy to all humanity. There is no other way. This is the law and order by which our soul/spirit live by the creative force.

We must always pay attention to our environments, in and out. We must cherish the life force that permeates all things. This form, which we care for so much will vanish into the formlessness of the cosmic lifeforce. So, allow all forms to exist until their time comes. Be gentle to your souls and all soul/spirit. When we harm a being emotionally or otherwise, one is harming or troubling the soul/spirit within. In turn, we harm our own soul existence. We do not need to speak about God, and how much we know God. If we all knew, we would not behave in such a way. Our talks are noise without action. The one witnessing our inner life is within and it is ever active. Pay attention! Be part of the change for peace and unity. Our Earth, we have all combined to push it to the edge of destruction with all the inhabitants on it. We are living for simple pleasures of eating and other indulgences. When will we start living for the soul, which longs for our transformation and ascension? See, I can write some flowery words. I will not do that, because if I do, I deceive myself and the readers as well. We are part of the whole and the whole is part of us. We must repair, wipe the tears of all the weeping ones; caused by our/human conduct. Take the path the sages took, the mystics took, they are least interested in talking about God, and rather they do their best to live for God's love. They see God in action in all creation. If our Earth is to survive the coming catastrophe, we must start acting, abstaining from many pleasures considered to be normal. Desire wisdom, direct knowledge, not accepting that someone said something. Humanity created everything that keeps souls in bondage so that they can keep their power, which will fall as if it was a castle built on the air in a matter of time.

My soulful thought for today is about suffering. There are all kind of sufferings. To rebel is the character of the animalistic nature, rebel against wrong, injustice, crime, evil. We have no choice but to rebel, because each one of us is contributing to other humans' or animals' suffering. A long, long time ago, the human soul/spirit plunged into the world of matter. They call it Adam and Eve and they sinned The creative power created souls/spirit, spiritual worlds and physical worlds by the will of the absolute. Humans are spiritual beings but have an animalistic physical existence. When we connected with total fleshly pleasures of eating and mating for the sole purpose of pleasure, we plunged into the great darkness. Then, we lost our light, we do not know how to get out, we, soul/spirit rebelled against the parents. Our pleasure cannot be satisfied, the more we do, the more we want. Hence, pleasure leads to great suffering for us and innocent animals as well. We are unable to use our faculties of empathy, compassion, love—which we are all capable of.

The pull of the dark power actively rules the physical world, and we allow this power to rule over our soul/spirit. So, we are slaves. Fighting all these dark entities, people do get mentally, and emotionally sick. Some people do not get sick, as long as they serve the master ruler of the mighty dark power. God is passively acting in the physical creation. It will not force anyone to come to the road which leads to eternal bliss.

People who seek the light, their journey is fighting the dark power all around. Humans are instruments of these good and evil forces. We have to climb the rugged mountain by clearing all the thistles, weeds, bushes etc. as we climb, using the love for divine. The destiny of the souls is determined by the way we live on the earth as physical beings. When we live for lust and gluttony, do not even dream that we can receive God's light. So long as we continue killing, devouring, raping, telling lies, falsehoods we have no chance to encounter God's light, until we clean ourselves, and become ready to receive the light. There is no wisdom with which we are living. We are ignorant and slumbering souls. No Messiahs, sages, or savant will help unless we long to be helped. The suffering will continue. People cannot stop evil, so they predict the end of time. Can you imagine billions and billions of galaxies, solar systems, planets, with countless spiritual dimensions beyond our comprehension? Can anybody understand the Creator and its power? These little men with their fleshly pleasures and ego-making noises, they may destroy the Earth and all its inhabitants but not the entire Creation. Stupidity all the way down.

Friends in spirit, the divine love is inviting each one of us to understand that the immortal is the God force and what it has created is also immortal. How foolishly have we lived, how many soul lifetimes we have wasted by engaging in the pleasures of these mortal bodies and their lowest nature? We fool ourselves by muttering words, reading some books. Reading is good, when what we read is applied to earn our spiritual food (the manna from Heaven) by transforming our inner lives and showing the outer transformation. All bodies are mortal, all spirits are immortal even those of animals or humans. What are we doing with our bodies and the bodies of other beings? I am telling, we are all in for a great surprise; the moment when we shed the coat called "body" and have moved or disappeared into the realms of the spirit. So, this teaching is coming to you, you may read it or forget it and continue the way you live, the way you lived yesterday, millions of soul's time, and will live millions of soul's time more. We are slow learners. We are not convinced about spirit. We think of this magic coat, which eventually will wear out, torn, wrinkled, cursed and then we wait for the death to ease the suffering. One day, the coat will come off no matter what, but the impression of all that we gathered through living a selfish/self-serving for glory goes with our souls, and we will go through torments, and we will not even have the ability to look for help as a soul. That much will be the weight on our souls. Nobody will hand you the heavenly paradise—if you think that you are fooling yourself. So, we have all lived to some extent badly or very badly. We need to recognize that and make amends with our soul/ spirit and listen to the call of the divine force and heal the world, or at least send out healing vibrations to all corners of the world. Pray for peace, and safety for all beings, including human children and others. Do not hurt any beings whether humans or animals. Animals have emotions, physical pains, fear of death. They want to keep their bodies for their spirit by the will of the absolute as well. Do not support evil and crime. Support the good and noble. The world needs such people to transform the course of events. Souls are in bondage.

Spiritual achievement while living is like climbing the mountain. If one can reach the summit of the Lord with our love for truth, justice desiring peace for all creation with our selfless living, we will have achieved something for our soul birth into the physical. We achieve lots of stuff here and with our thoughts of yesterday, we created today, today's thought, which will create tomorrow. What are we creating with thoughts and actions from selfishness, self-serving? Humanity started this way four thousand years ago and all beings live in terror and suffering. It did not happen by accident but by cruelty and serving

Lucifer. God stays in the mountains; we stay here till the end of time. By accident, I came across a movie, I saw a glimpse of it and fast-forwarded. It was one of those selfish movies produced about the end time. In it, God is so angry with people and causes killing, accidents, disappearances, and suffering. People are forced to pray and read the Bible. Read the Bible from the very beginning till the last page. Pray, it commands, but pray what? Let each one of us living be the prayer that should be pleasing to God. This kind of movie creates terror and fear of my God, or maybe their God, or our God.

Here, I will write about the sacred and the profane. There is nothing profane in creation because all came from the sacred. We make it profane by our attitudes, starting from the very first male and female, Adam and Eve. That was the first profanity to start by them. In a deeper sense, it is not profane. It was the will of the absolute that human creation must begin. Well, we got it all wrong and try to justify it, so we say all are profane. All moving animating or inanimate objects are in the subject itself. We must treat everything in creation as sacred. Every organ in our bodies and all bodies are sacred. Regarding our speech, when we speak incorrectly or to misguide, we are profaning the sacred ability of speech that God has given to us. Every function of our body will be kept going (in body, after body) until we achieve the purpose of the Creator. So, it is for all creatures. When we interfere with being and live thoughtlessly and force other beings to suffer, we are making the sacred into the profane. Humanity must be retrained to bring sacredness alive. Yes, we all have a great task to accomplish before the God force. The rivers, the oceans, the desert, the mountains, the flowers, the magnificent trees, all forms of life including us, all are sacred. Our current attitude towards each other, the divisions, war, violence are all profane. We must feel Sacredness within us in order to treat others as sacred. Until this happens, we separate ourselves from the divine. We give far more importance to the material. Also, we must treat everything with respect since they, too, play a part in our life. So, be conscious of everything, transform the world, by looking at everything with the sacredness of the soul/spirit/ heart. Let all be seen as alive and sacred in our eyes. Oneness of God will be the result of this attitude. We wasted many thousands of years in profane living and kept the sacred apart from ourselves. We praise God by giving gratitude for all our life, all lives and creation. See, we cannot live one day without the sun, air, water, trees, each other and so on. We are part of all, and all are part of us. God is one, from the one came all. So, all are sacred.

The Great Light
Jesus and His instructions...

What humans should do...

1. One day, just before I woke up, I was seeing this huge pulsating, emanating, dazzling light, like the sun, it filled the whole universe. And from the middle, I heard a voice saying, "I am perceiving as Jesus saying, 'Souls of humanity are stuck in the filthy swamp, and they are not even trying to pull it out.'"

2. A few days later, I saw the same light as mentioned above and perceiving as Jesus saying, "Humanity must change."

3. A few days later again, the same light as above and perceiving as Jesus saying, "People have to follow the immutable laws."

Instructions for prayers and worship:

In my vision, I was standing on the top of the mountain. Behind me there are also more hills to climb and below me is the valley. As I was standing on the mountain, on my left side there was heavy rain, thunder, and lightning. I was saying to myself, "Thank God I am not in it at all."

As I was looking down in the valley, there was all sorts of worship places, like a Jewish Temple, Mosque, Hindu Temples, Churches and hundreds of thousands of people coming to worship their particular buildings and praying to God and Saints. Then I hear the voice saying, "All these Saints and Sages have done their work and reached their places." Similarly, each of us has to do the same work to reach the place where they are.

About the soul continuous existence:

One day in my vision, I was in some country visiting some family where the mother had given birth to a new baby. She was trying to feed the baby and the baby refused to drink milk from her. At that point,

I was perceiving the child just remembering his past existence where he did very bad and painful things to others and he hated that he had great remorse and he didn't want to live anymore, so he was refusing to take milk.

In my writing, I often use quotes from Jesus because Jesus is my guiding light who instructed me in my life, and I follow the instruction that comes from this great light. Also, I use the Kabalistic Tree of Life and I found it is the most beautiful, spiritual/mystical path for all those who seek to journey to the ineffable and it is our work as soul/spirit in this world. It is the will of the Creator that we accomplish and fulfill our soul's purpose through the physical journey of compassion, love, unity, and peace with all creation. Without this, we achieve nothing much.

The destiny of the soul (instruction from the inner world) is determined by the journey through physical existence.

Solo is the journey of the soul (instruction from the inner world).

I would like to highlight a few points here. First of all, all my writings were finished some years ago. As one read, there were some writings such as 'take this as warning' and also elsewhere mentioning impending catastrophe, while I sit and write all these words come. Maybe it was for the COVID-19 virus situation or something else. Whatever that may be, all life on earth is living in constant fear caused by humans to humans and the rest of creation. Earth is being raped for resources, chemicals. Animals, they have no value, breed them, abuse them, and kill them. Overpopulation, children are abused, born in the street and abortion. Abortion is not the way to control population. Controlling the impulse should be the way.

I know some may feel furious when they read my book. They may use the 'F' word. Misuse of that word caused all these issues on the earth. They feel so powerful with that. A time will come when the body won't be capable of doing such things and will be finally worn out and die in flesh. Whether one believes in the immutable law or not, where one believe in soul/spirit or not, all humans have the heart to feel, minds to think of the consequences of our action and abstaining from it or ignore the gifts of comprehension and continue to do what we want to for our own selfishness sake.

If, what we do to others, imagine, if others done to us. Only humans have this ability to think and act. We must learn to and educate to control this fire, if not, this fire will consume all beings, which is now evident. Nobody wants to talk about it. It is a taboo subject. We abort babies, animals will not do that. Are we not better than animals?

Why did I write all these? If you do not like what you read, don't read. If you disagree, write your own book. My book is not for debate or arguments. Not for pleasing anybody. My awareness, I wrote it in this book. No offence meant to anybody.

Flowers of Wisdom Blossoms in the Garden of Life…

Poetry emanates from the Joyful Heart or Soulful Heart…

Read between the lines to know the poet [SOUL]

Rose

"If One decides to take the Spiritual Journey, do not forget to pack the food for the Soul Journey which is Love, Empathy, compassion etc." Rose

"Gather feather for the Soul Wing while in Physical Existence which is Goodness and Love." Rose

"Divine gave us life and engraved the Map in our soul. It is for us to open the map and navigate our soul journey through living." Rose

"I was a cast iron, went through furnace of physical existence and became a sharp steel blade. It will cut through ALL things. Soul Evolution." Rose

"The wise speaks in parables and in wisdom. The unwise make noises without any substance." Rose

"Do not ask others to carry one's burden. Life has given them enough of their own to carry. Have compassion." Rose

"Hate, kill or hurt a being, worship and love God - How is it possible?" Rose

"Do not create map for others where one has not journeyed." Rose

"Do not be a way shower, unless and until one saw and walked the Way." Rose

"Do not be 'Follow the Leader'. If one does, soon will recognize that the leader does not know the Way." Rose

"I enter the wind of time and traveled all four corners of the surface and finally the wind brought me back to the Timeless Zone." Rose

"When I wore garments of glitters, and the world was around me. When I wore the sack cloth, my friends and their world disappeared." Rose

"Do not worry about others judging you or praising you. These are the two sides of the same coin. They have done the same thing to ALL." Rose

"I sow the wind on Earth and harvested storm in Heaven." Rose

"God's love is greater than our faults." Rose "Fear prevent us from moving forward." Rose

"I am the Message and I am the Messenger of Love. Receive me into Your dwelling place (God)." Rose

"I am measured on Earth by my fine cloths, house, cars. People sought after my company. In Heaven, I am measured by my giving love, selflessness, compassion, empathy and unity." Rose

"The Earth is a school (prison) where souls learn their skills in order to travel the God's Universe made of LOVE." Rose

"After the physical death souls return to the Ether (Instruction from the Inner world)." Rose

"Even if people are bad, they are souls and they travel the path of Light. They are Light. (Instruction from the Inner world)." Rose

"In one of my dreams or visions, I was in a beautiful landscape, snow field and about twenty young men of their early twenties all passed on the other side. I had a long communication with them, and I asked them to explain what is going to be for the people who does wrong and crime while in the physical existence and dies.

They said, they are not allowed to disclose. I insisted they must tell me. Then they said, it is not going to be good for the people who does wrong and evil while in the physical. They experience great suffering while in the soul world. There is life after the physical." Rose

"Sexuality in Humans creates Bonds and bondage for the souls for countless lifetimes until all things are perfected and balanced." Rose

"A compassionate word on time can give hope to a troubled soul and save a life in crisis. Try, it is free." Rose

"Resolves and dissolve all emotional entanglement, if one does,

Journey of the Soul will be lighter and happier." Rose

"If one is dishonest to others, one is dishonoring oneself and dishonoring others as well." Rose

"Physical world and spiritual dimensions co-exist. One is visible to the physical eyes. Others are NOT. (Instructions from the Inner World)" Rose

"Do not try to know and comprehend God. It is not our Job. God is infinite and finite cannot fathom infinite (Instruction from the Inner World)." Rose

"Learn to live with and tolerate all beings and their place is creation. Thy Spirit will rejoice." Rose

"From the Mount Olive Master spoke. Birds flew over him. Angels sang. Disciples listened - HUMANS UNDERSTOOD HIM NOT." Rose

"LOVE IS THE LIGHT OF THE WORLD. THOSE WHO WALK BY THIS LIGHT WILL NOT STUMBLE AND FALL. THIS IS LIFE, LIVING BY LOVE." Rose

"Universal Mysteries are given to those beings whose hearts are filled with Love, Empathy, Compassion and Desire for Oneness and Unity in Creation." Rose

"Practice empathy, compassion, and love towards all Beings.

Thy soul will take delight, The Earth and Heaven will rejoice." Rose

"Love is the river of life that flows from the throne Of God Towards its Infinite Creation." Rose

We have one Earth as our garden that
include Us humans, animals, plants, waters,
mountains...

We have one Earth as our garden that
include Us humans, animals, plants, waters,
mountains...

All the best…

Rose

www.ingramcontent.com/pod-product-compliance
Lightning Source LLC
Chambersburg PA
CBHW051134120626
46547CB00012B/806